DAMAGED GOODS

By C. A. HOCKING

DEDICATION

For Kerry and her three beautiful daughters.
Wherever and whoever you are now, I hope you made it.

ALSO BY C. A. HOCKING

A PLACE IN TIME
HOME TO ROOST
OLD FARTS ON A BUS
THE SARAH ANN ELLIOTT SERIES
THE AUNT EDNA STORIES

CHAPTER ONE

The house came into view suddenly at the bend in the road just before the bridge.

Wide and white like a ship in full sail skimming across an ocean of cane fields with the mountains looming behind it like storm clouds. Gracious and elegant in the softness of a tropical morning haze. Raised high on vine covered concrete posts at the front and tucked into the side of the mountain at the back. Adorned on three sides by wide verandas garnished with timber lacework. Glowing with tinges of early morning pink and gold on the white.

Helen stopped the car on the bridge, turned off the airconditioning, opened all the windows and breathed in deeply. Sickly sweet cane. Rich damp soil. Hot wet air. And the smell of the rainforest after a Wet Season storm. That indefinable odour that she'd not smelled anywhere else in the world, so fragrant, so evocative of her past and so deeply disturbing.

She folded the tourist map she'd needed to find the road to her own house and surveyed the scene before her, registering a tremor of surprise at how beautiful it was. She had no memory of it as being beautiful. And not just beautiful, but impeccably beautiful. No weeds or peeling paint or run down outbuildings here, but rather a neat picture painted by numbers with the artist taking meticulous care not to colour over the lines.

The house had been built facing east to catch the morning sun, with views across the cane fields out to the Pacific Ocean. Designed with large airy rooms, tongue-and-groove timber walls, high ceilings and polished timber floors, it was the epitome of a gracious old highset Queenslander. Its only flaw, Helen remembered, had been the kitchen built along the back, dug into the side of the mountain, stinking hot on even the mildest days, airless, mildewy, an invitation for slithering and crawling rainforest creatures to trespass and lodge.

The original mango tree still shaded the northern veranda, but was now as wide and as high as the house, gnarled and twisted with age, its thinning foliage heralding its demise. Further down the slope were three younger mango trees and a small grove of tropical fruit trees.

A row of poincianas in glorious red display overhung the southern veranda, dwarfing the interplanted white frangipanis, their red and white petals creating a pink carpet on the emerald green grass below.

Together, the trees framed the house above manicured lawns that now ran clear down to the river, a luxurious green slope broken only by tall palms that stood sentry along the bitumen driveway.

Where there once had been stabling for a dozen tough mountain ponies two hundred yards north of the house, large modern galvanised iron sheds now clustered, their high sliding doors open to expose the heavy plant and machinery stowed safely under cover on concrete floors, with sealed bitumen paths giving them flood proof access to the other side of the bridge.

Bloody tractor's bogged again Dad, I'll get the ponies. Yeah, yeah, 'course I can manage, I'm not bloody stupid!

She heard the voice as clearly as if the speaker was standing next to her. A shock wave passed through her and she turned, expecting to see a grubby fourteen year old in torn baggy overalls with sweat stains under the arms and across the back, reaching up to remove the shabby, wide-brimmed hat and wiping the sweat from her face with the back of her hand, the black hair stuck to her scalp in wet greasy clumps, the mouth grim and tight beyond her years.

But Helen was alone on the bridge and the cane fields were empty and silent.

Then she noticed that the bridge was new, steel, two lanes wide, high and solid, and she remembered the rickety single-lane timber construction that had dipped low over the river and needed rebuilding after every major flood, that had cut them off from the rest of the world for weeks at a time, that had witnessed a mad scene to rival Lucia Di Lammermoor.

Don't Mum, come back Mum, DON'T!

Another voice, this time her own but from a different time. She felt weak and sick, reached for the bottle of water on the seat next to her and wondered again if she was being a fool. The voices in the middle of the night were one thing, but here they came at her in broad daylight. The place was full of ghosts and one of the ghosts was herself.

The voices had begun after the funeral, unbidden, a shock to her hard won sense of balance and order. They'd brought with them again the old fears, the nightmares that jarred her awake,

3

her ears keened for the sound of footsteps in the passage, her body rigid, her heart pounding, her mind scrambling for the present in order to purge the past.

Until the funeral she had believed herself to be liberated from that past, but the voices in the night made her liberation a lie, a veneer. They'd come faintly at first, as if from a great distance, then closer and closer until she now woke in the night with the sensation of the speaker's breath on her face and an unwelcome hand crawling over her body. Even through the sedative haze, the voices lunged at her, tearing at her mind and resurrecting the guilt she'd renounced, the betrayal she'd justified, until she'd became afraid to sleep.

The girls, Tina and Ria, couldn't help her at first because they didn't know, no one knew and she couldn't explain it to them. She'd kept her secrets safely locked away inside her for too long. To begin with, they blamed the change in their mother on the death of their father, but as she deteriorated, their concern became distress, and finally they gave up their own lives to care for her and she could never allow that. So she told them, her two beautiful daughters, after they'd come to her in the deepest darkness of a night that she'd shattered with her cries of terror. Shaking and weeping, she'd told them of her childhood. Some of it, anyway. Not all of it. Not even she could bring herself to admit to all of it. She'd told them a little about their grandfather and how she'd left after he'd died. But she didn't tell them the truth about how he'd died. That would have been too much for them. So the lie continued as did the nightmares, and finally, she'd told them about the ones she'd left behind.

They wanted her to have counselling, to talk to someone who could help, but Helen came from a generation who could not, would not talk about such matters. And there were things in her past that no one should know. Not her girls, not the family, no one, for they wouldn't understand. In desperation,

4

the girls went to their elderly Great-Aunt Maria for help and were surprised to learn that she and the rest of the family elders knew some of the truth. But not all of it. They didn't know of the ones left behind because Helen had spent a lifetime guarding that secret.

Aunt Maria was deeply upset that Helen had kept it from them all for so long. There was shock and heartache and a sense of time running out. Go back, her aunt had told her, go back and put it right while you can. Raymond had said the same words. Closure, her girls called it. Those lovely, clever girls of hers with their knowledge and degrees and wisdom and their safe, untainted upbringing. They thought they understood, but Helen was eternally grateful that they couldn't begin to understand.

But there was one who understood. Only one in the whole world. And as her torment grew, her need to be with that one again became an obsession until she'd finally agreed to go back. The girls wanted to accompany her, but she insisted that she do it alone. There was much to put right, but even more to protect.

They'd flown with her as far as Sydney where the family was waiting to greet her, and helped her pack the car for the trip north. Call us, they said. Let us know.

The three day trip had given her time to think, to rehearse, to prepare.

But she hadn't been prepared for the ghosts. It was as if the bridge marked a line between the present and the past. She'd crossed the line and plunged into a past that took shape in images she could hear, feel and smell, coming at her in savage shock waves that brought a tingling weakness to her body and an instinct to flee, as she had done once before.

She gripped the steering wheel to stop her hands from trembling and breathed deeply. Here was the moment in time when she could go back. She knew the nightmare behind her.

Could she face the unknown nightmare before her? Surely it couldn't be worse than what had been.

Could it?

Unfinished business is what Raymond had called it. Finish it, he'd said while he still had breath to speak. Go back and make amends. But it had taken two years and a nervous breakdown to get her here.

She tried to remember her two sisters as she had left them, girls of 21 and 15, and then to imagine the elderly women they were now. Sis would be 70 and Sweetypie 64. Would she even recognise them? Then again, would they recognise her now, at 67? And did they ever wonder about her as she wondered about them?

Raymond had been right, finish it and take what comes. If it's hard, if it hurts – well, it's what she deserved, she reminded herself, what she had long deserved.

After a moment to steady herself, she started the car and drove up the long slope towards the house. The wide driveway which had once been a narrow dirt track that stopped at the front steps was now bitumen running right up under the house where two vehicles were parked– a work worn Landcruiser utility and a late model red Holden station wagon.

A movement to her right caught her attention as two black bodies emerged from the shadows of the old mango tree. More ghosts? No. Of course not. Two Rottweilers instead of the German Shepherds, young animals with shine on their coats and spring in their gait, the latest in a long succession of dogs.

She would bet money on their names.

She pulled in behind the station wagon. The dogs leapt for her noisily as she stepped from the vehicle. Standing her ground, she pointed to the mango tree and commanded as she had done in her youth, "Prince! Lady! Tree!" They backed off and circled each other, glancing at her sideways, confused by this fearless stranger with the power of their names in her voice and the manner of their mistress in her actions. She yelled at them again and they slunk back to their shade and shelter.

A wide length of splintered timber suspended by two frayed ropes hung forlornly above them. The sight of it made her flinch.

An incongruous flaw amidst the pristine landscape.

Higher, Daddy, I want to go higher!

A shudder passed through Helen. Not that. Not yet.

She gathered up the bags and luggage from the back seat of the car and approached the house. The sound of clattering crockery and morning television came through one of the open front windows. The dogs must surely have alerted someone to her presence but as yet no one had appeared.

Standing at the bottom of the steps to the front veranda, the December sun already hot on the back of her bare arms and calves as it burned off the morning mist, she waited with a tremor in her body for the sound of bare feet padding up the passage, for the creak and bang of the front screen door . No creak came. Instead, the smooth silence of well oiled hinges and a muffled twang as the flung open door hit a padded doorstop.

"Did you bring my liquorice?" High pitched old lady-child voice. White-grey wispy hair above faded blue eyes and a big pink grin still dripping Weet Bix and cold milk from a bowl held under a delicately pointed chin.

Helen's heart contracted and the tremor within threatened to become an earthquake.

Oh god, not this. Not this sad creature before her with the oafish look of an aging idiot. Not this everlasting reminder of what had been and what might have been.

Helen had held close to her heart the image of pretty blonde hair and luminous blue eyes, but those eyes were now set in drooping folds of fragile sun-damaged skin. The childish grin framed crooked, stained teeth and the chin supported a sagging turkey neck above a stooped thickened body.

But she knew immediately who it was because of the pink. Pink patterned sarong tied too tight over a corrugated cleavage, garish pink toenails and fingernails with grime under the chipped rims, pink jewelled hippie bracelets on thick wrists, pink elastic bands catching the wisps of thin hair into two messy pigtails, and pink lipstick scrawled across her mouth like graffiti.

"Sweetypie." A whisper. A plea. For what once was. Creamy pink-white skin over a tiny frame, blue eyes alive with laughter and anticipation, golden blonde hair in neat beribboned pigtails above the pink organza.

Look at my pretty dress, Helly!

And those amazing pink, patent leather shoes and pink frilly socks.

Aren't I PRETTY, Sissy?

So innocent. So dangerously innocent.

Push me higher, Daddy, I want to go higher!

Then she saw that the eyes, although dulled with age, were as innocent and pure-souled as ever. Only the outer visage had changed. Inside, Sweetypie was as she had always been.

"Well?"

"Well what, Sweetypie?"

"Where's my liquorice?"

"What liquorice?"

A stamped foot sent milk splashing across the sarong which clung wetly to heavy breasts, revealing large misshapen brown nipples through the thin fabric. "You ARE a silly billy! MY liquorice of course!"

"She means the liquorice you promised to bring back from town for her when you left here fifty bloody years ago." The

8

voice came from behind one of the front windows, strong, harsh, unforgiving. A guttural beer and cigarette voice.

The shock of it caught at Helen's breath. She remembered that voice had once been low and velvety with a soft, warm smoothness that she'd envied, she with her high girlish voice and flippant laugh.

She looked towards the source and saw the shadow of a face in the window, unmoving, observing.

Behind the shadow, silhouetted against the window on the northern side of the house, she saw a suspended range hood and realised she was looking into the kitchen where she had expected the Front Room to be.

"Liquorice! Liquorice!" The childwoman before her was calling in her promise.

Helen went up the steps, noting that the veranda was tiled where once it had been timber. She dropped the bags at her feet and, with a catch in her voice that betrayed her uncertainty, addressed the source of the voice. "Come out, Sis. I'm not going to bite."

"But I bloody well might!"

Hostile? Certainly. But something else as well. Helen wasn't sure, and realised that she could no longer read the voice the way she once had. It had been too long.

"Have it your own way," she replied calmly, despite the turmoil inside her.

Turning back to Sweetypie, Helen nudged the group of parcels next to her suitcase with her foot. "I didn't bring you liquorice, little one, but I got you lots of other things, much nicer things. Presents. Pretty pink birthday presents."

The plastic bowl of unfinished Weet Bix dropped to the veranda floor. "Birthday presents? Ooh, pink presents! Come on, Sissy, come and SEE!" She flopped unceremoniously onto the floor and tore into the bags with such enthusiasm that Helen had to step back to avoid being tangled up with them.

Sweetypie flopped unceremoniously to the floor and tore into the prettily wrapped parcels with such enthusiasm that they had to step back to avoid being tangled up with them. They joined in the laughter of the other children, until they saw him watching her from the other side of the room. The laughter died in their throats. No, not today, not THIS day. It was too soon. She was still too little. Didn't he understand that?

Weakness overcame Helen as the unbidden memory washed over her and she gripped the banister railing to prevent her knees from buckling. Two large high-backed cane chairs and a low glass and cane table graced the veranda. She lowered herself into one of the chairs and waited for the weakness to pass, watching Sweetypie immerse herself in the joy of the moment like the small child she was. It was cruel to observe.

The sound from the television stopped.

The screen door opened slowly this time.

A manwoman emerged, barefoot, unlit cigarette in one hand, coffee mug in the other. Shapeless in cut off bib-and-brace overalls, unsupported breasts sagging heavily inside the black singlet. Sour faced under iron grey hair cut so short that the mottled scalp showed through. Wary eyes, dull brown, hooded. Skin dark and leathery from a life in the sun. The straight line of the lipless mouth, the big Roman nose squashed almost flat against her face.

He broke my nose again Helly.

Broad shoulders, still beefy at 70 after a lifetime of heavy hard work.

You look like one of them wog canecutters, Sis, shit you're an ugly bitch.

Short waisted, short legged.

10

**If you didn't have a neck, Sis, we'd think you were
a bloody frog!**

Hard faced. Tough. Intimidating.

Unless you really knew her.

Helen really knew her. Or had once. She wondered if it was wrong to assume she still did.

Sis put her coffee down on the table, lit her cigarette and sat back easily in the other cane chair, gnarled feet stretched out before her. Without looking up at Helen, she watched Sweetypie oohing and aahing over the sarongs, jewellery, sandals, mirror, brush and comb, bath towel and scarves, watched with a measure of pleasure that had nothing to do with Helen's presence and everything to do with Sweetypie's excitement. "Like the presents, little one?" The voice that had been so harsh a moment ago was gentle and amused.

"Ooh yes yes."

"But she forgot the liquorice, didn't she?"

"I don't care, I like these MUCH better."

"Good. Good girl. Now take them inside and put them in your room."

Sweetypie obeyed instantly, gathered up her treasures and went inside.

An awkward moment of silence followed. Then Helen said, "Well?"

"Well what?"

"No 'welcome home' for the prodigal sister?"

Sis drew long and deep on her cigarette and thought about that. "Is it?"

"Is it what?"

"Home."

"Of course. I still …"

"… still own a third of everything? Yeah, I suppose you do, even if you did sign the running of the place over to me half a century ago. But that don't make it home." The voice had a

11

cold, bitter edge to it, the eyes gazed fixedly on the tiles at her feet.

Helen sat unmoved. She'd been expecting this, but was surprised at how the doing was better than the expecting. Almost a relief. At least now she could run with it and let it play itself out. She felt the weakness pass and steadied her breathing, not sure how to continue.

"Do you want to hit me?" she finally asked, her voice gently taunting in a clumsy attempt to lighten the moment.

"Don't be so damn stupid," Sis snapped.

"Not pleased to see me, then?"

"Why the hell should I be? You're nothing to me now."

Helen felt as if she'd been slapped across the face.

Sis continued, "Jeez, if Sweetypie hadn't recognised you, I wouldna known who you was." She paused, then lifted her gaze from the tiles and turned hard eyes on Helen.

They confronted each other as the morning sun rose and dragged the light and heat away from them across the veranda.

Where someone else might have seen in Helen the clear brown eyes and smooth skin of good health, the confidence that belongs exclusively to the wealthy and successful, the tranquillity of one who has loved well and been well loved, the expensive clothes gracing a carefully maintained body, and the glossy mane of black hair drawn back from the classically beautiful face to rest in soft waves against the straight, elegant neck and shoulders, Sis saw something quite different.

Sis saw the cold blooded murderess and loved her for it. She saw the escapee and hated her for it. She saw the world and knew she could never have it.

She also saw the ultimate betrayal and understood, but didn't know how to say that she understood. Instead, the old pain and grief came at her in a rush, alarming her because she thought it had left her years ago. She suddenly wanted to raise her fist and smash it against her sister's face with fifty

12

years of unreleased anger, to hurt as she had been hurt, to quench the sudden surge of bitterness inside her with a simple act of violence. Her fist tightened with the thought and for an instant, she knew she could do it and not be sorry. Then she heard Sweetypie's delighted laughter from inside the house and knew she couldn't do it. Violence was no longer a part of their lives.

The need passed as suddenly as it had come. She relaxed her fist. Her face betrayed nothing of the conflict inside her.

Helen looked back at an enigma that an entire region, with the exception of a select few, saw as a rough, foul mouthed, hard as nails, ugly bitch who lived in relative seclusion with her retarded sister. She remembered the words of the man who'd filled her car with petrol as she asked for directions to the new road here – was it only an hour ago? He'd nodded and looked at her curiously, saying, yeah, he knew where that road was, but no one lived up there except for that old dyke and her crazy sister, you know, the one who looks like Bette Davis's Baby Jane on a bad day. Did you know she goes up into the rainforest every day and no one can find her, like a bloody animal for chrissake. Like a feral pig. But the ugly one – you gotta watch your step around her. Did you hear about the hairdresser she king-hit that time, and the new doctor she chased out of town? Bloody crazies, both of them, ought to be locked up. Still, the dyke can grow sugar, best damn cane farmer in the Far North, writes about it in those fancy journals. Last year's returns were the best in the district, no one can top her. To be expected I suppose, considering who her old man was, bloody good farmer before he came to grief in that cyclone. Pity about his daughters, though, one's mad, one's shitscary ugly and wasn't there another one – what ever happened to her? Then he'd asked her what business she had with them, a nice looking lady like her. She'd paid him in silence, turned her back on him and driven away.

13

Helen noted that the softening of features that accompanies the aging process in so many women was not apparent in Sis's face. In fact, the mask that she presented to the world was so rigid, so unrelenting, that there wasn't a trace of femininity left on any of the features. Neither was there anything feminine about her shapeless body, the muscled arms, the thick scarred legs, the cigarette hanging slackly from the corner of a grimly set mouth – yes, there was a woman in there somewhere, but you had to know that to see it.

Helen remembered, knew it and saw it. And she saw more. She saw the insurmountable wall of protection around Sis that had taken a lifetime to construct. She saw the nurturer who had devoted herself to the tender care of her youngest sister. She saw the girl who became a man to survive in a world where being a girl was fraught with danger. She saw the kindest, gentlest soul she had ever known, a soul incapable of hurting another human being unless provoked beyond human endurance. She knew that better than anyone.

And she saw a woman who was better in every way than she herself had ever been. A woman incapable of betrayal in any shape or form.

Love, admiration and a sense of her own unworthiness rose up in a smothering wave. She looked away for a moment. When she looked back, Sis was watching her closely, the mask giving nothing away.

"So how are you , Sis?"

"Alright."

"And Sweetypie?"

"She's alright."

"The farm looks good."

"Yeah."

Helen waited. Sis continued to watch her.

"I thought it would be raining. This time of year. It used to."

"Mmm."

"I heard the Wet Season has changed. That you don't get endless weeks of rain like you used to, but that you get more of it in the Dry now. The greenhouse effect, I suppose." She knew she was chattering inanely, but Sis's indifference wasn't helping.

Sis looked away.

Helen felt defeated. How do you pick up a conversation after fifty years of separation? She tried again, this time with a direct question.

"Does Bill Stewart come to see you?"

Sis glanced at her with a curious look in her eye.

"Bill? Yeah. End of the month, regular as clockwork. He's a bloody good accountant and a good mate. Why? What's it to you?"

"I just wondered if you ever saw anyone who knows you well."

"Jeez," Sis responded with a cynical shake of her head, "next thing you'll be telling me you give a damn. Don't bullshit me, Helen." She turned towards the door and called out, "Hey, Sweetypie, leave your bloody presents alone for a minute and get me another cup of coffee. And bring the kitchen sponge with you. There's a mess out here." She stubbed out her cigarette carefully in a covered ashtray on the low table, taking care not to let ash float onto the spotless tiles, pulled another cigarette from the packet tucked inside the bib of her overalls and lit up, her head bent forward, cupping the cigarette and lighter carefully between her hands as if to protect the small flame from a breeze. There was no breeze. The air was still and sticky.

They sat in uneasy silence, Helen remembering a time when, if the two of them were alone together, you couldn't shut Sis up. She sensed the continuing conflict within her sister and waited patiently for her to make the next move.

15

Sis stared out over the cane fields. "So." A deep drag on the cigarette and a pause as she carefully flicked ash into the ashtray. "So why now?"

Helen had hoped for a period of pleasantries, a period of grace in which to guide the conversation until the moment was right and she could ask for the forgiveness she so needed. She should have known better. It had always been Sis's way to get straight to the point.

"Raymond died."

"Yeah. Bill told me. Commiserations." Cold. Couldn't give a damn. "So? You got kids. You got friends. Not like you're alone or anything. So why now?"

"I made him a promise."

"To come back?"

"No. Yes. I promised him I would straighten things out, make it up to you."

"Bit bloody late for that, don't you think?"

"I hope not."

"How long since he died? Two, three years?"

"Two years."

"Jeez. We ain't getting any younger here! You might have missed your moment." The sarcasm was not lost on Helen.

"I thought about that. Maybe it took two years to get the courage to come back."

"You ain't never been short of courage. You wanted to do something, you always just up and did it. So what really made you get off your arse and come back?"

Helen straightened up against the wilting humidity. Her clothes were sticking to her in wet patches. She felt the pressure of interrogation adding to her discomfort. "I've been … unwell." No response. "After Raymond died, I started having … dreams." She paused.

"What are you talking about?"

"Dreams … about us. You and me and Sweetypie. After Raymond died, the dreams came back, bad dreams like I used to have in the beginning …"

"So you ain't sleeping so good. So take a pill." Sis squinted unsympathetically through the cloud of smoke.

"The pills don't help." She paused again, giving careful thought to her next words. "I started hearing voices in the dreams. Your voice. Sweetypie's voice."

"And what was we saying, me and Sweetypie?"

"You were calling me."

"Huh! I stopped calling you forty years ago! So you started having bad dreams and you feel all messed up. So you've come back to straighten yourself out? Is that it?"

"I want to straighten things out for myself, yes, and for …" Her words dwindled into a long uncertain pause.

"Go on. I'm listening. I been waiting fifty years to hear this."

"For the family."

"For your daughters."

"Yes. And for the rest of the family."

A moment to absorb. Then, "What family?"

Helen had rehearsed what she would say many times during the past two years, but what she hadn't counted on in those rehearsals was Sis's callous response, and now her penetrating gaze. It unnerved her. Words fell out of her mouth in an unrehearsed rush.

"Mine. Ours. Aunts, uncles, cousins. Lots of cousins." It sounded ridiculous.

Sis turned to face Helen full on. "What the hell are you talking about? We ain't got no aunts or uncles or cousins. There was only us for chrissake! Are you talking about Carrots' people? Make sense!"

"No, not Raymond's family. He finished with them over fifty years ago." Oh god, there was nothing for it but to launch headlong into it. " We've got relatives, Sis, lots of them. And

17

I've had them all to myself up until now. I only told them about you and Sweetypie a few months ago and they were very upset with me. Especially Tina and Ria."

"Your girls? But you named them after me and Sweetypie. How did you explain that to all those relatives?"

"That was easy. As far as everyone was concerned, they were named after Mum's mother, our grandmother, Sistina, and Mum's sister, Aunt Maria."

"Jeez. A grandmother and … but he always said Mum had no one."

"Yes. I know. I thought that, too, until …"

Sweetypie came through the door backwards, carefully balancing two cups of milky coffee on a tray. Conversation ceased, replaced by the awkwardness of important matters interrupted. She placed the tray carefully on the table, then put the cups one by one in front of her two sisters. "Made one for you, too, Helly." She was wearing one of the new pink sarongs and the sandals with the gold bows that Helen had bought for her. Every bit of jewellery she possessed jingled and clanked and dangled from her body and at least three different coloured lipsticks blazed trails across her face. Her smile was radiant as she pirouetted on her wrinkled pink toes to display her new clothes and trinkets. "Aren't I PRETTY, Helly?"

She picked up the sponge and hummed a tuneless melody as she bent to wipe up the spilled breakfast and splattered coffee, then dropped the sodden sponge onto the tray, sashayed across the veranda, down the steps and over to the dogs.

Sis stared woodenly out across the cane fields. Helen watched her, waiting. It was a lot to take in and she'd barely begun.

"Family, hey?" Sis finally muttered. "Mum had family. Then why …"

"She had her reasons."

"Like what? What could be so bloody awful that you would keep your own family a secret from your kids?"

"Dad."

Sis suddenly stood and pushed her feet into worn elastic-sided boots at the top of the steps. "I got work to do," she said with such force that for a second Helen almost lost her resolve. But not completely.

She took a deep breath and blurted out, "I want to talk about Dad." That was wrong, that was not how she'd planned it.

Sis spun around to look at her, the mask giving way to utter astonishment. "Dad? You wanna talk about DAD?! You turn up here unannounced after all this time and tell me you wanna talk about ... you've lost your bloody marbles, you have!" She lowered her head and directed a fierce, accusing gaze at Helen. "If you think it's alright to come waltzing back here when you feel like it so's you can sort out your messed up head at our bloody expense, you got another think coming!" She turned away in disgust. "Christ, I'm outa here!" She almost tripped over Helen's suitcase, kicked it savagely, then picked it up and threw it over the banister in a gesture of pure contempt. Without looking back, she spat, "Get outa here, Helen. You're not welcome." She moved towards the veranda steps and yelled, "Hey! Sweetypie! Up to the cubby! Now!"

Drawing on every ounce of whatever courage she had left, Helen stood and announced, "I'm staying."

Sis swung back to her sister with a look of pure loathing. "Oh no you bloody well ain't! I can't even stand to look at you! You better be gone by the time I get back or I'll throw you across the bridge myself."

"But Sweetypie ..."

"Sweetypie? Like I should believe you care about Sweetypie? Christalmighty, you got no bloody idea. Did you ever once think about her waiting here on the veranda for her damn liquorice every damn day for fifty bloody years? Every day! Right up til yesterday. And here you are today, and you didn't bring her the damn stuff." It sounded foolish and Sis suddenly clamped her lips together. She glanced at Helen for a second, then she turned her head a little as if to look into the house. Something flickered across her face that Helen couldn't interpret, as if she had suddenly remembered something, but wished she hadn't. "You mustn't stay," Sis said softly as if to herself.

"Mustn't?" It seemed such a strange word to use. "Why not?" Sis's sudden change from anger to introversion was confusing her.

Sis didn't reply, but instead continued to gaze at the house as if the answer lay there.

Helen was about to follow her gaze when a shrill scream rent the air around them. Helen flinched, her nerves already raw, and ran to the northern side of the house. Sis, relieved to be distracted, merely sighed heavily, grabbed the mangled Akubra from the hook by the door, jammed it down hard on her head, gave it a slap and strode down the steps to where Sweetypie, her naked breasts swinging to and fro, struggled to free something from between both dogs' jaws.

"My sarong!" she screamed. "Bad doggies, bad doggies!"

"Prince! Lady! Tree!" Sis ordered and the dogs dropped their mouthfuls of torn material and obeyed. She raised her hand to discipline them but Sweetypie screamed again, lunged towards the dogs and wrapped her arms protectively around both of them.

"Don't hurt doggies!" she pleaded and huge tears gathered and splashed down her cheeks. "Doggies are good doggies, nice doggies!"

The sight of Sweetypie's tears seemed to deflate Sis and the mask softened suddenly and unexpectedly.

"Jeez. Alright little one, it's alright," Sis soothed, "I was only going to give them a tap on the nose. You know I would never hurt Prince or Lady. Pick up your sarong and stop crying, there's a good girl. Go wash your face. Come on now, go and put your cubby clothes on. I gotta get some work done. Ahhh, come on darlin', no more tears now, no more tears."

Sis enfolded the weeping woman in her arms and stroked her hair tenderly until the tears stopped. Gentle, so very gentle. Then she gave her a squeeze, kissed her damp face, gave her a friendly pat on the naked wrinkled bum and pushed her gently but firmly towards the house.

Helen watched the strange sight of her elderly naked baby sister clumping heavily up the steps and felt oddly relieved. Her Sissy was still here, locked behind the mask, her soft and loving Sissy.

Helen went back to her chair. Sis strode past her without a word, the mangled sarong in her hands, kicked off her boots, put her hat back on the hook and went inside. When she came back, the mask was intact again. Instead of going to the chair, she sat on the top step, her back to Helen. She said nothing.

The silence between them was charged with tension. Helen wasn't sure whether a decision had been made about her staying or going, but didn't want to risk the situation by pushing it further. She understood that neither of them knew the rules here and they would have to make it up as they went along. For now, they needed to mull over what they had said and heard from each other. Helen leaned back in the chair and waited.

When Sweetypie emerged a few minutes later, she was wearing a pink singlet and huge, baggy pink cotton shorts, pink thongs and a battered pink straw hat. The jewellery was gone, but the pink lipsticks were still in place. No sign of the tears. Instead, she clumped cheerfully down the steps, called the dogs to heel and disappeared into the nearest shed. A motor fired up and she re-appeared on a hand-painted pink three-wheeler motor bike towing a home-made trailer piled high with flat rocks. She stopped in front of the house, hopped off the bike and pulled a mobile phone from her shorts pocket. Several of the buttons were marked with brightly coloured paint.

Sis stood, looked down sternly at Sweetypie and commanded, "Show me!"

"Alright, silly billy." In a bored singsong voice, Sweetypie recited, " If you talk to me, it goes buzz buzz buzz, then I press the green button, then when you finish talking, I press the red button. When I want to talk to you, I press the yellow and green buttons, then when I finish talking to you, I press the red button."

"And?"

"Don't get it wet, don't drop it, don't let the doggies eat it."

"Good girl. Now off you go and be careful. Be back for lunch when …?"

"When the shadow from the waterhole tree touches the big black rock."

"OK. See you then."

"Coming, Helly?"

"No!" Sis punched the word out. Then more slowly, "She's not going to the cubby today, little one, she's going to stay here and … and get us our lunch."

Sweetypie clapped her hands and cried, "Goody! Vegemite sangers for lunch." She came up the steps and enfolded Helen in a tight hug. The cloying scent of old lady sweat rose up in a cloud around them. Helen hugged back until she was released.

Sweetypie trotted back down the steps, mounted the bike, throttled gently and rode slowly up into the rainforest behind the house, Prince and Lady following in an orderly manner behind her.

Helen came to stand next to Sis and, in an effort to end the awkwardness between them, commented, "These dogs

seem as devoted to her as the German Shepherds used to be."
Silence. "What does she do up there?"

"She fixes the track to the cubby." Reluctant.

"The track? Are you talking about our track? Our secret track?"

"Don't need to be secret no more, does it, not since." Sis stopped as if the sentence was meant to end there.

"Since Dad died?" As soon as she said it, Helen wanted to take it back.

A veil fell across Sis's eyes, but not before Helen saw something there that caught her by surprise. A flicker of dread. An instant of pure fear. Fear of something that Helen didn't know about. She sensed it as completely as if Sis had said it out loud. It shocked Helen, because until that moment she had believed that they shared all the secrets there were. Now she knew there was more and she needed to know.

Sis saw the need in Helen's face and turned to leave quickly, but Helen's hand shot out to restrain her. "Don't go."

Sis pulled her arm from Helen's grasp, but instead of walking away, turned to confront her.

"What the hell do you want?"

"I want you to stay home today. I want to talk to you."

"About him? Jeez, you don't waste time, do you? You just turn up here and expect to pick up the conversation where we left off fifty years ago?"

"Yes. I didn't come back for small talk."

"Well, you got that bit right. Now tell me why you really came back, no bullshit about dreams and voices this time. And if you say it's because you missed us, I'll bloody deck you."

"The dreams and the voices are true, Sis, but what they served to do was confront me with my betrayal of you, something that I have avoided confronting all my life. What I did and why I did it – it all seems so abstract now, like it happened to someone else." Suddenly, the rehearsed words

23

came back to her. "I came back to clarify some memories and some truths. I came to talk to you, to explain some things, to try to understand others, to put him into some sort of perspective in our lives, yours and mine and Sweetypie's. I came back to finish it."

Sis narrowed her eyes. "We finished it fifty years ago. Remember? And I haven't spoken his name since. Not since the day of the memorial service."

"Memorial service?"

"Oh, you didn't know about that, did you?" And suddenly, words were pouring from Sis in an bitter gush. "Well, everyone thought you and the old man was dead. I reckon every bloody Catholic in the district turned up here, one after the other, to offer me and Sweetypie their condolences and encourage us to go to church again. I ain't set foot inside that building since the memorial, see? But I don't reckon I was real nice to them 'cos they only ever came once and then they never came again. Gave up on me as a lost cause, I suppose. Except for the Stewarts. They was always good to me and Sweetypie. But then there was the memorial service three months after the cyclone. Figured I gotta go to that. So I leave Sweetypie here dosed up with so much laudanum she didn't wake up for two days and I go into town for this bloody service and the postmaster comes up to me and hands me this letter from Sydney and I seen it was your handwriting and I rip it open and there you are, you ain't dead at all but having a fine old time in Sydney, not a word about how you got there, just that you got a job and you'd be home soon. So I tell everyone about your letter and hallebloodylulah, everyone's rejoicing and it's only the old bastard I gotta be sorry about. Oh, I was good, let me tell you! I was a great grieving daughter, quiet and miserable, thanking everyone for their kind words. And didn't they go on! About what a fine man he was, what an example he was to us all as a husband, a father and a good citizen, and

24

what a loss he was to me and Sweetypie and how good it was that I now had the reunion with you to look forward to and wouldn't that lift my spirits. Oh yeah, lift my spirits alright. When I got home, Sweetypie's out like a light and I'm all alone and the only spirits I lifted were of the amber variety. I tied one on, let me tell you, I had a hangover for a week, and I vowed … I vowed never to say his name again, and I ain't." She took a step closer to Helen.

"I'm so sorry, Sis, I didn't know …"

"Course you didn't know!"

Helen flinched and unconsciously backed away.

"You wasn't bloody here, was you? And there's other things you don't know about, like Sarge coming here and giving me a hard time 'cos he never believed our story. What did you say to him to make him not believe us? You said it was gunna be easy. But it wasn't, Helen, it wasn't easy. He kept coming back. He had his blokes crawling all over the place for years looking for something, anything because they never found the bastard's remains. He never gave up and it didn't stop til he died. It wasn't like you said it would be. It was a bloody nightmare on top of a nightmare!" She was shouting, the last words lashed out with such venom that her voice cracked and she began to cough violently.

Sis dropped heavily into the chair and reached for the coffee, slurping urgently until the coughing abated and her breathing eased. Leaning back into the chair, she closed her eyes and let her shoulders sag while she regained her composure. Helen was shocked at how suddenly old and tired she looked. When she opened her eyes again, the mask had dropped back into place. Pulling out a cigarette, she lit up quickly with trembling hands and inhaled deeply several times. The outburst was over.

Helen noted the trembling hands and wanted to comfort her sister, but she needed a moment herself to recover from the attack. Her own hands were shaking as she sat down. She didn't remember ever seeing Sis like this. Fifty years had done much to change them both.

Finally, she said cautiously, "They didn't find anything of him?"

"Nope."

"Why would they expect to? Floodwaters, crocodiles ..."

"That's what everyone kept telling him. Christ, more than a dozen went missing without a trace in that cyclone. But Sarge was like a dog with a bone. He got an idea in his thick head and wouldn't let it go. He didn't like me, for starters. And he always carried on like he knew the bastard better than we did." She snorted scornfully. "What did he bloody know? Anyway, enough of that. I ain't gunna talk about any of that and that's final."

Helen was quiet, then she reached over, hoping the moment was right, and gently stroked the spiky hair. Sis pushed her away with startled embarrassment. Helen withdrew her hand. She couldn't seem to get this right. She searched for a shared memory that had brought them happiness, and said softly, "There were some good times. No, not with him, never with him, but for the three of us, there were some special times. Do you remember ...."

"No! Don't start the 'do you remembers'."

".... the day Sweetypie was born?"

"Jeez." Softly. Forlornly. Sis stared out over the cane fields. "What was good about that day, Helen? Tell me that. What the hell was there to remember about Sweetypie's birth that was good?"

"I remember the way she looked at us both, the way that look enslaved us, how beautiful she was, so tiny, so fragile."

"Damn it, Helen, you were only a baby yourself. You can't possibly remember any of that."

"I remember the noises. We were playing in the rainforest, weren't we? Then we heard the noises. But no, I suppose I don't remember much else. Tell me."

"No. I told you, I ain't going back there." She started to stand up but flopped back into the chair as if winded, stubbing out the cigarette with still shaking hands.

Helen seized on the moment. "Tell me, Sis, tell me what you remember."

Sis leaned forward, pulled the mangled pack of cigarettes from her overalls and lit up again. She hung her head and shook it slowly from side to side as if in defeat, blowing smoke out through her nose in a long slow stream. "Dunno if I can," she said simply.

"Do you remember much of it?"

"Every single moment, like it was seared into my brain. But it's not something I wanna be remembering. Or anything you wanna be knowing."

"I was there too, Sis. Please, tell me, it's my story, too."

Sis nodded silently, thoughtfully. "Yeah, I guess it is." She looked up towards the bridge, then at her watch. "Jeez, Stubby'll be here any minute." She glanced uncomfortably across at Helen and back to the bridge, then pulled a mobile phone from her pocket and jabbed at the numbers. "That you, Stubby? Listen, mate, don't come today. Nah, I ain't giving you the bloody day off. My sister's turned up out of the blue. Yeah, that one. Yeah, I'm taking the day off. Nope, I ain't bloody dying. You go get those parts, make sure the bloody thing gets fixed today, you hear me? Yeah, yeah, 'course I trust you. Yep, do that. Nope, don't do that. Nope, don't drop it off here. I don't want anyone coming here, so spread the word. Alright, mate, I'll leave it on the other side of the bridge. The rest is up to you. Yeah, 'course I'm alright. But thanks for asking anyway. Yeah, yeah. Leave a message. OK mate. Bye." She turned the phone off and shoved it back into her pocket.

27

They looked at each other, Helen with anticipation and Sis with reluctant resignation. Sis obviously didn't know how to begin, so Helen gave her time to think about it. "I could do with a coffee, a real coffee," she said, pointing to the remains of Sweetypie's untouched muddy concoction going cold in the cups on the table. "Have you got any real coffee?"

"Yeah. I got beans. You know, the kind you grind. I got one of them grinders. You like that stuff?"

"Oh yes, Sis, I like that stuff."

"I ain't had my breakfast yet. Can't get going without breakfast. You want something else besides coffee?" Helen nodded.

Sis went inside. Soon the delicious fragrance of fresh coffee and toast came through the window. She emerged with a laden tray. While they sipped and munched in silence, they fortified themselves physically and mentally for the conversation ahead.

Finally, Sis wiped crumbs from her mouth and said slowly, "So. The day Sweetypie was born." The words came almost painfully. "That woulda made you three and me six. We didn't even know Mum was pregnant, maybe she didn't know herself. She was so bloody fat, who could tell?" She looked away to the south where the mountains rose and fell as far as the eye could see. "Yeah, we were playing in the rainforest up behind the house when we heard the noises."

CHAPTER TWO

"What's that noise, Sissy?" Three year old Helen straightened up from the pile of stones she was collecting to build a castle. She wanted it to look like the one in the story book Dad had brought home from town the day before, but the stones were too round and wouldn't stack on top of each other.

Above her, six year old Sis sat on the lowest branch of the climbing tree, her legs swinging to and fro, doing nothing in particular. "Dunno." She lifted her head and listened intently. "Sounds like an animal in pain. Where're Prince and Lady?"

Helen called out, "Prince! Lady!" The German Shepherds bounded up to her and sniffed around the stones at her feet. "Here they are. It's not them. Ooh, there it is again! It's scary, Sissy. What is it?"

"Must be one of the ponies. Come on, let's go see."

Sis leapt from the low branch to land with springy legs on the steep slope and trotted down the hill, skirting ferns and bushes until she broke free of the rainforest just above the

29

house. She turned back to locate Helen who was slipping down the steep track on her bottom. "Come on, slow coach, keep up." She was about to go north towards the stables, but a howl erupted from directly below her, stopping her cold. She waited until Helen caught up, grabbed her by the hand and the two of them cautiously approached the house.

They slipped deftly through the narrow space between the mountain and the veranda railing at the back of the house and stopped. A strange noise came from the middle window along that side of the house. Mum's room.

First, a low moan seemed to slide out through the window, then an odd sort of squealing, weak and high pitched, mingled with the moan. The girls waited, frozen with fear. The moaning stopped. A moment later, the squealing also stopped, and then they heard a more familiar sound.

It was Mum sobbing.

Sis pulled Helen towards the window, but the curtains were drawn and she couldn't see in. She called out, "Mum? You alright Mum?" There was no response. The sobbing continued, but it sounded wrong to Sis, who was accustomed to Mum's weeping. There was a sort of helplessness, a sadness in the sound, a weariness that made Sis's stomach knot in a fear she didn't understand. Then the sobbing stopped and there was silence.

Sis was even more scared by the silence.

She dropped Helen's hand and ran around to the front veranda, opened the screen door and stepped into the passage, waiting a second while her eyes adjusted to the change in light. It was always dark and cool in here. She hadn't wiped her bare feet on the mat first, but it didn't matter, because Dad wasn't here to tell her off. He was out in the cane fields and wouldn't be back until lunch time.

She could see Mum's bedroom door open. She didn't like Mum's bedroom. It always smelled funny. Sweaty and rancid.

Dad never went in that room. He called it the pigsty. His bed was outside on the veranda. Sometimes, he would slam the door shut as he went past Mum's room. At other times, he would stand in the doorway and yell at her. Sis liked it better when he just slammed the door and walked away.

Sis took a few steps and stood in the doorway. The bedroom was full of shadows and the smell was particularly bad. Sis recognised sweat and urine and faeces, but there was something else, something earthy and cloying. She held her breath against it and stepped into the shadows, Helen just behind her.

Luisa Downing was sitting up in bed, her huge naked body undulating around her in waves of sweat-soaked fat. Her short black hair stuck to her scalp in greasy strands. She was leaning forward, her legs spread wide, her hands busy with something in front of her, oblivious to the presence of her two daughters. Her arms stopped moving, she lifted her head and Sis saw tears streaming down her face. Then she sighed heavily and fell slowly back onto the pillows, her arms flopping to her sides. Sis saw that she held the big sewing scissors limply in one hand and watched, mesmerised, as they slipped from the chubby fingers and clattered to the floor. There was blood on the blades.

The girls stared at it for a moment, then looked back up at Mum. She was very still. Too still. An alarm went off inside Sis's head.

They were accustomed to finding Mum in bed when they came back from playing on the mountain. Dad always said it was because Mum was a lazy fat wog slut, whatever that meant, but Sis knew it was because Mum cried a lot and didn't like Dad seeing her cry. It made him cross and sometimes he hit her when he was cross, and then she cried more. So it was alright for Mum to stay in bed and let the girls look after themselves, at least that way Dad didn't get cranky. Except when he came home at the end of the day and found his tea *wasn't ready. Then he yelled at Mum and she pulled the sheet over her head and cried again.*

But that was getting better because he was teaching Sis how to cook the chops on the wood stove and she was almost big enough to do it by herself, and he was teaching Helen how to pull a chair up to the sink and peel the potatoes for tea. It took her a long time and she was a bit scared of the sharp knife, but Dad said she was a good little cook and that she'd soon do it without him helping her. Then he would teach her how to mash the potatoes the way he liked them and they wouldn't have to get Mum out of bed when she wasn't feeling good, and everything would be better. Dad said so. Dad said his girls were the cleverest girls in the world and they liked that.

Dad taught them things all the time. He said Sis was almost old enough to use the big copper in the washhouse with the washing stick and the washing board that was almost as big as she was and the blocks of soap and the cubes of blue for the whites. But the best thing was when Dad showed them how to polish the furniture with the nice smelly wax. Sis did the top of the furniture and Helen did the legs, only they had to do it right or Dad would get cranky if he found streaks.

Mum didn't like doing any of those things. The girls weren't sure why, they thought it was fun, except for the wood stove, which was too hot and made their hands so slippery with sweat that they dropped things. But Dad said they could go for a dunk in the river after they finished and that was always fun.

So they knew it was alright for Mum to be in bed in the daytime, and it was alright for her to cry and stay out of Dad's way.

That was normal.

But this was not.

Sis gently pushed Helen aside and approached the bed. "Mum? What's wrong Mum? Should I go get Dad?" Silence.

She climbed onto the bed by her mother's head and shook her by the shoulders. "Mum, should I go get Dad?"

Luisa's eyes opened slowly and she stared up listlessly at the small face of her eldest daughter. She whispered hoarsely, "Mia bambina. Bella bambina."

"Don't talk that funny talk, Mum. Dad says you're not allowed to, it makes him cross. Should I go get him? Dad? Do you want me to go get him?"

Luisa's vision seemed to clear and focus, the question penetrated and she gasped and jerked. "No! Not him! Not the papa! Keep him away, keep him away!" A sob erupted from her, then a deep sigh as she turned her ashen, tearful face away, closed her eyes and whispered, "Mama very tired. I sleep now."

Sis heard the breathing change and knew Mum was sleeping. It was then that she looked down and saw that the sheets were wet and stained, and that something lay wrapped in a white towel between Mum's legs.

Helen clambered up onto the bed beside Sis and they stared at the bundle.

"What is it, Sissy?"

"Dunno for sure." She poked at it with her fingers. There was a tiny face with a little nose, a little mouth and two slits where eyes should have been. "I think it's a baby. But it don't look right. It's a funny colour." She poked it again. "And it ain't moving."

Helen pointed towards the placenta next to the baby and wrinkled her nose distastefully. "What's that? It's yucky, I don't like it."

Sis poked it. She didn't like it either. Something was sticking out of it. She reached down and took the end of the umbilical cord between her fingers. It had been tied off with a shoelace. She didn't understand any of this.

She held the cord up to show Helen, who recoiled from it. "Yucky, yucky! Make it go away! I don't like it!" Helen

33

backed away towards the edge of the bed until she was perched precariously, and then she tumbled backwards, her hands reaching out wildly for something to hold on to. As she fell, one hand found the end of the towel wrapped around the baby and gripped it instinctively. In a split second, Sis realised that the baby was about to follow Helen over the side of the bed. She leapt forward to stop it, but was too late and the momentum of her movement carried her over the side of the bed with Helen and the baby.

They lay in a tangled heap, Helen sprawled on her back, Sis above her, and the newborn infant sandwiched between them.

Sis felt a quiver under her, rolled off Helen and sat back. "It's moving," she said in amazement. Helen lay frozen in terror, her wide eyes only inches from the baby's head. Suddenly the little creature inhaled, a jerking wet sound that Helen responded to by thrusting it off her. It unravelled from the towel and hit the floor with a dull thud. A feeble cry rose up from it.

"It's alive, Helly. It IS a baby! Ooh, we've hurt it. Look, it's going all pink and – aaw, it's crying. Get up, come on, we gotta do something for it. It's so little."

"Did we squash it?" Helen pulled herself to her knees and gingerly touched the squirming baby.

"Yeah, I reckon we did."

The baby was crying lustily now. Sis touched its belly, seeing the end of the newly cut and tied cord without understanding what it was. "Feels cold. Maybe it doesn't like it out of the towel." She spread the towel on the floor and rolled the baby onto it. Helen saw what was intended and held the end of the towel over the squirming infant. Together, they rolled the infant in the towel until it looked the way they had first found it. It still cried, but it didn't sound so intense. They looked down at it, their mother temporarily forgotten, and thought about what they should do next.

"It smells bad in here, Sissy," Helen announced with wrinkled nose. She jumped up and ran from the room.

Sis heard a snuffle come from the bed. Mum. She left the baby crying on the floor and went to her mother. She was still sleeping, but colour had returned to her face and she was breathing deep and easy. In fact, she breathed like she always did when she was asleep. Yeah, Mum was alright. She was just tired, that's all. When she woke up, she'd be fine. Then Sis would tell her about finding the baby.

Sis turned back to the baby. The crying bothered her. She picked it up carefully and followed Helen out onto the veranda. They sat side by side on the top step and stared at their new sibling.

"Why is it crying, Sissy?"

"Dunno. Maybe it got a fright when it fell off the bed. Look, it's opening it's eyes."

Both girls watched in wonder as the tiny creature's eyes opened from a slit, then a bit more and even more, until it was looking right into Sis's eyes. It stopped crying.

Sis took a deep breath. "It's beautiful," she said, "it's looking right at me. Oh, what a little sweetypie." She looked deep into the baby's eyes and fell in love.

"Is it a boy puppy like Prince, or a girl puppy like Lady?" Helen asked, not able to take her eyes off the miracle before her.

"It's not a puppy, silly billy. It's a proper baby. Like you. Only littler."

"I'm not a baby. I'm this many," and she held up three fingers. "I'm a big girl."

Sis grinned at her. Helen was a big girl compared to the tiny infant in her arms. She began to unwrap the towel to inspect the baby. "I reckon it's a girl 'cos it hasn't got a soldier like Dad. See, it looks like us, only littler."

"She's so teeny-weeny. Oh, she's looking at me now. Hello baby." The baby wound a tiny fist around her finger and Helen also fell in love.

Sis wrapped her up again. "She's such a little sweetypie." With an instinct she didn't even begin to understand, Sis hugged her new sister tightly and began rocking backwards and forwards. "A real little sweetypie. Our little sweetypie." The crying eased and stopped. Sis looked down. "Sweetypie's asleep. Look how pretty she is, Helly. She's all pink and her hair is as white as a frangipani. Oh, she's sooooo pretty." She hummed tunelessly.

They sat there on the step, the three of them, in absolute contentment, Sis hugging and humming, Helen looking on and sometimes stroking the towelled bundle gently, Sweetypie safe and snug in the arms of her saviour and protector. They could have happily sat there all day, but for the rattle of hooves on the bridge.

Dad was coming home for lunch. He tied his horse to the post under the mango tree where the dogs were resting in the shade and approached the house. Sis stiffened and held the baby closer to her, not quite sure why she did so.

Dad stood at the bottom of the steps. "What have you got there?" he asked casually, lighting a cigarette and removing his sweat soaked hat. "Playing with your dolls, are you?" He climbed the steps and was about to pass them when his downward glance arrested his progress. He stared in disbelief, then his face darkened. "Girl or boy?" he asked.

"It's a girl puppy, Daddy, and she's a real little sweetypie," Helen answered in wide-eyed innocence.

Harry Downing froze for a moment, then with a sudden angry gesture he tossed his cigarette away and threw his hat onto his bed at the end of the veranda. The door slammed behind him and they heard him call out, "Luisa! Where are you? Oh, marymotherofgod, what a stench! Wake up! Wake up you slut!

36

Why didn't you tell me? A man gets drunk and too stupid to know what he's doing three times in his life and you spit out a brat every time. And it's another bloody useless girl. You can't even give a man a son. You're a useless fat bitch, no good to anyone. Don't you start the tears again! It doesn't do you any good. Get out of this pigsty and clean it up. Do you hear! Clean the bloody place up. I'll go eat with the men, but when I get back, you better have this place sorted out. You hear me?"

They heard the whack of knuckles on soft flesh and cringed back as Dad flew past them, untied his horse and galloped away.

Sis heard her mother's sobs, rose and went inside.

Standing at the bedroom door, she offered the baby in her arms to Mum and said encouragingly, "Don't cry, Mum, look what we found. She's real pretty, a real little sweetypie. Look." She brought the baby to Mum who reached out and took the bundle from her arms. Sweetypie woke suddenly and squealed. To Sis's astonishment, Mum manoeuvred the baby until it appeared to attach itself to her breast. "Whadya doing, Mum?"

"She's hungry, Sistina, she wants her milk."

"Milk? Outa that?"

"Si, mia cara. Like the calves and the foals." Mum wiped the tears from her face with the back of her hand and tried to smile at Sis.

"Oh. Hey, Helen, come see this. Sweetypie is drinking milk from Mum like she's a horse or a cow." They stood and watched. The suckling infant seemed to calm Mum down better than anything.

After a few minutes, Sweetypie slept and dropped off the breast. "Sistina, put her in Helen's old cradle, then come help me clean up before the papa gets home."

By the time they heard hooves on the bridge again, it was five o'clock and everything was in order. Mum had even dressed and was sitting on the veranda, but she began to shake uncontrollably as Dad approached. She needn't have been afraid. He walked past her as if she wasn't there. He went straight into the house where he stood silently over the cradle. After a moment, he called out to Sis, "Get yourself and Helen ready for a bath. Yeah, I know it's early but do it!"

Sis and Helen jumped to obey.

CHAPTER THREE

Sis suddenly stopped talking. Helen thought she was pausing to light another cigarette, but instead she jumped up and threw the smouldering butt over the banister, then leaned forward with her hands gripping the timber railing so hard that her knuckles turned white.

"Go on, Sis, I'm listening," Helen urged, but Sis ignored her and leaned forward as if she was gagging. For a brief second, Helen thought her sister was going to vomit. She rose and stood by her side, looking into the averted face, trying to understand what was happening. "Please ..."

"NO!" Sis spat the word out with a viciousness that made Helen flinch. She stepped away, trying hard to recall what it was that Sis seemed so afraid to remember, but this was obviously not her memory. It belonged to Sis alone.

"What happened next, Sis? What was so terrible that you can't speak of it?"

Sis turned to face her and Helen was shocked at the distressed eyes and pinched mouth fighting to control the twisted mask her face had become. "Let it be!"

"But why?"

"You don't wanna know, you don't want that in your head. Shit! If this is what you came back for, Helen, you're bloody mad." She lit another cigarette and inhaled noisily.

"I'm sorry. I knew it wouldn't be easy. But surely, after all these years …"

"I spent the better part of those years doing my best to forget the past, to get on with the business of getting up every morning and doing whatever had to be done, and I done a pretty bloody good job of it. Without any help from you!"

"Yes, but …"

"But you don't wanna stop, hey? No matter what it costs? I can see it in your face."

"No. I don't want to stop. I … I need to know. To explain a little more. Put another piece in the puzzle. To … to understand."

"What's to understand? He was a malicious bastard and no amount of talking about it is ever gunna change that. Or what he did to us."

They stood in rigid silence for a few seconds, then Helen asked, "Wouldn't it be a relief … to speak about it, out loud, in the open?"

"Jeez, you're bloody crazy." Sis was sucking on her cigarette as if it was a life support system. "No, it wouldn't be a relief. I already feel like shit just talking 'bout Mum. An' now you wanna go back through every sordid bloody detail of our lives with HIM!" She angrily stubbed out her cigarette and lit another quickly, her hands shaking.

"Please, Sis, I have to know."

Sis hung her head in defeat and muttered, "Damn you, Helen, damn you for coming back." She looked up and

40

searched Helen's face. "You're like a dog with a bloody bone, you are. You always were. You'd get something between your teeth and weren't nothing in the world gunna make you let go of it. You might look different on the outside but you ain't changed on the inside. So you just rock up here unannounced and expect us to talk away like it was the good ol' days, hey?"

"We don't have to do it all at once," Helen said, trying to placate her agitated sister.

"Oh, thank you, how kind of you. Can we take a tea break now?" Sis replied with bitter sarcasm. She took a deep noisy breath and turned her back to Helen. "I gotta take the harvester to the other side of the bridge. Stubby'll pick it up there. That way we won't be disturbed and god help us, I don't want no one overhearing any of this." She took her hat, shoved her feet back into the boots and walked heavily down the steps to where the suitcase lay on the grass. "You shouldna come, Helen, you shoulda let it be." Helen didn't respond. Sis looked up at her thoughtfully, drawing deep on the cigarette, her eyes shaded by the wide hat brim. The simple act of getting back to the business of the day had steadied her trembling hands. "You ain't gunna go away, are you? So how long you planning to stay?"

"I haven't decided yet. Is it a problem?"

Sis scoffed angrily as if Helen had said something patently stupid. "Look, Helen, I dunno if I ever got over you leaving the first time, but if you're just gunna stay for a while, stir things up and leave again, then go sooner rather than later. Alright? There's just so much a person can take, and I reckon I've taken more 'n most." She picked up the suitcase and placed it at the bottom of the steps. "As for Sweetypie and what your leaving again might do to her – well, we can figure that out when the time comes for you to go. But don't you go poking around," she added vehemently, emphasising her words by stabbing at

41

the air with her cigarette. "And stay outa my face. I got things to do."

She turned away and strode towards the big sheds. A moment later, Helen heard the sound of heavy machinery. The harvester appeared, Sis high atop it in a small cabin, steering effortlessly with one hand while the other rested on the open window, the ever present cigarette clutched loosely between her fingers. She did not look towards the house.

Sis was right, Helen thought, I am like a dog with a bone. Raymond used to say much the same thing. When she decided she wanted to do something or know something, she couldn't rest until she had what she wanted. And now she wanted to know what it was that Sis wouldn't tell her. She'd work at it, wait for the right moment, and try again later. She'd always been able to bring Sis around in the past. She hoped that, like herself, Sis might look different on the outside but had remained the same on the inside.

A sudden wave of hot fatigue washed over her. The confrontation had taken its toll. She sat for awhile and waited for it to pass, then rose wearily, collected her suitcase and went inside.

Helen stood inside the doorway while her eyes adjusted to the change in light and breathed in the scent of clean and fresh. Very Sis. That much hadn't changed. There was a faint hint of new paint as well, although she couldn't see where it came from. She looked down and saw white tiles where she expected polished timber floors.

She closed her eyes and pictured it the way it had been and suddenly she was seven years old, down on her knees, dipping the damp rag into the big flat tin of honey coloured wax, wiping it over the already spotless floorboards in large circles and then polishing with the dry rag. Polish, polish, polish until there were no streak marks and the light coming through the front door reflected back from the floor in golden rays. When Dad was out of the house, the three of them would put on their Sunday socks and skid up and down the slippery passage with squeals of disobedient delight.

Helen opened her eyes. The mahogany hall table supported a large vase of tropical flowers and the big gilt-frame mirror above it reflected the white paint and collection of small prints on the opposite wall. Just as she remembered it.

But something was different, askew, out of kilter. She felt it instinctively, but couldn't immediately pinpoint it.

Three wide oak doors off each side of the passage opened into large rooms, with the exception of the middle door on the left which had been her bedroom. That door was closed. The door at the end of the passage that had once opened into the kitchen was gone and ferns in hanging pots under a skylight replaced it. It looked as it should, except that …

What was it? Something in the balance of the passage had changed. She knew it was different, knew it in the same way she would know if the lines on her hand were to change. You wouldn't quite remember exactly how they used to be, you would just know they had changed. She gave herself a moment to focus on the feeling, but the answer eluded her. Perhaps it was just a change in energy. When she had last stood in this passage, the energy had been charged with uncertainty and fear. Now, it was peaceful, settled.

But no, it wasn't the energy. She sensed it was something physical, something dimensional. Perhaps it was because of the tiles or the skylight at the end of the passage.

It really had been too long. It didn't matter. She was exhausted. She let it go.

Dropping her suitcase, she turned into the first room on her right, the new kitchen that had once been the Front Room.

She well remembered this room as it had been fifty years earlier. It had always been formally called the Front Room, as if you could hear the capital letters when you said it. There

43

had been several big cane chairs, yellow cotton curtains, an ornate polished mahogany sideboard and coffee table, and a large Persian rug which had made it as comfortable as she had ever known a room to be as a child. It had rarely been used, though, as the veranda was where most of the living had taken place.

Now it contained every mod con imaginable, a country kitchen of some splendour with a round cane and glass table in the centre and four elegant cane chairs. As in the passage, white ceramic tiles replaced the timber floor, but the tongue-and-groove walls remained. Two recliners in front of a big screen TV took up one corner. An expensive sound system on shelving next to a glass fronted cupboard stacked with CDs filled another corner. A large modern split-system air conditioner dominated the space between the northern facing window and the back wall.

Helen opened the glass fronted cupboard and ran her fingers idly down the CDs. All classical music. Another surprise.

"She burned it down."

Helen spun around. She hadn't heard Sis return. She was standing in the doorway, hands on hips, watching her. The hat and boots were gone.

"The old kitchen?"

"Yep. Three times. '58, '67 and '75. Same cause every time. She sets the fat in the frypan alight and stands back to watch it because it's 'so PRETTY Sissy'. Shit! Came close to losing the lot the last time. Decided I'd better do something about it. Demolished the back of the house, turned it into a fernery and converted the Front Room into the kitchen. Look." Sis pointed upwards to the high ceiling. Helen looked up and counted eight fire sprinklers. "They work bloody good, too, saved our arses a few times already. She thought I'd turned them on so she could play in the water. Had a bloody ball, didn't she? Keeps asking me to turn them back on. Thank christ she doesn't understand the connection between them and the fire or she'd be lighting up regularly." She suddenly looked uncomfortable, as if she'd given too much of herself when that hadn't been her intention.

She looked over Helen's shoulder, strode past her to the sink and pulled a tall glass from the overhead cupboard. She filled the glass with water and drank it quickly without offering any to Helen, then put the glass into the dishwasher and walked back past her sister as if she wasn't there. She was back in control and saying, without words, I can take you or leave you Helen, I don't care. You can talk, I can talk, but don't forget, I'm the boss here, you're just a visitor, so know your place.

She took a key from a hook by the door, re-hatted and re-booted, and without another word, trotted down the front steps. Helen heard the Landcruiser start up.

Helen stood at the window and watched her sister drive toward the sheds. A hollow feeling inside her made her realise how much she cared that Sis didn't care. Or at least made a show of not caring. She thought, I have hurt her too deeply, why should she care. Sis wasn't lying when she said I meant nothing to her now.

She turned away from the window and picked up her suitcase, crossed the passage and opened the door to what had been her bedroom. She stopped in the doorway, uncertain of what she saw before her. Was she seeing the present or the past? It took a moment to sink in.

Her room had been preserved.

Every detail as she remembered it remained intact. The high single iron bed with the plain white damask bedspread, the dressing table with six drawers and the three-part mirror, her tortoiseshell brush and comb and a vase of fresh flowers on pristine white doilies, the round rug with six rings of different coloured green, the narrow wardrobe in the corner with the wall tapestry hanging next to it, the pretty white lace

45

curtains that floated briefly in the breeze created when the door opened.

No modern white tiles here. The floorboards were polished to a gleam. And on the bedside table was the eight sided glass and a jug of clean fresh water. That had always been Sweetypie's job before they went to bed at night. Fresh water on the bedside tables. Every night without fail.

It was a moment before she realised that the dressing table mirrors were missing from within their frames. Odd. But perhaps they hadn't survived fifty years of humidity as well as the rest of the room.

It all looked as fresh as it had been on the day she left. Not a trace of dust or mould could be seen and it smelled sweetly of the frangipani outside the window.

A memorial to a lost loved one. A loved one whose return was expected at any moment. The truth of it hit Helen hard and she felt a rush of emotion rise within her, but stifled it quickly. It was too difficult, especially on top of what she had just dealt with out there on the veranda. Why waste the energy, she instructed herself, particularly in this heat. There was enough to contend with here already.

She put her handbag on the dressing table, dropped the suitcase next to the bed and went to the south facing window. She touched the curtains, realising as she did so that the fabric was new, but a good match for the original, as were the bedspread and the recently painted walls. She looked out and saw the Moreton Bay Fig down by the river. It had looked huge to her as a child and it still looked huge to her now, its surface roots climbing the slope towards the house like giant serpents, its aerial tendrils hanging from the massive lower branches like long agile fingers trying to reach the water.

They used to fish from there, sitting on the wide surface roots, tossing their home-made lines into the deep waters of the river, worms in the tin at their feet, bread and fruit in the dillybag.

Simple farm girls who thought the world began and ended at the boundaries of their cane fields, and that everyone else lived just as they did. They had been in their teens before they understood that their own lives weren't normal.

She turned away and went to the wardrobe, wondering suddenly if Sis had preserved the contents as she had the rest of the room. She gasped softly as the door swung open to reveal her clothes exactly as she had left them. With disbelief, she examined the soft cotton, now limp with age, but still clean and fresh. Sis would have to wash and press them regularly to keep them like this. Two pairs of shoes at the bottom of the wardrobe were looking far less well preserved. She suddenly remembered a third pair - they weren't here. Where ...? Then she remembered. Of course. Slung over her shoulder that day on Ginger, and then at the top of the pole.

She pushed the memory away quickly. She was feeling a little short of breath and blamed it on the heat.

She went to the dressing table and opened each drawer. Before leaving the farm as a young woman of eighteen, she had never felt she lacked for anything in the way of clothes or shoes or female bits and pieces, but compared to her daughters' wardrobes, her things here looked pathetically poor and sad. Homemade cotton knickers, the elastic long ago perished, lay next to yellowed cotton socks and faded shorts that looked as if they would disintegrate if they were touched.

A white silk scarf that Dad had brought her from town when she was sixteen caught her attention. She lifted it carefully and held it up to the light, remembering how captivated Sis had been by its shimmering silver-whiteness. Dad had been angry when Helen had let Sis wear it. He'd torn it from around Sis's neck and told her she looked like a fool in it. Girls like her didn't wear such things, he'd said. Helen knew that when Dad said girls like her, he meant ugly girls, but Helen thought Sis was beautiful with her smooth olive skin and liquid brown eyes. But Sis didn't think she was beautiful. As Dad placed the scarf around Helen's neck, Sis had drawn the mask of indifference over her face and gone off to do something in the sheds as if it didn't matter. Helen had known that it mattered a lot, though, and that night she'd wrapped the scarf around Sis's neck and kissed her gently before they drifted into sleep tangled in each other's arms. After that, Sis often slept wearing the scarf, her fingers entwined in its softness.

Camphor blocks littered each drawer. Like the wardrobe, the contents of these drawers were tended to regularly. It was too much. Helen closed the drawers and looked up at the framed tapestry landscape next to the wardrobe.

The tapestry had faded but its colours were still legible. A sunlit valley with rows of green against the gold, a tree-lined road climbing the far hill to a blue house with red shutters. With a jolt, Helen recognised her own home in Tuscany. She took the tapestry from the wall and stepped nearer to the window, holding it in the light to examine it closely. Yes, there were the eight windows across the front of the villa, the portico above the red door, the low stone cottage to one side, the grove of olives trees below and the pencil pines escorting the road to the top of the hill.

She'd lived with this tapestry every day for the first eighteen years of her life, but had forgotten it the moment she'd left. It had meant nothing to her back then.

Turning it over now, she saw a name and a date scrawled in faded black ink. It was Nonna's name and the date was the year after Nonna had come to Australia.

How had it come to hang in her bedroom?

A wedding present to Mum perhaps?

Don't Mum, come back Mum, DON'T!

48

Helen felt the faintness return. She scrambled in her handbag for one of her many tablets, swallowing it without water. Tablets to make her sleep, tablets to keep her awake, tablets for the headaches, tablets for the dizziness, tablets to counter the side effects of tablets.

She wondered how long a person could go on swallowing pills like this before something serious gave way. Like your sanity.

Turning on the ceiling fan to create some air movement, she lay back on the bed and waited for the faintness to pass.

It passed. She poured herself a glass of water, rehung the tapestry and went to explore the rest of the house while Sis was out.

Where Mum's bedroom had been across the passage from her room, there now existed a modern office with computer, fax and modem. A yellow Post-It with the name of an internet service provider and a password had been taped to the base of the computer. Helen smiled. She had done the same to her computer at home so that she wouldn't forget her password.

Open shelves covered two entire walls and Helen noted how everything on one wall was collated, numbered, filed and neat as hell. Sis's touch was evident in everything. Strongly built shelving that wouldn't come down if you hung from it. A mahogany desk so highly polished that Helen could see her darkened face in it, the legs elaborately turned in just the way Dad had taught Sis. Even the chair was Sis-made with turned legs to match the desk. Books on computer software were lined up close to hand and below them were volumes on modern cane farming techniques. Two volumes had coloured bookmarks in them. Helen opened them and found to her great surprise articles written by Sis, and her name mentioned in the Foreword as a ground breaker in new cane farming techniques.

Sis had made her mark without the education she had so craved and without having ever left the farm. Helen felt a sense of personal pride swell within her, wondering at the same time what Sis might have achieved had she not been denied the basic right to education that their father had denied all of them. She put the two volumes back with satisfaction.

The second wall of shelving held National Geographic magazines and books, mostly travel books. The National Geographics went back to the 60's and the travel books encompassed the planet. Testament to unfulfilled dreams. A born traveller who had never left home.

She went into the third room on the northern side of the house. It had been the formal dining room, never used as far as Helen could remember, with a large cumbersome table, eight straight backed chairs and heavy red velvet drapes that had always smelled musty. Very Victorian and completely unsuited to the tropics.

It was now a modern bathroom, big enough to swing a cat and its kittens in, with extraction fans in the ceiling to keep the room from becoming a mould trap and a washing machine and tumble dryer close to the window. Most of the back wall above the bath had been cut out, opening the bathroom directly into the fernery which Helen could see went the full length across the back of the house. The display of tropical orchids, ferns and plants was impressive. A bath in the rainforest.

The passage opened directly into the fernery. It was cool and sweet. As a child, Sis had always made a fuss about the plants they found on the mountain and around the river. Here, she had developed her natural eye for beauty into a stunning display. Helen shared her passion for plants, but she had nothing like this in Tuscany. She wondered how many other people had ever seen this and suspected very few, if any, even knew about it. Most people would never think such beauty possible of tough old Sis Downing.

She crossed the passage, looked through the doorway of the back south-facing room and knew it was still Sweetypie's bedroom immediately. Pink double bed with a pink mosquito net hanging from the pink ceiling, pink furniture, pink curtains, walls, rug and floor tiles. Even the split-system air conditioner in the wall was pink. Helen wondered how Sis had managed that. A big-screen television and DVD player took up one corner in front of a recliner covered in pink cabbage roses to match the curtains. A large full length poster of Fat Cat was fixed to one wall between laminated prints of Miss Piggy and the Teletubbies. An assortment of pink underwear, outerwear and the remnants of Helen's gifts lay scattered across the floor amongst the discarded jewellery and everyday toys. Very Sweetypie.

She walked past her own room and went into the front bedroom. Sis's bedroom, but nothing like she remembered the austere room of their childhood.

It was white. Pristine. Immaculate. Downright virginal. No objects on the hand-carved Italianate dressing table from which the mirror had been removed, and only a single reading lamp on the bedside table. White lace at the windows. White tiles and a silver and white rug on the floor.

Not a mirror to be seen. Helen realised there hadn't been one in the bathroom either. The only mirror in the house seemed to be the old gilt frame mirror in the passage. Odd that Sis had kept that when she obviously couldn't tolerate a mirror anywhere else.

Helen shook her head in disbelief at the sight of the bed. Instead of the replica of her own neat little iron bed that she remembered sharing with Sis on so many occasions, there was now an ornate monster taking up the centre of the room. Mahogany. Four poster. Richly carved. King size at least. Four pillows across the top of the bed, cushions scattered atop the pillows, white brocade, white tassels, white embroidery, white lace, a white silk embroidered bedspread, and draped from the four high bedposts was the most elaborate mosquito net Helen had ever seen or could ever have imagined. Layers of luxurious frills, lace and netting, falling, draping, cascading in a shower of froth and romantic decadence. It would have done justice to any romance novel cover.

And everything was spotless. Sis had always been obsessively houseproud, even as a little girl, and with good reason. If Dad felt it hadn't been done well enough, they had to do it again, and again and again, until it met with his approval. If it was Helen's chore, he'd just tell her to repeat it. But if it was Sis's chore, she'd get a beating, told she was a lazy wog slut like her mother and made to repeat it many times over, long after it had been done to anyone else's satisfaction. He'd taken a vicious pleasure in watching her scrub a triple-scrubbed floor again. So she'd learned quickly to do it well, better than well. No streak marks on the polished floors, no finger marks on the white walls - she scrubbed, polished, cooked and arranged to within an inch of her life, and one beating in particular, the last and most vicious beating which Helen suddenly remembered with an unpleasant shock, had almost taken her to that point.

She quickly turned her mind away from that memory and instead thought how difficult it must be to maintain all this whiteness. She wondered if Sis still bathed several times a day and slept with clean white socks on her feet so that she wouldn't soil the sheets.

Helen was certain that no one other than Sweetypie had ever seen this room. Not even Bill Stewart. She knew no one would believe it of Sis, even if they did see it, for there was opulent sensual femininity here amongst the pristine decor.

And a longing fulfilled, unlike the travel books in the office.

I'm gunna have a pretty room like yours when I grow up, Helly. Bugger Dad. Just you wait. It'll be even prettier.

Built-in cupboards lined one wall, the doors peculiarly padded with white vinyl and silver knobs. Helen was suddenly curious about what Sis kept behind those doors and opened one. She almost reeled back with the shock of what she saw.

A vision of shimmering snowy softness - evening dresses, day dresses, tailored suits, blouses, even an elaborate wedding dress complete with veil and tiara – gorgeous clothes with designer labels in small sizes that could never have fitted Sis – silk, lace, linen - the very best that money could buy. And every single garment in white. White on white. Sparkling, soft, diaphanous white.

Each garment appeared to have its own pair of shoes below it, dainty shoes with jewelled trimmings, bows, straps and delicate heels. Shelving above the hanging garments held hats, bags, gloves and shawls. White upon white upon white.

The shimmering white scarf of their childhood had become an obsession in adulthood.

Helen opened the next door, and the next and the next. The same behind each door. She took her reading glasses from her pocket and inspected the clothes more closely, realising they represented every decade of the last fifty years. And it was obvious that none of them had ever been worn because the labels, receipts and shipping instructions were still attached. She saw catalogue names on some of the earlier labels and internet mailing addresses on the more recent purchases. Sis had never been further than the local town, but she shopped all over the world.

So was this the secret inside the house that Sis had been afraid she would find?

Poor Sis, Helen thought, poor dear Sissy. I have been wearing beautiful clothes like this for forty years without a thought, but she could only dream of such things, could only possess them in secrecy to look at, touch and adore.

She wondered briefly what a psychiatrist would make of all this. But then, what would a psychiatrist make of any of them? That was one profession she had carefully avoided all her life.

She was curious about where Sis kept her everyday clothes and went to the mirrorless dressing table. Yes, there they were, neatly folded inside the drawers – worn overalls, shorts, singlets, socks, baggy cotton underpants, the trappings of a hard working life. She assumed that the oilskins and heavier items for the Wet Season would still be downstairs on hooks under the house, as they had always been. You didn't bring rain soaked items into the house to go mouldy, you left them to air – an ingrained part of growing up in the tropics that she still practiced to some extent in Tuscany.

Three wardrobe doors remained unopened. The first revealed floor to ceiling shelving that stored accessories, jewellery, scarves and lingerie. Delicate lingerie that appeared to have been handled, even washed, but never worn as they were sized for a much slighter woman than Sis. Helen examined some of the jewellery and estimated there must be many thousands of dollars worth lying unsecured here. Still, who would think it of Sis. Her persona kept it safer than a bank vault.

The bottom shelf was stacked with expensive makeup, none of it opened, and dominated by lipsticks sealed in their original packaging. All red. Dozens and dozens of bright red lipsticks. Sis's skin had never known the feel of makeup and lipstick was something she had openly sneered at in her youth. Helen was truly taken aback, but suddenly remembered catching a teenage Sis in church staring at the girls who wore lipstick and thinking at the time that she'd detected envy in her sister. When she'd broached the subject to Sis later, Sis had merely said those girls looked like trollops, which was a word Dad had used to describe girls who wore makeup on Sundays. At the time, neither of them had known what a trollop was, but the way Dad said it, it must be bad.

Helen opened the last two doors together, gasped and took a step back. For a moment she couldn't make sense of it, then she moved forward for a closer look.

A pair of elaborate silver candelabra on a shelf stood sentinel on either side of a collage of photos. Photos of Helen. Helen and Raymond, Helen and the girls, Helen and a host of famous people, but mostly just Helen, at her most glamorous, her most elegant, her most public. Paparazzi shots.

Sis was lying when she'd said she wouldn't have recognised Helen if Sweetypie hadn't done so first. She would have known exactly who it was standing at the foot of the stairs.

The candelabra were covered in many layers of wax. They were not merely for show. These candles had been burned often.

It was an altar. An altar to Helen. She was shocked and deeply touched.

Helen recognised most of the photos, but a few were unfamiliar to her. She realised she was looking at pictures cut from magazines – Woman's Weekly, New Idea, Woman's Day, Cleo, Cosmo, Vogue, etc. Under each photo was neatly written the year it was published, nothing more. Helen traced the photos back to 1961, a photo of herself and Raymond with a Hollywood screen goddess at the opening of their Paris nightclub.

Under the altar were shelves stuffed with bundles of letters. She took a bundle and with a jolt recognised her own handwriting. She took another bundle. The same. She counted them in silence. Twelve letters per bundle. Each bundle neatly tied with white ribbon. She didn't need to count the bundles to know how many there were. Fifty. They were the letters she had written to Sis every month since she'd left home. And not one of them had been opened.

"What the hell!" Sis roared behind her, almost knocking Helen down as she flew past her to slam the doors shut. Slam, slam, slam! Then she turned on Helen, her eyes aflame, her fists clenched, the violation more than she could bear.

"Sis, I'm sorry, I'm..." Helen backed away, for a split second really afraid that Sis would hurt her. Then she saw the embarrassment and the confusion behind the anger and reached forward as if to put a reassuring hand on Sis.

Sis recoiled. " Get away from me!" She unclenched her fists and glared furiously, seeming to loom over Helen even though Helen was the taller of the two. "I told you not to poke around. This ain't your place no more. It's mine! Mine and Sweetypie's, and you got no right. Jeez!" She was breathing heavily, fighting to regain control of her emotions. Then suddenly, unexpectedly, she sagged, shaking her head from side to side. Her next words came almost in a whisper. "You shouldna done that, Helen. You shoulda minded your own business."

Helen felt a sudden surge of shame. Her snooping had desecrated probably the only intimate part of Sis's life. She wanted desperately to make amends. "Sis, I didn't mean to pry, it was just ... such a surprise ... this..." she indicated the bed and the furniture, "...all this. It is beautiful, so very beautiful."

Sis took in a quick breath and the anger evaporated. Just like that. Helen was finding it hard to keep up with Sis's sudden changes of emotion and struggled to understand what she had said to change the mood so suddenly. Then she remembered a much younger Sis staring at the white scarf with one simple word on her lips. Beautiful. That was the key. She followed up on it quickly. "The furniture is gorgeous. The bed is sensational. You made it yourself, of course? And the clothes! I've never seen such divine clothes."

"Yeah?" Sis responded doubtfully.

"Yes, Sis. Why, if I'd known you loved such exquisite things, I would have sent you some from home – from Italy. From all over Europe. From everywhere. Oh, I wish I'd known!" As soon as she said it, Helen knew she'd gone too far.

Sis raised suddenly hard eyes to meet Helen's. "Well, you didn't, did you? If you'd come home, you mighta known. But you didn't."

And there it was. The mountain, the ocean, the abyss that lay between them.

"Yes," Helen said quietly, feeling like a chastened three year old. "But I tried to stay in touch … the letters…" It sounded feeble and it was.

"Stay in touch? Don't bullshit me, Helen. I got the phone on in '71. Bill said he gave you the number but you didn't ring, did you? Not a damn word from you."

"Sis, I thought about it, but…"

"… but you had a life and you didn't want me and Sweetypie spoiling it for you. That was it, wasn't it? You was ashamed of us."

"No, Sis. Never. It wasn't like that at all. Why do you think I kept writing, even when you didn't write back? I didn't want to lose you completely."

"Lose us? You never bloody lost us, we didn't go nowhere, we always been right here. You gave us up. That's what you bloody well did!"

"No, that's not it at all." Feeling unable to explain herself in the heat of the moment, Helen held up the bundle of letters in her hand. "You didn't read any of these letters. But you didn't throw them away."

"I kept them. So what?"

"Why, Sis?"

The mask pulled and twisted with unaccustomed emotion. She didn't answer immediately and Helen didn't push her.

She let Sis do it in her own time. When the reply finally came, it was in a cold hoarse voice.

"I read the first one," she said, "the one you sent from Sydney. Like I told you, it arrived the day of the memorial service. I read your letter, maybe a hundred times, and it made me happy and it made me angry. Happy 'cos you'd got out, you escaped. Angry 'cos I knew I was trapped here forever and there weren't no choice about that with Sweetypie to look after. But mostly it gave me a pain," she tapped her chest, "here. 'Cos you weren't here with me, see? A letter meant you weren't here. So when the next one came, I put off reading it 'cos I knew it meant you weren't coming home yet, and the next one and the next one, til one day I realised I was never gunna read any of them. But I couldn't throw them away, 'cos … they was all I had of you." She paused, thinking something through, her intense eyes never leaving Helen's face. "But you didn't know I hadn't read them, 'cos you told me just today about this family we got, like I didn't know about it. So you didn't tell the truth in them letters, did you?" She let the accusation hang for a moment between them. "So what bullshit did you write?"

Confronted with her own deceitfulness, Helen looked away, the shame that had haunted her for fifty years rising up like bile in her throat. "I wrote," she said, trying to explain but knowing it was too soon for Sis to fully understand, "about where we'd been, Raymond and I, what we'd done, what new business we'd bought, about the birth of the girls, what they were doing - a child-raising travelogue really. Impersonal when I think about it now, but at the time I believed I was being … protective."

"Protective? Of what?"

"Of you and Sweetypie."

"That don't make sense, but shit," she said, her gaze relaxing, "it don't matter now. Too much water under the bloody bridge for it to matter anymore." Sis was regaining control of herself, the mask settling back into its harsh cold lines.

"It matters, Sis. But why didn't you write back, even a few words? I always put a return address on the back of each letter. Believe it or not, I looked for a letter from you almost every day of my life. Why didn't you write?"

Sis opened her mouth to answer, closed it, then tried again. "Because I had nothing to write about. Every day here is the same as the day before. So what should I write? That we blew out the candles? That she got the sickness again? That she had another nightmare? Nah. I had nothing to say. Besides, if I had written that something was wrong, that I was going stir crazy in the Wet, that Sweetypie was my reason for living but sometimes I wished us both dead, would it have made any difference? Would you have come home?"

Helen lowered her head in shame. "No, probably not."

"And you never gave a street address on the back of your letters, always a postal address. I figured that meant that you didn't want me turning up unexpectedly. True?"

Helen sighed, contrite at confronting her own betrayal. "True." She felt the need to repeat her apology, "I am so sorry Sis. I saw you looking at the house when we were outside, like there was something here you didn't want me to see. I'm truly sorry I poked around when you especially asked me not to. This is your personal space and I have violated it. More than anyone else in the world, I should know better."

Sis was suddenly calm. Too calm. If Helen had thought Sis had been angry because her secret had been exposed, in this instant she knew instinctively that this was not the secret that Sis feared being discovered. She had dismissed it too quickly.

The hairs on Helen's arms tingled and she wondered why she felt so disturbed.

Sis reached for a cigarette, then put it away. No smoking inside the house.

Helen suddenly remembered something Sis had said earlier. "Did you really wish yourself and Sweetypie dead?"

"Yeah. Sometimes."

Helen took a step closer to Sis and looked into her face. She needed to begin the real apology, the apology she had come all this way to make. It wouldn't happen with just a sentence, the damage was too big, too deep. But she had to make a start. She'd been imagining the words for fifty years, but when they came, they came uneven, unoiled, like a gate rusted with age and neglect. "I'm sorry, Sis. I shouldn't have done it. I'm sorry."

Sis thought she was apologising again for being nosey. She pushed the last of the wardrobe doors shut and said easily, "What the hell. I don't give a shit."

"No, I mean I am sorry for leaving you. For leaving you here alone with Sweetypie, for … deserting you."

Sis snorted with disdain. "Well, one of us shoulda had a life, Helen, it may as well have been you, so don't go beating yourself up about it. Alright?"

Was this forgiveness? Helen wasn't sure. It didn't feel like forgiveness. It felt like indifference.

Sis reached for the packet of cigarettes again. Her need was urgent. She turned her back on Helen to go outside, but paused in the doorway to fling over her shoulder, "No more sticking your nose into stuff that's none of your business. You got that this time?" She strode away before Helen could answer, but the point had been made.

Helen went into the kitchen and helped herself to a cold drink from the fridge. When she joined Sis on the veranda, a six pack of chilled beer sat on the table, the first bottle already consumed, the second well on the way. She took her place in the other chair and wondered where to go from here.

Sis drank and smoked in silence, staring fixedly out over the cane fields to the ocean. Helen wondered if it was normal

60

for her to get into the beer so early in the day. It was barely nine o'clock.

The silence began to feel like punishment. She wanted to change it's direction. She opened her mouth to say something, but Sis cut her off abruptly with, "Give it a rest, Helen."

So she leaned back in the chair and tried to relax, her body sagging in the heat. She closed her eyes and let her mind go back to the last time she had seen her sisters, the house, the mountains. It had been raining hard and the house had dissolved into the rain as she'd headed up into the rainforest, the mud squelching under the hooves ...

She felt something cold being pushed into her hand. "You look bloody crook, get this into you." Sis was standing over her. The cold thing in her hand was a stubby of beer. Was that concern in Sis's face? If it was, it disappeared as soon as it was recognised. Sis sat down again. "Thought you were gunna cark it for a moment, you went white as a bloody sheet."

Without thinking, Helen brought the beer to her lips and sipped. It was icy cold and as delicious as she could ever remember a beer to be. She drank slowly until she'd emptied the bottle. After a moment, she felt a little energy return.

Sis was watching her out of the corner of her eye. "You sick or something, Helen? Is that why you've come back? One of those last-journey-home-before-you-die things?"

"No. I'm not sick. Or at least, nothing that will kill me. I just don't sleep well."

"Yeah? Well, I don't have that problem. I work til I drop. That's the trick. Wear yourself out good and proper. Get yourself too bloody exhausted to think about anything."

"You can't keep that up all the time, Sis. You must have times when you can't help but think about ... things."

"Not if I can bloody help it. Takes a bit of practice but I got it down pat."

"So you never think about me, about us, all of us here together all those years ago."

"Only when I get those letters of yours, but it don't last long. Jeez, I run the biggest family owned cane property in the Far North, it's not like I got nothing to do."

"Does that mean you have forgotten it all, Sis, wiped it from your mind?"

Sis thought about that. "It's here," she said, pointing briefly to her head, "I just don't get it out and look at it any more." She swigged from her third bottle.

"Have you forgotten about us in those last days."

"Depends what you wanna remember, don't it?"

"Well, for instance, what is the very last thing you remember about me all those years ago, Sis?"

Without hesitation, as if the memory had been held and cherished, Sis said, "The back of you and Ginger disappearing into the rainforest, up the track, like you just melted into the trees. I kept looking for you, but you was gone. I still see that sometimes, when the light is just right and the air is heavy and hot after a lot of rain."

The emotion behind the words caught Helen off guard. She looked at Sis with open astonishment. Sis pretended not to notice and continued. "It took a month for the river to drop low enough for anyone to get up here. I heard hooves on the bridge, like when we was kids, and I looked out, expecting to see you and Ginger, but it was Sarge and a couple of his boys. He thought you was here, that you'd made your way back. I told him you hadn't come home. He said you'd disappeared from the hotel where everyone was holed up, no one had seen you leave, and they'd all figured you'd gone home, found some way to get through the floods, a boat or something, and come up over the mountain. When he saw you wasn't here, he said you must have come a cropper. Sorry, he said, but he wasn't. Then he got into me about … him. Kept wanting to cross check my story against yours. Kept saying it didn't sound like the old bastard at all, like he knew him better than we knew him because they was mates."

Sis leaned forward and dragged deeply on her cigarette. Helen sensed she hadn't finished and waited patiently. "I been wondering about something all these years. I been wondering what happened. I wanna know. 'Cos it never made sense to me, see? I never could figure out what happened between you leaving here and then running off that changed everything. It shoulda been so simple, like we planned it." She turned her cold gaze on Helen. "So tell me, Helen, tell me what happened after I waved you goodbye. I was sure you'd get into town alright, as long as you went high enough to clear the waterhole and then stuck to the ridges all the way."

Helen leaned back, kicked her sandals off her sweating feet and remembered. It wasn't hard, the going back, even after fifty years. After all, she had been rehearsing this part for two years, ever since that promise she'd made to Raymond to go back and make it right.

She'd had plenty of time to put the fragments of memories together, to retrieve details from that place in the back of the mind that stores them safely in the little pigeon holes of the subconscious, to examine them, juggle them and join them to make the memory whole and the telling of it complete.

CHAPTER FOUR

"Take Ginger, he's sure footed, he'll get you through."

They surveyed the scene before them. The cyclone had left little remaining of the stables, but the house and equipment shed which were tucked into the side of the mountain remained intact. They could hear the ponies whinnying nervously inside the shed.

Debris from the rainforest lay scattered across the expanse of muddy grass down to the river. The bridge had disappeared completely and the water was already halfway up the slope to the house. It flowed fast and deep and there was more to come.

Even though the wind had dropped to a flapping breeze, the rain continued to pelt down and they could see little beyond the flooded river. But they could see enough to know that every cane field in the district was flattened and submerged. There would be no crop this season.

Sis helped Helen into the oilskins. "Go right up to the waterhole, Helen, that way you'll clear the river, then across to Stewart's Ridge and follow the road in from there. You'll be safe that way. Stay clear of the flats. I reckon it'll take several days for them to drain, the way this rain is still coming." Her hands trembled.

Helen, steely eyed, took the trembling hands in her own and held them tight. "I know what to do," she said, "don't you worry about me. It's you that has to get it right. Can you do it?"

"Yeah, 'course I can." Sis didn't sound as convincing as she hoped.

Helen gripped her by the shoulders. "Sis! You have to do it just right. Everything we talked about, can you remember it all? Can you do it?"

Sis straightened her shoulders and pushed Helen away from her. "Get going," she said, "you worry about what you gotta do, I'll worry about what I gotta do. Alright?"

"Yes, alright."

Sweetypie flung open the screen door and bounced towards them. "Cyclones are fun!" she announced, her mouth smeared with biscuit crumbs. "EEEEEE!" she squealed, mimicking the scream of the wind. "EEEEE."

"Sweetypie!" Sis's nerves were on edge. "Quiet! We've had enough noise. And don't pout. Go down to the washhouse and clean your face. Go on, go!"

Sweetypie stopped at the top of the steps. "Where you going, Helly?"

"Into town, darling."

"Oh, liquorice, liquorice! I want liquorice!"

"Sure darling, I'll bring you liquorice." Helen waited until Sweetypie had disappeared under the house before turning to Sis and pulling her into a fierce hug. "It'll be over soon," she said, " and then you'll see, we'll be free and happy and no one will ever hurt us again. I promise. Alright?"

"Yeah." Sis returned the hug. "Be careful and get back as soon as you can." As Helen reached the bottom step, Sis suddenly cried, "Money! You got any money on you? You gotta bring some liquorice back for Sweetypie."

Helen ran back up the steps into the house and took a pound note from Dad's money pot in the kitchen. She shoved it into the coat pocket but it went straight through. The other pocket was also torn. She needed something to put the money in so that it wouldn't fall through.

She went into Mum's room, skirted around the bed with averted eyes and opened the wardrobe door. She knew there was a purse somewhere, a black one, she'd seen Sis use it once when Dad had bronchitis and he'd sent her into town to shop. She looked in the wardrobe and the dressing table. Nothing. She rummaged through the chest of drawers, still feeling that strange disturbance of the heart whenever she touched any of Mum's things.

She didn't find the black purse, but found instead a brown leather handbag tucked away in the back of the bottom drawer, wrapped in a black lace shawl that Helen had never seen before. Mould had attacked both the shawl and the bag over the years, but the bag was still useable. She flicked the corroded catch open, shoved the pound note in, pushed the bag into the pocket of the coat and went back outside.

Sis watched nervously as Helen trudged through the mud to the shed, a pair of shoes slung over one shoulder to keep them clean for town, and waited until she emerged with Ginger saddled. He was jumpy, having been spooked by the cyclone. "Be gentle with him!" she called out. "Don't let him throw you!" She knew Helen had never been thrown from a horse in her life, but she needed to say it anyway, as if the saying would invoke protection for her.

Helen mounted the pony, rain pouring from her wide-brimmed hat, her wet oilskins hanging heavily down the pony's flanks, her small, bare muddied feet sticking out below. She tied the shoes by their laces to the saddle horn, turned Ginger towards the cubby track and waved to Sis.

"Be careful!" Sis called again, waving back. "And hurry home!"

The steep track was awash, rivulets of flood water cutting gutters across the narrow path, but Ginger knew this track better than any of the ponies. Helen only had to give him his head and gentle him on. He picked his way up through the saturated rainforest until they cleared the waterhole and reached the ridge where it started to become more difficult.

She knew the way across the mountain top to the Stewart's place, but in this heavy rain it was impossible to pick out the usual landmarks. At one point she reined Ginger in and looked around her carefully. For a second she thought she might be lost and felt a flicker of panic run through her, but the thought of Sis and Sweetypie and what they had done and what they still had to do came rushing at her and there was no room, no time for panic.

If she didn't do this right, they could lose everything.

With courage born of fierce determination, she pushed on, heading north as the morning became afternoon and the watery light began to wane, until she came to the break in the ridge where the boundary of Stewart's place began. She turned east and followed Stewart's Ridge down until she saw a windowless house at the base of the slope, then a second house with its veranda hanging in tatters, and a third with its roof gone and she knew she was almost there. Many hours of riding after the sleepless night had exhausted her, but she forced herself out of the slump she'd fallen into, berating herself for feeling weak and tired. She thought, not long now, it'll soon be over and then I'll be home safe with Sis and Sweetypie and no one will ever hurt us again.

Urging Ginger on, she rode down to the flats, despite Sis's warning, for it was impossible to find the road to town from Stewart's place under the sheet of water spread out before her.

Total devastation confronted her wherever she looked. It was worse than she could have imagined. Whereas she had been protected to some extent from the full ferocity of the wind by the mountain behind her house and high enough to escape the flooded river, these timber houses on the flats, some no more than shanties, had taken the full force of the winds and floods. They lay scattered across the flats, roofless, de-walled, water up to the roofline in some while even those highset houses still standing had water washing through them.

People in small boats or on pieces of floating timber paddled their way through the wreckage, looking for whatever they could salvage. Ginger, slowed to an awkward walk by the water swirling around his body, shied as dead animals and debris floated past him. Helen held the reins firmly and nudged him on until she saw the hotel in the distance.

The three storey hotel was built on a raised area in the centre of town with only a few inches of water through the lower floor. The police station was further down the road, a highset Queenslander which stood above the floodwater. She tethered Ginger to the post outside the hotel and waded through the water to the police station. She left the shoes, knowing they would be a waste of time until the flood waters receded.

Sarge was standing on the veranda, taking a break and watching the town, his town, begin to put itself back together. He leaned his lanky frame wearily against the veranda post. It had been a bad night, the day had held horrors of its own and he knew it was far from over yet. Holding a cup of tea in one hand and the inevitable cigarette in the other, he looked down at the bedraggled figure knee deep in water and pushed his hat back on his forehead. "Young Helen Downing, is that you? What the hell ...?" He dropped his cigarette into the flood and met her halfway up the stairs, catching her around the waist as she suddenly sagged with exhaustion. "Girl, what are you doing here? How the hell did you get through? What ...?"

"It's Dad," she said, weary but well rehearsed, "he's gone." Suddenly her knees gave under her and she began to tremble violently. It looked to Sarge like a case of shock, but Helen knew her nerve was threatening to fail her.

"Gone? What do you mean, gone?" He pulled her up to the veranda and called out, "Kath, get out here! It's young Helen Downing." Sarge's wife appeared at the door and immediately sized up the situation.

"Oh my dear, what has happened? Oh you look terrible. How did you get here? Everybody's cut off everywhere. Oh my dear ..."

"She said Harry's gone." They helped her inside and lowered her onto a kitchen chair. Around her were signs of the recent crisis – broken glass from louvres shattered by the fierce wind, torn curtains and waterlogged flooring. But the signs of recovery were also apparent. Sarge's three teenage daughters wielded mops and buckets while his two sons nailed strips of timber over the broken windows to keep the rain out. The stove was fired up with wood from the watertight tin wood-box in the corner and a large black kettle boiled water from the store of buckets lined up against the kitchen wall, their tin lids tied down with rope to prevent debris from contaminating the contents. They had prepared well, they were safe and there wasn't anything here that couldn't be mopped up, dried out or repaired. They were lucky.

Kath called to one of her daughters to get dry clothes and make young Helen a cup of tea. She peeled the oilskins from Helen and led her into a bedroom. Between them, Kath and her other two daughters changed her into dry clothes and wrapped a light blanket around her shaking body. Helen was grateful for the time it took and for the hot cup of tea because it gave

69

her a chance to gather her wits and her courage. When Kath called Sarge in, she was ready.

He pulled a chair up to the bed. "Alright girlie, tell us what happened."

"Dad's gone, Sarge." Her voice was a whisper of fatigue. She hoped it sounded like grief. "He tried to cross the bridge and got washed off. We tried to get to him, but he got carried away so fast. We saw him go under but he never came up." She looked Sarge in the eye with a bravado that was barely skin deep.

Sarge looked her right back in the eye. "What was he doing trying to cross the bridge in the middle of a cyclone? He knows better than that."

Helen's mouth opened and stayed open. This was not supposed to happen. She was supposed to tell her story, Sarge was supposed to be sympathetic and then he was supposed to go look for Dad and find what was left of him in the river. She would go home to Sis and Sweetypie and it would all be over. She didn't know what to say. She hadn't prepared for doubt or questions.

She dropped her gaze, unable to answer. Sarge's eyes narrowed. He lit up another cigarette and said soothingly, "Come on now, I know you've been through a lot, young Helen. Just calm down and think. What was he doing trying to cross that damn bridge in a bloody cyclone?"

"I ... I don't know. He was ..."

"Sarge," Kath admonished, "give her a minute to collect herself. She must have been through a terrible time to get here. Look at her, poor thing, she's still shaking." Sarge, knowing who the real boss was in his house, sat back and gave Helen an appraising look.

"Sorry, girlie. It's been pretty hard on us all and we can't do much more until the water goes down. Now, just take a deep breath and try to tell me exactly what happened."

70

Helen couldn't look him in the eye at all now. She would have to wing it and he was smart enough to detect that. She was scared. She stammered, "He went outside because ... because we could hear the ponies and ... and he thought the stables were going and they might run off ... might run off so he went out to the stables and got the ponies and took them into the shed but one of them ran off and he ... he ... he followed it over the bridge and ... and the water was around his knees and then a tree or something came rushing down in the water and knocked him off and he got carried away and ..."

"Alright, young Helen, I get the picture." But the look he gave her was less than convinced. "Here, stop that shaking now. I'm sorry. I didn't mean to upset you. Just trying to get the picture straight, understand? I'll get someone out there to look for him as soon as I can. Don't you worry now. Harry Downing is a champion swimmer, if anyone can survive that, he can. What about your sisters? Where are they?"

"At home."

"Anyone hurt there?"

"No."

"How did you get through?" She told him. "Blimey! I don't know anyone else that could have done that in these conditions. You must have been mighty determined to get here to help your father, hey?" He was watching her intently. She felt it like an accusation. He suddenly patted her trembling hand. "You're a brave lass and one hell of a horsewoman. Don't you worry. If Harry came off the bridge like you say," he paused almost imperceptibly as she flicked her gaze up through her lashes and dropped it quickly again, "he'll be alright. He's a tough old bastard. Now, you rest, Kath and the girls will look after you and I'll go see what I can do." He rose and left.

Had he believed her? Was it over?

She allowed Kath to fuss around her, feed her and bed her down. "You sleep dear, don't you worry about a thing now.

71

And by morning, if the water is down enough, we'll get you home and see to your poor sisters as well. Sleep now, that's a good girl."

Helen lay on the bed and watched the dim light become darkness. She felt herself slip into an uneasy sleep, knowing there wouldn't be the dreaded footsteps in the passage tonight, that despite her uncertainty about Sarge, at least the true horrors of her life were over. One way or the other, when she woke, it would be to a new life, one she and Sis could only imagine. She suddenly felt as if she could sleep forever and gave in to it.

It was only a few hours later that she woke into blackness and a sound she was only too familiar with. She rolled out of bed and opened the door. Kath and the children were gathering around the kitchen table with a single kerosene lamp between them. Sarge was absent. Kath was jollying her children along, but it was clear she was frightened. Helen rubbed her eyes and yawned. "What's happening?" she asked, raising her voice to be heard over the howling wind and the rain drumming on the roof.

Kath turned towards her. "It's backtracking," she said, "and we think it's picking up speed."

"The cyclone? It's back?" She couldn't believe it. It simply was not possible. It was not in the plan. It should be over, finished. All of it.

Sarge suddenly flung the kitchen door open. He was soaked and frantic. "All of you," he commanded, "over to the hotel now. Come on, move! The water's rising fast, we've only got minutes."

They reached for oilskins hanging by the door and someone threw Helen's to her. She pulled it on quickly over the borrowed nightie. He marched them all outside and down the steps. The water was already waist high with an undertow that nearly

72

knocked Helen off her feet. One of the boys held her firm as Sarge shepherded his little group towards the hotel.

The front bar had completely disappeared under water and as they climbed the stairs to the first floor, the wind changed from a howl to a high pitched scream. The cyclone was upon them again, more ferociously than before.

They took shelter with about thirty others in the long first-floor passage, mattresses laid end to end, buckets of water and food in tins and jars lined up along the wall. Helen had no time to think, everything seemed to happen so fast.

This was not like it had been a couple of days ago, when she and Sis had sat with their arms around Sweetypie in the stone washhouse, singing and telling her funny stories to ward off her fear, waiting out the cyclone with the sort of stoicism that only those born in the cyclone ravaged tropics can feel. She had felt safe there, their backs against the mountain, measuring the howl of the wind against the thickness of the stone walls around her and knowing them solid enough to meet the challenge.

But here, amongst frightened strangers in a strange place, their screams mingling with the scream of the killer wind, with no one to cling to when the veranda tore away from the front of the hotel with such a shattering screech that they all truly believed they had breathed their last, and every window in the place blew in with an explosion that sent shards of glass through walls as if they were made of butter, with nowhere to go but up to the second floor passage when the flood water reached the first floor, no one around her who even knew her name when she realised she had become separated from Sarge's family, when the dreadful realisation hit her that Sis and Sweetypie were in the middle of this too – then she knew a fear that made her heart feel as if it would tear from her body.

The cyclone hovered over the town for two days and two nights. Helen thought that she would lose her senses if the screaming wind did not stop. She was certain she would die. She was sure Sis and Sweetypie already had.

Then, just as the second day dawned, the old man lying on the mattress in front of her did die. Exhausted, he simply lay back, crossed his hands over his chest and gave up the ghost. Helen sat and stared at his dead eyes for a long time before anyone else noticed, and then someone leaned over, closed his eyes and left him there.

What else could they do? The cyclone rendered everyone helpless. They must wait it out.

Helen saw a huddle of people form around someone in the middle of the passage. She crawled towards them in the dim light, more to escape the dead man than out of curiosity, for he was already starting to smell very bad in the suffocating heat and humidity. She reached the group and pushed her way in. No one noticed, no one cared.

A young woman lay on her back giving birth, the baby coming easily and the blood coming even more easily after it. The new mother kissed a blessing on her baby's forehead, then silently bled to death. Her husband cradled his newborn son and pulled his wife's dress up over her white face so that he did not have to see her empty eyes. In doing so, her bloodied lower half remained naked and exposed, but that didn't seem to matter.

The group moved away a little from the congealing pool of blood, but there really wasn't anywhere to go, so they sat around the edges of it, their faces turned outward. Another young woman with an older baby took the newborn and put him to her breast. He would live.

Food was handed around from time to time, but little was eaten. Fear drove out hunger. When Helen could no longer contain her bladder, she moved to the end of the passage, pulled her panties to one side and did what she had to. Others shit and peed where they sat, too afraid to move.

At dawn on the third morning, the sound of the wind changed and Sarge pushed a door open, fought his way through the debris in one of the bedrooms and looked outside. He stayed there for a long time and when he came back his face was streaked with dirty tears.

By noon it was over. The rain beat steadily on the roof, but the wind had abated. They could not go downstairs, but they could open up the top floor and let some air in. Some of them moved the mattresses back into the bedrooms, ignoring the glass and debris, and collapsed onto them, exhausted beyond human endurance. The children and the women first, then finally the men.

Helen joined Kath and her brood in one room. She tried to stay awake at first and think of Sis and Sweetypie, but her wretched body won over her shattered mind and she slept.

She woke to a gentle prodding. Kath was standing over her with an enamel mug. "Drink this, dear." Helen sat up slowly, her body aching in every joint and muscle and took the cup. It was water, but it tasted of mud and mildew. She drank it anyway. Kath moved on to someone else and Helen went to the window.

Water lapped halfway up the first storey, washing freely through the gaps below her that had once been windows. This hotel was the only solid stone three storey building in town and had survived with walls and roof miraculously intact, but without its graceful veranda and balcony. Almost everything else around it had been blown away or was buried under the flood. But even as she peered down, she saw movement in the level of the water. It was dropping fast.

She collapsed onto the nearest mattress and slept again.

The rain stopped. The wet air was suffocatingly hot. A thumping sound woke her. She went into the next room, treading carefully between shards of broken glass and timber, and peered out to see what was banging up against the side of the hotel. It was Ginger, his body bloated and stinking. The hitching post was still standing and he was attached to it by the tangled leather reins. Her shoes hung limply from the top of the post. She stared at them for a long time.

Then a flash of colour in the distance drew her attention. A small child in a bright red dress floated face down in the water, her blonde hair spread around her head like a halo. Helen watched as she drifted toward the hotel, she watched mesmerised until the little body washed up against the corner of the hotel, watched without breathing as it nudged its way along the wall until it was directly below her.

It was not Sweetypie. She breathed.

The stink drove her back inside, but it was no better there.

Sarge went downstairs and found a dinghy in one piece slapping up against the side of the stairs. He gathered the strongest of the men and they set forth to survey the damage. Some of the men who remained began cleaning up. They dragged the bodies of the old man and the young woman into the furthest bedroom and shut the door. They could not be buried yet and would have to wait. The needs of the living were more immediate.

They erected a blanket across the end of the passage and set up a makeshift toilet. Then they cleared the passage and began sluicing the filth away with buckets of water. Water was something they had plenty of. Even so, the stench would linger for many weeks to come.

The women began the business of tending to the children and the poorly. It would be at least another day before they could leave the hotel. Helen helped where she was instructed to and where she could see she was needed. Clothing and bodies were dunked in water downstairs, washing away the personal evidence of fear and chaos. Cleaner water from the buckets was splashed across faces and swilled inside mouths. Food was distributed and eaten, each of them knowing how lucky they

76

were. Many locals had not survived and those who had would suffer much hardship while cut off by the floodwater. Enough food remained here to keep them all for at least the next few days.

Eventually, Helen found herself in a corner of a room with the newborn baby asleep in her arms. The nursing mother slept on a mattress in the middle of the room, her own baby tucked into her side.

That was when Helen met Beryl. She had seen the woman before, a big fat woman in her fifties whom she knew to be the owner of the haberdashery shop. An obnoxious, loud mouthed woman who seemed to dominate whatever space she was inhabiting at the time. She looked in through the doorway, saw Helen with the baby and sat down heavily next to her.

Helen knew she smelled unwashed and sweaty herself, but the waft of body odour from this woman made her gag. She turned towards the window space and gulped for a breath of fresh air. She was rewarded by the stink of rotting flesh and vegetation. There was no escape.

"You're the little Downing girl, aren't you?" the woman demanded rather than enquired in her ear shattering voice. "Which one are you? Not the ugly one for sure. Are you the mad one?"

Helen was shocked by Beryl's belligerence. She stared at the rough skin and bad teeth, the greasy colourless hair flattened against the sweating square skull, the voluminous bust swelling above the strained neckline of the filthy floral print dress, the mottled skin on the elephantine legs that stuck out from under the pendulous belly, the gnarled feet with their blackened split heels, and thought she would kill herself before she ever allowed herself to look like that. As if reading her thoughts, the woman bellowed a laugh and said "I was young and pretty like you once. Hahaha, just think. With a little time and effort you can end up looking just like me. Hahahaha!"

77

The woman on the mattress woke and turned a disapproving face towards them. "For goodness sake, Beryl, keep it down." She reached for the baby and Helen handed him over.

Beryl opened her mouth to add to her previous insults, but Helen sprang up, grabbed the oilskin coat she had been sitting on and headed towards the toilet. It stank, of course, but it wasn't as bad as what she had just experienced. She pulled the blanket across behind her and sat on the damp plank suspended over a bucket.

"You gunna be long?" Beryl was on the other side of the blanket. "Come on, girl, other people gotta go too." Helen finished and pulled the blanket aside to let Beryl through, but instead of going through, she turned and followed Helen up the passage. "Whatcha got in that bag, girl?"

Helen stopped. "What bag?" she responded without thinking.

"This bag." Beryl leaned forward and pulled it from the coat pocket before Helen realised what she was up to. She leapt to snatch it back, but Beryl whizzed it behind her, then turned to open it and look inside. Helen was stunned. She had never witnessed such oafishness before.

"Money. That's a good start, but a pound won't get you far." Beryl dug into the bag and pulled a handful of things from it. "Handkerchief, two shillings, a letter and lipstick." She wound the lipstick up. It was empty. "Fat lotta good that'll do you," she said, dropping it all back into the bag and thrusting it towards Helen. "So what's your name?"

"Helen," she said, taking the bag and pushing it deep inside the coat pocket again. She turned to go, disgusted and impatient.

"Hey, Helen, come back here. Got something to ask you."

With her back to Beryl, she sighed with resignation, for this woman was not going to give up until she had what she wanted. "Ask."

"Oooh, aren't we the stuck up little smartypants," Beryl snapped with a nasty edge to her voice. "What I wanna know is this. I hear your Daddy drowned. Sarge told me. So why aren't you crying? When my old man died, I was about your age and I cried for weeks. Where are the tears for Harry Downing, huh?"

Helen stood rooted to the spot, suddenly feeling as if all eyes were on her. She had forgotten to cry, damn it. Was that why Sarge had seemed unconvinced? She had plotted and planned, but she had failed to include a session of weeping. It hadn't even occurred to her, for it had been so long since she had cried that she had overlooked the fact that other people still regarded it as an essential part of grief. She turned, looked into the curious, sly face of Beryl and tried to give her what she wanted.

She thought of Dad, but could not summon up a single memory that was worthy of her tears. Then she thought of Sweetypie and Sis and, unbidden, the memory of Sweetypie's sixth birthday and the following weeks in the cubby came to her. And even though she'd made a pact with Sis never to cry again, she exhaled slowly and turned on the tears.

Kath appeared behind Beryl. "Beryl! What do you think you're doing? Oh my dear girl, you mustn't let Beryl upset you. Beryl, you're a wicked woman. Get out of my way." Kath pushed the big woman aside as if she was a naughty child, embraced the weeping girl and led her away.

Helen turned off the tears, then dismissed the episode as nothing more than being useful in helping to convince everyone of the truth of her story. She threw herself into helping the others and managed to avoid Beryl for the rest of the day.

Kath told her it would be at least another night before the flood waters abated enough for them all to leave the hotel. Her own house had washed away, leaving only the stumps and the *floor. Helen wondered if she would find the same when she got home.*

By nightfall, someone had rigged up a fireplace on the second floor inside another bucket and they burned furniture, boiled water, drank sweet black tea and cooked damper with what was left of the dry flour and salt. The next few days would be spent scrounging for whatever food they could find.

Helen spent another night sleeping spasmodically, deeply disturbed by the stench coming in through the windows and from the room at the end of the passage. That would be tomorrow's first job — move the dead. But it would be days, maybe weeks before they could be buried in the soggy earth.

Helen woke just before daylight and visited the toilet. When she emerged Beryl was watching her with something in her face that Helen found oddly familiar. She skirted around the obese figure, collected her coat and went downstairs. Sarge and three men were already up and getting ready to go out again, this time on foot. The tide surge brought by the cyclone was ebbing and the flood waters were draining into the Inlet and out to sea. Helen stood in the doorway and waved them off, donned her oilskins and went outside.

The heart of the cyclone might have moved on, but the tail of it still hung over them. She didn't recognise anything. Squelching black mud under an eerie, sagging green-black sky. Rotting stinking cane flattened beneath the sucking grasping mire. The distressed sea, filthy brown and spewing up the dead and the dying onto a gouged shore to join the wreckage of boats, buildings and lives. The silence of the dead. The despair of the living.

The horror around her was as impossible to absorb as the sight of her shoes on the hitching post. It was there but it meant nothing. It was just there.

She ducked and weaved through the debris until she came to the remains of Sarge's house. His two sons were already at work clearing rubbish away from under the floor. They didn't see her and she kept going, not sure exactly where she was heading, but drawn towards the Inlet where the air coming from the ocean might be sweeter than that coming from the land.

As she reached the end of the street, the edge of the cyclone's tail parted from the distant horizon to reveal the sunrise, dispelling the gloominess and colouring the sky in pastel greys and pinks. Turning her face into the sunlight, she breathed in the untainted breeze from the south-east until it cast out the stench in her nostrils. She followed the breeze towards its source until she stood at the shoreline, the Inlet to her right and the town to her left.

A wet, shuffling sound behind her made her turn. Beryl was hurrying after her, knee high in the mud, the bottom of her skirt dragging behind her, sweat pouring from her face. "You saw it," she puffed, "you saw it too?"

Helen was annoyed. Would this insufferable woman never leave her alone? "Saw what?" she responded irritably.

"The sails, of course. It's the SEA BEA. Look." She pointed towards the mouth of the Inlet. "There she is, and ain't she a beautiful sight? I got half a dozen crates on board, but they can throw the lot into the drink for all I care. I'm finished here. That was my third bloody cyclone and I'm sick of cleaning up and starting all over again. Except there's nothing to start with this time – it's all gone, every last needle and thread of it. But there's my way out and I'm gunna take it. When she leaves, she'll leave with me."

Helen turned just as a white angel appeared around the headland, her bow cutting through the heavy swell as if it was melted butter. Her sails caught the pink morning light and threw it back across the water. A three-master, glorious against the sunrise, turning into the Inlet where the wharves lay damaged and barely visible above the ebbing tide surge.

Helen had never seen a ship before and thought it the most majestic sight imaginable. It filled her with an unfamiliar longing, a pang of discontent that confused her. Beryl was watching her face and said suddenly, "Come with me."

"What?"

"Come with me. I got passage for both of us. Look." She reached deep into her bosom to produce a small purse and opened it. It was bulging with notes. "My last week's takings. There's plenty here, enough to get us to Brisbane on the SEA BEA. I'll pick up a car there and we'll drive down to Sydney. I got a little house I been renting out in the city. I'll kick the tenants out and we can move right in." She reached across and gripped Helen by the arm. "Come," she urged. "What is there to stay for? You never been off the farm, I can see that. Girl, there's so much for you to see and do, a whole world waiting for you. What reason does a pretty little thing like you have to stay here?"

Helen pulled away from her. "My sisters..." she began, but Beryl cut her off.

"Your sisters will be alright. I seen you all coming into town every week with your old man, seen you all filing into church like the good little Catholics you are. That ugly one, I heard she was as good a cane farmer as your old man. She doesn't need you. As for that other one, the mad one..." Helen turned away but Beryl reached up and roughly turned her face back towards her. "... she don't need you there, either. She's got the ugly one to look after her. And what will you have if you go back there?" Beryl was talking urgently now, as if it really mattered to her. Helen thought she was quite crazy and more than a little frightening. She turned to trudge away. "Hey, I ain't finished!"

"Well, I have," Helen announced. "Go away. Leave me alone."

With a sudden agility that left her breathless, Beryl came after her and grabbed her from behind by the coat. "If you come with me, you can see your friends in Sydney."

Helen stopped. "What are you talking about?"

"That letter in your handbag. It's addressed to someone in Sydney, not too far from my own house. You can visit them. Hey, what's the problem? You're a beautiful young girl. You could have the world at your feet. There's nothing here for you. Come with me."

Helen pushed her away with disgust and went back to the hotel. People were leaving, going out to see what was left of their homes and their lives. Kath and her family appeared to be setting up house on the top floor. It would be some time before they had a home to go back to.

Helen didn't know what to do. Ginger was gone and she wasn't sure how she would get back home without him. She could walk, of course, but it would take more than a couple of days with the roads cut off and many of the cane fields between town and home still under water. She'd need food and good walking shoes. She had neither.

She went into one of the bedrooms that overlooked the Inlet where she could look out at the SEA BEA. Someone had swept, tidied and thrown a rug to dry out over the empty window sill. She found a stool that hadn't yet been used for firewood, pulled it up to the window and leaned out over the rug. The ship had anchored offshore and put out a small boat with three men in it. She watched for some time until she saw them reach the shore where Beryl greeted them. They seemed to know her.

It was getting hot again, so she took off her oilskins and threw them onto the bare mattress. Then she remembered what Beryl had said. She took the handbag out of the coat pocket, opened it and stared at the contents.

They were Mum's things, they had to be.

She'd been six when Mum died. It was strange to see these things, such personal things, to touch them and feel them. The lipstick had been bright red, she could see that from the discoloured remains inside it, but it didn't look as if it had ever been used. It looked, rather, as if it had been broken off and discarded.

Helen had never worn lipstick. Dad always said only wicked girls wore lipstick.

The handkerchief had once been white linen with hand embroidered lace around the edges. Carefully folded, it was now spotted with black mildew, the edges of the lace yellowed and curled.

Two shillings. Twelve years since Mum died. Twelve years that pathetic two shillings had been sitting in the bottom of this bag. Dad never let Mum have any money, Sis had told her that, so she must have hidden this away for something special. Maybe for a new lipstick. Two lousy shillings. She pushed them all to the bottom of the bag and took the letter out.

The paper was mildewy and soft, but the writing on the envelope still clearly legible. A childish uneven print to a Sydney address, as Beryl had said. Addressed to Mrs Benotti. Helen had never heard of Mrs Benotti. She wondered why it hadn't been posted. It didn't have a stamp on it. Perhaps the two shillings had been for a stamp.

She opened it. The date at the top gave her pause for thought. It was dated only days before Mum died. Then she saw that the letter was not in English. Dad always called Mum a wog, whatever that meant, and would get very angry when she talked "wog talk". Maybe that was what this writing was — wog talk. But she understood who the letter was directed to, she understood that first word.

"Mama."

At the end of the single page was carefully printed "Luisa". To Mama. From Luisa.

Mrs Benotti. Mrs Benotti in Sydney was Mum's Mum.

Suddenly, Beryl's invitation took on a whole new meaning. Beryl seemed to know where this address was. And if there was a Mama, she would be Helen's grandmother.

This was an entirely new concept. As far as Helen knew, she had no relatives. She had asked Dad once about relatives after the Stewarts had visited with their elderly parents in tow, and Dad's reply had been simple. "Dead," he'd said, "all dead long ago." That was the end of that.

Helen stared at the letter again. She wanted to know what it said, but could think of no one who might be able to translate it for her. Then it occurred to her that maybe she didn't want anyone else to read it anyway. It was from Mum and it was all she had of her. She hugged the letter to her and thought hard.

Beryl came into the room, her dress even filthier than Helen thought possible, mud caked to her knees, sweating profusely and breathing heavily. "Well?" she queried, as if picking up the conversation without a break. "Coming or not? They're leaving now. The cyclone threw them off schedule, so they gotta head back to Brisbane right away."

Helen looked up at her. "Why do you want me to come with you?"

"Why not?" Beryl answered, narrowing her eyes as she looked down at the girl. "I could do with some company and you're as good as any."

"I don't have much money, I ..."

"You let me worry about that. I told you, I got passage for both of us, and you can earn your keep by doing a few things for me. You know," she looked down at her dress, "laundry and such."

"Is Sydney far?"

"You don't know where Sydney is? You even heard of it before now?" Helen shook her head. "Talk about a dumb bush hick. Well, Sydney's big, bigger'n you can ever imagine, not a

85

bloody hole in the bush like this. And yes it's far. A few days sailing, then a few days driving. You'll love it."

Helen showed her the envelope. "When we get to Sydney, can you show me how to get to the address on this letter?"

"Course I can. Sydney born and bred I am. You're coming, ain't you? Good girl. Now get a move on. You got any luggage or are you as I see you?"

Helen looked down at her shabby nightie, ancient oilskins and filthy feet. "This is it." She looked up. "I don't want to stay in Sydney very long, just long enough to visit this address. How will I get home?"

Beryl smiled unexpectedly, a crooked sort of smile that did not quite reach her eyes. "I'll help you out there," she promised. "I'll pay you a little for looking after me on the trip, it'll be enough to get you back here. You only need be gone a week or two, about as long as it'll take for that river up your way to go down. No way you're gunna get back home before that happens, is there? Why, you'll be back in no time at all. And I'll get you some nice new things to wear, pretty you up a bit. Those crates on board the SEA BEA are jammed full of goodies, everything you'll need and more."

"I'd have to let Sis know ..."

"Don't you worry your pretty little head about that. I saw Sarge heading back here, I'll talk to him before we leave. He'll take a message out to your sisters if you don't get back before the floodwaters go down. Now, hurry up or we'll miss our boat." She reached across and pulled Helen up from the stool. "You make your way down to the wharf right now, they're waiting for you."

Beryl pushed her along the deserted passage, continuing to cajole and encourage. There was no one downstairs to say goodbye to. They passed the remains of Sarge's house where his sons, as before, were too busy to notice them.

By the time they reached the Inlet, Helen was convinced she'd be back home before the floodwaters receded. The thought of a little money of her own and some new clothes was enticing. And maybe she could find something in Sydney to bring back for Sis and Sweetypie, something pretty like Beryl kept talking about. Nice things that girls should have.

At the wharf, Beryl pushed her into the dinghy with the three sailors and unexpectedly turned away. "I'll be along in a few minutes. I'll make sure I get a message to Sarge for your sisters. Don't let these buggers leave without me," she called out as she made her way back to the hotel.

The sailors were jovial and chatty. They asked her about the cyclone, where she came from, where she was going. They eyed her admiringly, but without intent, for she was with Beryl and they all knew what that meant.

Beryl joined them, a small battered suitcase under one arm. The sailors rowed out to the ship and, with each stroke of the oars, Helen felt a mounting excitement. The air smelled sweet and salty, the breeze cooled and dried the sweat on her face. She trailed her fingers in the waters of the Pacific Ocean and felt the horrors of the past week melting away from her.

Welcoming hands hauled her aboard the SEA BEA and there was more joking and laughter. While Beryl busied herself below, she stood astern and watched the town disappear behind the headland, then turned her face south into the clean fresh breeze and looked towards the new horizon.

As the sky cleared above them, the tail of the cyclone moved over the mountains, leaving the decimated slopes in deep shadow for a short time. Sunlight bit into her damp skin and the southerly breeze seemed to refresh her spirit as well as her body. The memory of her home and what she had done and the life they had lived seemed suddenly surreal, dark, distorted, far away, as if it had happened to someone else. Reality was *here, in this moment, in this clean sunlit moment, on this ship with laughing sailors and a promise of better things to come.*

She would return soon, very soon she promised herself, and sent the promise across the water and the flood soaked cane fields, sent it flying through the bright sunlight right up to the front door of her home, right into the heart and soul of Sis and Sweetypie.

She was not deserting them. She was just having a little adventure. She'd be back before they knew she was gone.

CHAPTER FIVE

"Some little adventure. It lasted fifty bloody years," Sis remarked cuttingly. "Well, Sarge didn't tell me because that bloody bitch Beryl didn't tell him. Nobody saw you go." She flicked the lid off the last stubby and gripped it with both hands, staring at it hard, remembering. "Jeez, I reckon those four weeks before Sarge got through were the longest in my life. Hell, I was starting to think me and Sweetypie was the only two people left on the planet."

"I'm sorry, Sis. I caused you so much anguish, but that was never my intention."

"No?" Sis turned and looked at Helen piercingly, trying to remember the girl she once knew so well. "No, I suppose it wasn't. I don't reckon you wished anything bad on us. Then again ..." Helen opened her mouth to say something but Sis held up her hand to stop her. "Hang on, give me a minute here. I'm still trying to get my head around what it must have been like for you, coming from what you knew, which was nothing at all outside the farm, to seeing all that stuff going on. Birth, death, love, grief – like all of life rolled into a few days. Enough to change anyone's view of the world. Right?"

Sis's insight surprised her. "I suppose so. Now you put it like that, I can see it. But it was still wrong."

"Jeez, don't worry about it. Alright? You were young for chrissake and I had … well, I had other things on my mind." She upended the stubby and swigged noisily.

"Yes?"

"Don't matter now," she answered evasively.

There it was again. A secret. "Please, Sis. You said you'd been wondering all these years. Well, so have I. What happened?"

Sis sniggered, as if Helen had said something amusing, then paused before saying with a strange sense of finality, "Sarge turned up." Helen immediately felt the gap, the bit left out, the four weeks that Sis obviously didn't want to discuss. There was something there that she didn't want Helen to know. And it made Helen desperate to know. "What about before he came, what was it like here for you and Sweetypie?"

Sis looked away toward the tranquil waters of the river and frowned against the sunlight, etching strained lines across the mask. She took a couple of swigs again and sat quietly for a moment, as if needing time to choose her words carefully. "Sarge had search parties out for everyone missing in the cyclone. All up, over a couple of hundred people not accounted for. Bloody nightmare for the whole district. What a monster that cyclone was, but what a bloody godsend it turned out to be for us, hey, backtracking like that. No one but Sarge doubted that Dad died in the cyclone. Everyone else said if he'd managed to survive the first onslaught, he sure as hell couldn't have survived the second. It's a wonder anyone survived. Me and Sweetypie, we waited it out in the cubby, hardly knew it was going on, but jeez, what a mess when we finally came out. Trees tossed all over the mountain like bloody

90

matchsticks, not a leaf left on any of them and there was mud and shit everywhere. I was amazed the house was still here, all the window louvres gone, floodwater right up to the top step, two feet of stinking mud from the mountain through the passage. Took weeks to clean up the rubbish and months to dry out the damp. Just about had to rebuild the house. " She swigged, smacked her lips and said unexpectedly. "So you cleared out. Bloody strange, that, now I think about it."

"What's bloody strange?" The booze was loosening Sis up in body and tongue and Helen was having trouble keeping up with the changing direction of conversation.

"How I felt, once that letter turned up. About you being gone. Angry 'cos you weren't here with me. But kinda relieved 'cos you'd flown the coop. Found a way out."

"Did you ever wish it was you who had … escaped?"

"Nah. Never."

"Didn't you want to get out, too, Sis?"

"What the hell for?"

"To have a life, to find out what was out there."

"There was nothing out there for a dumb ugly bitch like me, Helen, I always knew that, but there was everything out there for a beautiful, smart young girl like you. And someone had to stay to look after Sweetypie and the farm. I always knew it would be me."

"Sis, you were never a dumb ugly bitch. Never."

"Christ, Helen, look at me."

"You look like the person you want the world to think you are, Sis, but you can't fool me. Even after all this time. I see who you really are."

"Yeah? Then you'd be the only one."

"You only need one."

"Jeez, you're getting too bloody profound for me. You need another beer. I'll get it." Sis began to rise.

"No, thanks. I'm already a little dizzy. I've had enough. Coffee is normally my beverage of choice in the morning. Why haven't you got any mirrors in your bedroom?" she asked suddenly, catching Sis off guard with her own change in direction.

Instead of answering, Sis said contemptuously, "Dizzy? On one piddly stubby?"

Helen pushed the empty bottle across the table towards Sis. "I'm not a drinker. Two glasses of fine wine with a meal is more my style, and my limit. Raymond always called me a two pot screamer."

"Yeah? Well, I dunno the difference between good booze and bad booze, it all makes me feel the same. And I can drink any man under the table."

"I'm sure you can. But you couldn't do that last time we shared a drink on the veranda. If I remember, it was tea back then. When did you start drinking?"

"Not that it's any of your damn business, but I started having a drink or two after the cyclone. Dad had a box of wine and some beer someone'd given him stored under the house. Found it when I was cleaning up. Figured if you can't cry, you can drink."

"I see."

"Yeah."

"But we didn't grow up with alcohol when we were kids, did we?"

Sis shook her head thoughtfully. "Nah. The old bastard didn't drink at home, did he? Only drank at those bloody parish meetings he went to occasionally and the odd Christmas do. Then he'd come home at some ungodly hour, pissed out of his brain, noisy as hell, knocking over the furniture. Only happened two or three times that I can remember. Nah, like you, he couldn't handle it either."

"The mirrors?" Helen repeated, never distracted for long.

"Jeez, Helen, why do you think? I don't like what I see, never have, never will."

"I like what I see."

"Huh. You really are a two pot screamer. And what do you see?"

"I see my big sister, my Sissy, my protector when I was little, the one who took the punches for me when I was older, the clever one who plotted and planned to keep Dad away from Sweetypie." She saw a shudder go through Sis and quickly reached out to rest a reassuring hand on her shoulder. Sis didn't pull away. "It wasn't your fault, Sis. You kept her safe for six years, but he was determined. No one could have stopped him. And it was the only time. It could have been worse."

"No," Sis said coldly, turning her head to meet Helen's gaze, "it couldn't have been."

Helen drew her hand away. This wasn't going as she had planned. She hadn't meant to sound as if she was accusing Sis. She said again with conviction, "But it wasn't your fault. You did everything right, everything you could possibly have done. You always did."

"I'm no bloody saint, Helen."

"As far as I am concerned, that's exactly what you are."

Sis gave her another look, one that, for a second, Helen couldn't fathom. Then, with a sudden flash of enlightenment, Helen thought, your secret, Sis, you want to tell me but you don't know how.

As if reading her mind, Sis leaned closer to Helen and said, "There are things, Helen, things I shouldna done but ..."

"Yes, Sissy?" Helen responded earnestly, her body language replicating Sis's until their faces were only inches apart.

A loud noise cut between them like a knife severing a cord. Sweetypie's motorbike. It was noon.

Sis and Helen snapped apart and turned as one to the source of the interruption, the moment of unplanned intimacy dissolving in a second. Sweetypie turned off the motorbike at the base of the steps and grinned up at both of them, the dogs coming to heel on either side of her.

Sis rose quickly and ordered Lady and Prince to their tree. She trotted down the steps with the visible relief of a claustrophobic leaving an elevator and filled their water bowls from a tap under the old mango tree.

Sweetypie bounced up the steps and reached for Helen's hand. Then, in a gesture that bridged the fifty years faster than anything else could have, Sweetypie kissed the fingertips of her free hand and pressed them briefly against Helen's lips. The smile that had always followed this gesture came involuntarily to Helen and she leaned forward to wrap her arms around her elderly baby sister, feeling the sweaty heat rise up around them.

Sweetypie pulled away and frowned at the empty stubbies on the veranda table. "Where's my sangers?"

"Oh, Sweetypie, I forgot. I was supposed to make the sandwiches today, wasn't I?" Helen laughed, relieved to be able to do so, and said, "Come on, little one, let's go inside and you can help me."

"No you don't," Sis ordered, striding up the steps. "She makes too much bloody mess. I'll do them. You two clean up the table. I gotta freshen up and check the answering machine for messages."

Sweetypie pouted and said, "You're such a bossy boots, Sissy."

Helen put her arm across Sweetypie's shoulder, pouted with her and said in her best Sweetypie voice, "Oh, please, Sissy, I promise I'll clean up afterwards."

Sis stopped with her hand on the door and turned to look at them both. Her dull brown eyes seem to metamorphose and a

94

twinkle appeared. A crackle began in her throat, it deepened and became louder, and suddenly, Sis Downing was laughing. The laughter became a chuckle and she said, "Alright, make the bloody sandwiches, only don't let her use any sharp knives. I've run outa bandaids." She continued to laugh as she went inside. Within seconds, they could hear the sound of the shower running.

Helen led Sweetypie into the kitchen and asked, where is this, where is that, is that enough, what do you like to drink? Sweetypie answered every question with, "You know, silly billy." She thought it was a game and giggled.

Sis appeared in fresh singlet and shorts, answering Helen's unasked question about whether she still bathed several times a day. She brought another chair out from the kitchen and they ate on the veranda. Sweetypie chattered about her morning's work, going into extraordinary detail over every rock, every bush, tree and fern, every noise, every birdcall. Sis listened with equally extraordinary patience and devoted interest, and Helen did her best to keep up.

As soon as they had cleared up, Sweetypie called the dogs, fired up the bike and headed back into the rainforest. Helen and Sis resumed their seats in awkward silence, the mask settling back over Sis's face. Another six pack of beer had appeared and Sis was settling in with a new packet of cigarettes.

Helen, wanting to make a start, asked Sis, "Is she always like this?"

"Always," Sis replied with an edge of bitterness to the resignation in her voice, the smoke forming a cloud around her face. "Every interminable bloody day. Just think what you have missed." And then quickly, in Sweetypie's defence, "But I'd hate it if she ever stopped."

Helen sat quietly and let the realisation of what Sis's life had been like for the past fifty years really penetrate her consciousness. Finally, she thought, poor Sis, what have I done, and then she thought, thank god I escaped. She might regret Sis's life, but she had no regrets about her own.

The siisshhh of a newly opened stubby broke the silence, then Sis said, "So you toddled off with Beryl. What was her game? Did she fancy you?" There was a touch of malice in the question.

Surprised again by Sis's insight, Helen replied, "You got it in one, Sis. I was so stupid."

"You were never stupid, Helen. Just naive. We both were. I still am. Christ, I never been off the bloody farm." She paused and Helen sensed another change in her mood. Before lunch, she'd been unwilling to talk, but now she was opening up. Helen decided it was probably the beer but hoped it was more. She held her tongue and let it happen.

Sis continued, her gaze following the line of the cane fields down the slope to where new suburbs were springing up around the base of the mountains. "Best thing that ever happened to me was getting the power and phone put on here in '71. First thing I did was put up the aerial tower and buy a bloody television. Better'n all the National Geographics and travel books put together. Reckon the Wet Season that year I was waiting to be rained in so's I didn't have no excuses not to watch it. Day and night for about three months. Never seen anything like it. Shows about animals and countries and people so damn different from us, I couldn't hardly believe my eyes. Then when colour came in, I reckon I was the first in line to get one. Made it easier here, you know, like, I couldn't get out there but I could let the world in through the box." Sis paused as if she had gone too far, revealed too much of herself too soon, then hardened her voice and changed direction again. "So she wanted you. Bloody Beryl. Did she get you?"

Helen chuckled as she remembered. "She came close, god she came close!" Then she chose a new direction of her own. "You haven't asked me anything more about the family."

Sis dragged deeply on her cigarette. "Yeah. I wanna know, but jeez Helly," the childhood familiar slipped out without her realising it, "you're back here five bloody minutes and you dump that on me. I wanna know, but I dunno where to start."

Helen felt them drawing closer again, as they had before Sweetypie had interrupted them. It was an unconscious thing, tangible only in its comfort, but had once been as natural as breathing for both of them.

A sudden wave of fresh guilt swept over Helen. She'd known this sort of intimacy with Raymond. She'd known it and enjoyed it for almost fifty years. She wondered what her life would have been like without it. She couldn't imagine.

She had withdrawn this precious thing from Sis fifty years ago and not given it a thought until this very minute.

She hoped with all her heart that there was still time to make it up to Sis. But there were shocks in store for her sister before she could do that.

"Sis," Helen tried to choose her words carefully, "what I have to tell you next may turn everything upside down for you. It is one of the reasons I didn't write to you about the family and didn't tell them about you. I don't expect you to ever forgive me, but please, just listen quietly and try to understand."

"That bad, is it? Shit." Sis opened another stubby, lit a cigarette, drew her chair towards the edge of the veranda and swung her feet up onto the banister. She squinted into the light, leaned back and commanded, "Go ahead. I'm listening, and don't you leave nothing out. I wanna hear it all."

CHAPTER SIX

Beryl took a bath on deck in a small tub, right out in the open, her fat body vibrating in waves as she scrubbed her hair, her breasts, her armpits, her inner thighs. The crew sat around and watched with disinterest. Helen was so embarrassed she had to go below. When Beryl insisted it was her turn to bathe and handed her the soapy sponge, the captain took pity on her and offered her his small cabin and a robe.

After she'd bathed, Helen came back on deck to see her nightie and the coat floating away to starboard. The handbag lay up against the mast. She looked around for Beryl who, now clothed in loose cotton slacks and a man's shirt, was giving two crew members directions as they ripped open a crate with her name on it. She pulled several items of clothing out and threw them towards Helen, who went back down to the cabin and changed into lacy underpants and a soft pink cotton dress. She heard a clatter behind her and found a lacy black brassiere and suspenders, sheer stockings and pretty leather sandals on the floor. She put the sandals on but left the other items. She knew girls wore such things, but she had only ever worn home made cotton knickers and wasn't sure exactly what to do with the rest. When she came back on deck, the crew whistled appreciatively, but politely. She blushed and slipped the sandals off. They were tight and, anyway, bare feet were better for a rolling deck.

Beryl gave her a look of pure pleasure and took her hand. She led Helen to a pile of dirty underwear and the filthy dress she'd been wearing, pointed to a basin of clean soapy water and said, "You can start with that. And don't worry about these boys, they ain't gunna touch you, I can promise that." She grinned up at her sailor mates and winked.

For the rest of the day, Helen was Beryl's slave, fetching and carrying for her, preparing her food, cleaning up after her, heeding her every whim. The crew made jokes about her slave status, but eyed her sympathetically.

Even so, as obnoxious as she found Beryl to be, the big woman appeared to be very popular with the crew. As the light faded, a singsong began and a flagon of plonk was handed around. Beryl drank, told stories and sang dirty ditties until she had the crew rolling around with laughter. The night was humid, but the sky was clear and Beryl insisted she and Helen sleep on deck, so a collection of bedding was brought up for them and, by midnight, all but the watch were asleep.

Helen woke as the sky changed to soft grey. Something heavy and damp lay between her thighs. She turned her head. Beryl, soundly asleep, had moved her bedding closer through the night and it was her sweating hand that lay between her legs. She pushed it away carefully and rose to meet the dawn.

While Beryl continued to snore heavily, Helen told the captain she wanted to be useful, so she was given cotton trousers and a shirt to wear and the crew initiated her into the joys of sailing. After eighteen years on the farm, climbing

99

trees and roaming all over the mountain, she was strong and agile, surprising the crew by taking up the challenge of going up the mast as if she had been doing it all her life. She found it thrilling and it kept her out of Beryl's way.

The younger members of the crew spent a lot of time teaching her the finer points of sailing. She'd never known the company of people her own age before, other than her sisters, but found herself falling easily into their jokes and games. By the second night she was exhausted, as much from the laughter as from the work, falling asleep long before the drinking and singing were over.

She woke in the dark to the feel of Beryl's boozy breath on her neck and a hot hand on her breast. She tried to push her away, but Beryl was insistent, so she rolled onto her front, face turned away and arms tight to her sides. Beryl sighed and pulled away, heaved with alcoholic lethargy and drifted into sleep.

The next night, Helen waited until Beryl was asleep, then made her bed up at the other end of the boat. She slept fitfully, waking many times to check on the fat woman's whereabouts, but she lay splayed out like a beached whale at the other end of the deck until dawn. By then, Helen was busy with the crew.

When they reached Brisbane, Beryl did as she said she would, found a car and headed south. She was jovial and the many friendly pats on the knee seemed part of the mood. They booked into a guesthouse for an overnight stay in two beds in the same room, and that night Beryl became very insistent. Helen fought her off, and again the next night, but by the time they got to Sydney, Beryl was losing patience.

They drove straight to the little terrace house where Beryl proceeded to abuse the tenants, fabricating reasons why she wanted them out on the spot. The couple and their three children gathered up their meagre possessions and Helen watched sadly as the forlorn little procession left.

That night, after another tussle fueled by Beryl's heavy drinking, Helen fought back. When she pulled away, Beryl grabbed the young woman by the hair, pulled her onto the sofa and held her fast.

"None of your little tricks tonight, girl. You know why you're here and I know why you're here."

"I came to see my ..."

"Enough! I don't want any more of your silly games. You know what I want and I ain't about to let you go until I get it."

"And if you don't?"

"You're out on your ear, my girl, and what will you do then, hey? Tell me that. You got no one here but me, and a bushie like you will starve on the streets without someone to look after you."

"I got ..."

"The letter? Huh! That address is right across the other side of the city and you ain't never gunna find it without me."

"You said it was close to here."

"I said a lot of things. It ain't close. Now, get that nightie off. I wanna look at you."

Helen slapped Beryl's hand away and jumped up.

Beryl struggled to heave herself off the sofa as Helen ran into the bedroom. "Don't you run from me. Get back here!" She stood, out of breath. "Bloody hell. I've had enough. You don't cooperate, you're out, you hear me?" As Helen reached for her clothes in the wardrobe, Beryl screamed, "No you don't! I paid for them, every goddamn one of them! You want out, then you go in your birthday suit!" She staggered into the bedroom and made a lunge at Helen, tearing the cotton nightie across the shoulders. Helen made a desperate grab for her brown handbag and sprinted to the front door, Beryl's laboured breathing right behind her.

She ran from the house, hugging the remnants of the nightie around her, the handbag clutched desperately to her chest. She ran into the night and kept running, knowing that if she ran fast enough, fat old Beryl couldn't possibly keep up with her. She ran until she was sure Beryl was far behind her and out of sight, she ran until she could run no more and found herself under the shelter of the Sydney Harbour Bridge.

The night was balmy and clear, there was no one else around and she sank to her knees, exhausted and shaken.

The nightie was torn across the front, exposing her breasts. She slipped it on backwards and wrapped it around her as best she could. Then she leaned against the concrete pillar and looked out over the water. She thought the lights of Sydney were beautiful. So different from the blackness of her farm at night. She thought of Sis and Sweetypie, sending them love on the breeze, and sank into a deep sleep.

She was woken by someone tugging at her handbag. She snatched it away from the thieving hands and looked up into a wretched, ancient face. The old man backed away and shuffled off.

She watched the morning arrive and looked around her for inspiration for her next move, but all was unfamiliar, foreign, daunting. Finally, hunger drove her from under the protection of the bridge. She opened the bag and looked for the pound note. It was gone. Bloody Beryl. But she still had the two shillings. Her mother's two shillings. Her fist closed around the coin and she felt the link with Mum, as if she was reaching out with a gift to help her on her way.

She looked around her. Where to go? Where did one find food in a city? If she was on the farm, she'd know what to do, but Sydney was a mystery to her, a huge jungle of roads and houses and buildings that were as alien to her as if she had just landed on another planet.

As the sun rose in the sky, the empty roads gradually filled with buses, cars and noise. She followed the road across the bridge, holding her nightie tightly around her, the breeze along the Harbour threatening to lift it and bare all.

Once across, she headed up an alley that seemed less exposed than the roads and saw clothes hanging on a line – dresses, panties and those items that Beryl had thrown her on the boat. With one eye on the house and another on the alley, she pushed open the gate, took a dress and a pair of panties and fled. The alley ran into an even narrower alley between high walls with no windows. Here she changed and suddenly, in the ill fitting cotton dress, felt her confidence return. At least she could go out in public and ask someone for directions.

A milk bar in the next street advertised fresh bread. Two shillings bought her a loaf, a bottle of milk and a block of Cadbury's Chocolate. She took them down to the water's edge and ate half of everything. Then she went back to the milk bar and asked for directions. The owner looked doubtfully at her baggy dress and bare feet, but drew her a rough map with a pencil on a piece of butcher's paper, saying it was a long way, did she have the bus fare. Helen looked blank. She didn't know what the woman was talking about. What was bus fare? She thanked the woman, folded the paper in her bag and began her journey.

Helen walked all day, stopping to rest twice when she felt herself slacken. As night fell, she knew she was hopelessly lost. This never would have happened at home. No matter how far into the rainforest you went, you knew that the mountain range ran north-south and that the mountains were to the west and the ocean to the east with the flats in between. If you stayed on the mountain too long, or wandered too far, you just climbed a tree, looked for the sun and, if it was the morning, you headed towards the sun, but if it was the afternoon, you headed away from it. In the middle of the day, you just waited a bit longer until a shadow appeared. There were so many landmarks to guide you. The river that cut a swathe across the base of the mountain before it headed down to the flats and the Inlet, the waterhole, the tree split by lightning, the patch of tall palms, the triple-crested summit, the fallen tree, the twisted tree, the spiral branched tree – it was so simple.

But here, there was no sense of north south east or west, no up, no down and she was exhausted.

She stopped at a vacant block with two big gum trees at the back of it in a street of partly built red brick houses and sat cross legged under the spread of the trees. It was as close as she could find to familiar surroundings. She ate the rest of the bread and softened chocolate, but the milk had soured in the summer heat. Thirst made her feel ill. Clouds had been building up during the day and she smelled rain in the air. Lying back against the tree to think about her next move, she sank into sleep.

The storm hit shortly after midnight. Helen huddled against the tree for awhile until she was soaked through, then ran across the road and fell through a glassless window into one of the unfinished houses. There she crouched and shivered until, during one of the many flashes of lightning, she saw a chipped enamel mug in the corner of the room, left by one of the builders. Leaning out of the gaping window, she held it under the overflowing gutters and drank her fill. Back on the bare timber floor, she curled up and slept again.

The morning was overcast and humid, more like home, and she felt a little of her energy return. She approached a couple of early-bird builders across the road and asked once again for directions. They perused the map, told her she'd taken a wrong turn somewhere and that she had a long way to go back to get on the right road. They marked the map with landmarks to look for – "the pub with the green double doors here, Smith's fish and chip shop there, can't miss it, girlie".

The walk back to where she had made the wrong turn took her all morning. She found the pub, the fish and chip shop, the other landmarks and knew she was getting close. But she was getting slower, too. So hungry she felt dizzy, she kept walking, even when the southerly buster hit and drenched her. Her throat became sore and her breathing laboured, and when she began to cough, she thought she would faint. Helen, who had never had a cold in her life, knew she was getting sick. She felt the fever take hold, but still she kept walking, for there was nothing else she could do.

Everywhere there were people, so many people, in cars, on buses, in shops and houses, on the road, on the footpath. She had never imagined there could be so many people in the world. And yet she had never felt more alone. She moved among them as if she was invisible.

More rain came and went, and just before sunset she stood under the street sign she had been looking for. Clinging to it for support, she rested for a few moments until the dizziness passed, then checked the number she was looking for on the envelope. The street sloped steeply upwards and she just knew the house she wanted would be at the top. She dragged herself up the footpath until she reached the crest and stood shakily before the house, her breath coming in wheezes.

The house was large and, she decided, rather grand. Two storeys, many windows across the front, red brick with a terracotta tiled roof and six pillars gracing a wide veranda and balcony. The top storey and the veranda looked newer than the bottom storey, the bricks not yet weathered in. A row of tall pencil pines lined either side of the path to the front door. She knocked and leaned against the door while she waited for a spasm of coughing to pass.

And so it was that she fell into Gino Benotti's arms as he threw the door open, expecting his son, but instead finding a thin, dirty adolescent girl in a sodden ragged dress lying limply in his arms.

"Maria!" he called, "Maria! Come quickly!"

Helen looked up into his concerned, confused face, pushed the letter towards him and fainted.

When she came to, she was lying in a warm bed in a clean nightie. Her hair and body had been washed and something smelling of eucalyptus steamed close by. Three men and three women sat on chairs around the bed. As she opened her eyes, she was aware of a collective sigh. The women murmured something and the men left.

Helen and the women surveyed each other silently, then Helen, feeling desperately weak, whispered, "Who are you?"

One of the women, an impressive looking brunette with a long slim waist and beautiful even features, said in a velvety voice, "Are you Luisa Downing's daughter?"

"Yes. I'm Helen Downing."

All three gasped. The woman caught Helen by the hand. "And your Mama? Where is your Mama?"

"Mum died. She drowned when I was six."

The woman released her. "We were told she had died, but we so hoped it was not true. Drowned," she said slowly. "He lied to us." She hung her head forlornly, then looked up at the other two women, who seemed to be waiting on her to make the next move. They whispered amongst themselves, then they moved towards the bed and arranged themselves around the edge of it. The woman who had spoken said, "Dear girl, if you are Luisa's daughter, then I am your Aunt Maria and this," with a kind smile as she indicated the second woman, "is your Aunt Maria, and this," nodding towards the third woman, "is also your Aunt Maria." When Helen did not respond, she continued, "I am your Mama's sister and these are the wives of your Mama's two brothers, Gino and Sonny. You can call them Aunt Gino and Aunt Sonny, all the nieces and nephews do, it is less confusing." And quite suddenly, she was weeping and then all three were weeping.

Helen shrank back a little. "I don't understand," she said.

Maria calmed herself. "Do you speak the Italian, Helen?"
Helen shook her head. "Then you do not know the contents of
the letter you brought with you?" Again she shook her head.
"I would like to read it to you. Are you strong enough to hear
it, or would you like to sleep now and I'll read it to you later?"

Mum's letter. As weak and ill as she felt, this could not
wait. "Now," she said. Maria took the letter from the pocket of
her dress and translated.

"Mama, I am well. The baby was born, it was a girl but
she died. This is right as she was unholy. But she is just
an innocent little baby so I call her Sistina after you.
I bury her in holy ground because the priest does not
know she is unholy. My husband does not know she
is unholy. But my husband provides for me, Mama,
we have a nice house and I now have a little girl my
husband named Helen, and another little girl I called
Maria after my sister, but we call her Sweetypie. They
are good little girls and very pretty. Helen has black
hair and brown eyes and looks like my sister. I miss
my sister very much. Sweetypie looks like my husband
with yellow hair and blue eyes. My husband is very
busy and does not always have much time for me and
my little girls. I want to come home to visit. Please
send me some money so I can come home. Sometimes,
my husband is like Papa and I think I should come
home. Please send me money to come home soon.
Luisa."

Maria wept again. Helen closed her eyes. What was that all
about? Sis wasn't dead. She wasn't unholy. She hadn't been
buried. What was it that the priest and Luisa's husband didn't
know? Why did she write to her own mother that her firstborn
was dead? And she said that Dad was like Papa ...

She opened her eyes and struggled into a sitting position. Maria leaned forward and adjusted the pillows behind her. "Who is Papa?"

"My Papa. Your grandfather. He died many years ago."

"What did she mean about Dad being like Papa?" Helen thought she knew but she had to be sure.

"Oh, it doesn't matter now. It's all in the past, Helen." Maria looked away. The other two aunts looked down. Helen saw shame and guilt in their faces. What was going on here? She had to know.

"Please, tell me."

"Perhaps another time, when you are well and strong."

"I'm alright. Please. I want to know. Why was Dad like my ... grandfather?"

Maria straightened a little and looked uncomfortably at the other two aunts. "Helen," she said carefully, "when you came here yesterday ..."

"Yesterday?"

"Yes, when you came here yesterday, you were very ill and you have been asleep. We were all here because it was Gino's eldest son's birthday and we were planning a surprise party for him. Gino called the doctor, who came and told us to sponge you down with cool water because you had a very high fever. So we," she indicated all three women, "undressed you and then we saw." She paused, reached out and gently touched the area of Helen's groin. "We saw the scars and we called the doctor in and he told us what it meant. Tell us, did your Papa do that to you? Did he hurt you like that?"

Helen nodded. There was no reason not to, for weren't all girls like she was? Weren't all fathers like her own?

The women stared at her with grim faces. One of them said something in Italian. Maria said, "No, English, always the English or we will frighten her. Helen, how old are you?"

"Eighteen."

108

"That is old enough. We were all married at eighteen. Eighteen is a woman, not a girl. You are old enough to know the truth. But are you well enough to hear it now?" Helen nodded and prepared herself for she knew not what.

Maria gave her a long penetrating look. "You are strong, like me. I think you even look like me when I was your age. But it is maybe not a good thing that you hear this so soon after arriving. You have not even met the rest of your family yet. And you have obviously been through a bad time. You are sick and very thin. Perhaps I should tell you a little now, and later, when you are well again, I will tell you everything ..."

"No!" Helen exclaimed, her voice hoarse with inflammation and emotion. "Tell me everything now. Please. I have to know."

Maria looked at her sisters-in-law for their assent. One of them said quietly, "You must tell her, Maria, she will not rest until you do. But it is your story. We shall wait for you in the kitchen."

Maria nodded her agreement. Aunt Gino and Aunt Sonny stood and kissed Helen on the cheek, both saying, "Welcome, niece," before they left the room.

Maria took a glass of water from the bedside table and offered it to Helen. "Drink," she said, "then lie down again and you shall hear your mother's story. It is not a happy one. It will not be easy to tell it." She waited until Helen was comfortable and took her hand.

Helen thought how soft and smooth was the hand that held her own and noticed that the long blood-red nails matched the lipstick her new aunt was wearing.

"First, before I tell you about your Mama, I must tell you about our Mama, your Nonna. She is back in Italy now. She is the only daughter of a wealthy wine making family in Tuscany." She saw the question in Helen's eyes. "You do not know of Italy? It is a country in Europe. No? Did you go to school, Helen?"

"Dad wouldn't let me go to school because there was too much work to do at home. But he taught me to read and write."

Maria shook her head in disgust. "No matter. You have much to learn and we will teach you. Your Nonna's family owned a large vineyard in Italy and they made very good wine. Your Nonna was a wealthy young woman who should have made a good marriage, but she fell in love with one of the vineyard workers and when her Papa opposed the match, she ran off with this man and married him. They came to Australia to flee her Papa's wrath and they had four children, Gino, Sonny, me and Luisa. Our Papa was a hard worker and became a builder. He made the money and built part of this house for his family, but he was not a very nice man, Helen. He drank too much wine and he used to hit our Mama. When I was about six and Luisa was five, he hurt his back and could not work any longer. Gino was fourteen and went out to work. Then a year later, Sonny joined him, they worked hard and eventually started their own building business. Between them, they made a lot of money and supported us all. This made Papa very unhappy because he thought he was no longer a proper man and he drank more and more. He hit Mama a lot until one day Gino hit him back, then he never hit Mama again. But his mind was not good after that. He lived outside in the shed. Sometimes at night we could hear him crying, but when Mama tried to go to him, Gino and Sonny would stop her."

Maria paused, finding it difficult to go on, then inhaled deeply and continued. "Then one night, when we were all at mass and Luisa was home with a cold, he came into the house and went into Luisa's bed. We came back from church and found him there. He had done the business and was asleep, but Luisa," she shook her head sadly, "Luisa cried very much. She cried for many days. Gino and Sonny were very angry, they took Papa away and he never came back. The police came one day and told us that they found Papa's body washed up on

110

some rocks in the harbour. I never asked Gino or Sonny about that, but they were not surprised when they heard. Sometimes it is best not to know."

Maria turned her face away and continued as if talking to herself. "Then Mama came to me and said, Luisa is sick in the morning since Papa did the business. He ... he had made a baby. It was very shocking to us. Luisa was a little girl, eleven years old, almost twelve, I was just thirteen. I told Gino. He was very angry. He said the child was unholy and should not be born. I said it was more sinful to harm the child than for it to be born. He said the shame on the family would kill our Mama. He went away. Then he and Sonny came to Mama and said they knew someone who would marry Luisa, a good Catholic man who liked young girls. They said they knew a priest who would fix it and a way to make the man think the child was his. So they brought this man to the house. I had seen him before at mass. He was a very handsome man from up north and kept talking about a farm in Queensland and the house he had built there. He was here to sell some property and then he was going back to Queensland."

Maria closed her eyes for a moment and shook her head slowly back and forth, as if seeing something she couldn't quite believe. When she spoke again, her voice shuddered with unwept tears.

"Gino and Sonny got him very drunk. They gave Luisa some medicine to make her sleep, then they put this man in her bed and left him there. He did the business. Then Gino and Sonny went back in and beat him for committing the worst of sins and said they would kill him if he did not do the right thing. They kept him drunk and brought the priest around. This priest was a bad man who did bad things to children and Gino and Sonny threatened to expose him, so he fixed all the papers, married Luisa to this man and it was done. When Luisa woke up properly, she was on her way to Queensland with a husband

and a marriage certificate saying she was seventeen and had her mother's consent." Suddenly, Maria looked heavenward and wailed, "She was eleven! What were we thinking?" Then she put her head in her hands and wept.

Helen lay very still, her gaze fixed on her aunt. The story was monstrous, but familiar. So Mum's Papa had "done the business". So what? There was nothing new here. Except that she suddenly understood that her mother was not the woman she had appeared to be. She found herself doing a quick calculation. Mum would have been barely twelve, fifteen and eighteen when she gave birth to each of her daughters. And just twenty-one when she died.

Mum had been the age she was now when Sweetypie was born. She tried to imagine herself having a baby at twelve, and three children by this age. A child having children. It was unthinkable. She turned her face away.

Maria's weeping ceased. The room became silent. After a few minutes, Maria said quietly, "Your Papa, was he kind to our Luisa, Helen?"

In a very small voice, Helen replied, "No. He hit her a lot." A leaden silence followed.

Then Maria said, "He was a very bad man, Helen. We did not know how bad until after he was gone and Gino came to me in tears and said he had done a very foolish thing, that Harry Downing had done something terrible to a very small girl, only three years old, and that we must find Luisa and bring her home because she was not safe with him. And Mama kept saying that Luisa was not married before God, that what the priest had done was illegal because Luisa was too young. So Gino and Sonny tried to find Luisa. They went to Queensland, but it is a big place and they did not know where he came from. They came back and wrote many letters to many places, but it was five years before they were given an address. We were so excited. We wrote to Luisa to tell her that we were coming to

112

get her, but a letter came back from Harry Downing saying that our Luisa had died in childbirth and that he hoped we were happy with the result of the wicked trick we had played on him. Gino and Sonny have never forgiven themselves. But now here you are, and the unholy child died, which is perhaps for the best, and you have a young sister with blonde hair and blue eyes. So where is your sister, the one called Sweetypie? And your Papa?"

"Dead," Helen said, meaning Dad was dead. And suddenly, she meant Sweetypie too, for what would this new family make of her sister with her lost mind and strange ways? To explain Sweetypie, she would have to explain the birthday party to them. If she told them about that, she would have to tell them the truth about Mum, that it wasn't just drowning but murderous suicide. She felt weak with the memory of it all. "Dead," she repeated, "in the cyclone last week."

She thought she should correct them about Sis, but suddenly Sis should be dead too. Unholy they called her. That meant her grandfather had sired her by his own daughter. She had heard that spoken of in church. Unholy. Worse than death, worse than divorce. They would not love her or accept her. And if they would not love her, Helen would not let them have her, for Sis already knew enough of hate and rejection. No, she would not give her beloved sisters to people who would not love and accept them, even if they were family. She kept her mouth shut.

"And so you have come to us," Maria continued. "This is a good thing, Helen, or you would be alone. We will light candles and say prayers for your Mama and your sisters at mass. And what about the farm, is that yours now that your papa is dead?"

Helen suddenly saw complications if they thought the farm was hers. It would mean having to contact someone up north to decide what to do with it. No. That would mean discovery. She must protect Sis and Sweetypie at all costs.

113

"No," she replied, the first of many deliberate lies coming easily, "Dad was only the manager. It was never ours."

In that instant, Helen cut herself off from the truth and from her past.

CHAPTER SEVEN

Sis lowered her feet to the ground and swung around to level her gaze at Helen, something beyond revelation or accusation in her face, unreadable, unmoving, and silent for so long that Helen felt compelled to urge, "Well, say something. I know it's a shock, I know I betrayed you and Sweetypie shamefully, but you must have something to say."

Without a word, Sis rose, pulled Helen up with her and, not stopping to put on her hat or her boots, led her by the hand down the steps and up the slope towards the rainforest. "What is it, Sis? Where are you taking me?"

Sis didn't answer, but tightened her grip on Helen's hand and pulled her along.

Helen was not afraid, there was nothing threatening in Sis's behaviour, but she felt such intensity in the hand grip that she steeled herself for whatever was in store.

They entered the hushed world of the rainforest and found the path that Sweetypie had spent most of her life laying and repairing. Helen wondered if they were going all the way to the waterhole and worried that she might not make the steep climb, but Sis stopped about fifty feet up the track, parted two bushes and pulled Helen through. They walked a dozen paces and stopped in the damp muffled silence, the thick canopy overhead creating a low light which Helen took a moment to adjust to.

Sis released her hand and silently pointed down to a large flat-topped rock with marks scratched into the surface. Helen looked down and back up, confused. "Look," Sis said simply, her voice tight with something Helen didn't recognise.

Helen squatted next to it and saw that the marks were roughly hewn letters. Rubbing the leaf litter away, she made out the words, "Stewart Downing" and a date underneath. Confused, she looked up at Sis and was shocked to see the carefully constructed mask cracking, the bottom lip trembling as if she was about to cry. She knew Sis didn't, couldn't cry, as she herself didn't, couldn't cry.

"What is this?" she asked as she stood and put a comforting hand on Sis's shoulder. The hand was pushed away and Sis replied in a small, tired voice, "My son."

Dismayed, Helen said, "What are you talking about? What happened here?"

"My son," she repeated. "Born seven months after you left."

Helen gasped. The possibility had not even entered her mind during her fifty year absence. And suddenly she remembered that final beating and rape, and she voiced her thoughts. "The fight?"

"Yeah. The fight. I didn't give it a thought afterwards. Hell, what he did then, he'd done a thousand times before. Why should that time be any different from all the other times? I didn't even know, I was so bloody dumb."

Shocked, Helen put her hand back on Sis's shoulder and said, in the gentle voice that she'd always used when one of her girls was upset or when Raymond had been in terrible pain, "Tell me, darling." Her hand was not pushed away this time.

Sis looked down at the rock and waited a moment. Then she whispered darkly, her voice coloured with anguish, "I'd put on a bit of weight. Didn't pay much attention to it. Thought I was having the most godawful wind rumbling around inside my gut. Went on for months. Thought I'd got one of them parasites you get from the water. Didn't give it no mind, figured it would pass. I was so bloody busy, it never registered that I wasn't having periods. Then one day I got bad pains, thought I had food poisoning. Sweetypie got scared 'cos I was moaning and groaning so much. Ended up knocking her out with laudanum to get her to sleep."

"You didn't know you were in labour?"

"Nah. Not for a minute. Not til I started pushing and then the penny dropped. I was shit scared. I didn't know what to do, but it was all over real quick and there he was, lying between my legs making noises like a kitten." Her breath came in a sudden catch. "Beautiful he was, all this black hair and the sweetest little face." Her mouth twisted with emotion and she paused.

"Go on, Sissy. I'm listening." Helen, remembering her own difficult labours in a modern hospital with doctors and nurses and her man by her side to love and encourage her through it all, felt overcome by deep, helpless sympathy towards Sis. With the instinct of the children they once were, she moved closer to Sis, wrapped an arm around her waist and rested her head on the muscly shoulder. Sis did not respond, but neither did she pull away.

"I sat up and I held him. I thought and thought. Didn't know what to do. Then I remembered that bloody fight and it hit me. It was his, the baby was his. And it made me sick to think about it."

117

Helen felt a shudder of revulsion pass through Sis's body. Then she was still again.

"Like Mum said about me in that letter, I thought he was unholy. Father O'Keefe used to preach about it. Remember? It was a sin. The worst kinda sin."

"Father O'Keefe? He had no right to talk about sin in others."

"Yeah, but I didn't think about that then. All I could think about was he was Dad's. Dad's and mine. He was unholy." She paused and Helen gave her a little squeeze of sympathy. "But when I looked at him, Helly, he was so little and so helpless and it wasn't his fault who made him. He was innocent. And he was mine. He deserved a name. Stewart, after our neighbours, because the Stewarts were the best people in the world."

Sis shuddered again, the sort of shudder that usually precedes sobbing, but she didn't cry. Instead, she stared down at the tiny memorial, her voice raised itself above the whisper and she suddenly cried, "And now you tell me it wasn't so! That bastard wasn't my father after all! My son wasn't unholy, but I am? Jeez, I expected some surprises, but not this." She squirmed, thrust Helen away from her, turned and fled.

For a moment, Helen felt unable to move. She let Sis's revelation penetrate, really penetrate and the shock of it made her put her hand over her mouth to stop the cry that rose up in her throat.

She had left Sis to this nightmare all by herself. She had stepped onto the SEA BEA and not given a thought to what she might be leaving behind. Was it stupidity or naivety or selfishness that had made her so sure that Sis and Sweetypie would be alright?

No, it was none of those.

Standing there in the damp stillness with the smells and colours and noises that had once been her world, feeling the sensations of her childhood flood unbeckoned through her,

Helen saw clearly, for the first time in fifty years, that her life here had been terribly small, claustrophobic and aberrant.

How aberrant, only she and Sis would ever know.

Her memories of it now were coloured in shades of black. Dark, dirty, moody memories that made her want to walk into a fresh breeze in the sunlight to cleanse herself of them.

That was what had made her leave. Going into the light. Never going back into the darkness.

She hadn't even been aware of that darkness in her mind and her soul until she'd been forced to spend those nights away from home during the cyclone. First with Sarge's family. Boys and girls her own age, but with an openness and a freedom that Helen had not understood back then.

Then in the hotel where, in spite of the uncontrollable horrors going on outside, inside only kindness, generosity and decency were shown.

And that shock when, after the cyclone had passed and the mothers took their small children downstairs to bathe them in the flood water, Helen had seen no maiming, no scarring, no evidence of injury or suffering.

Until that moment, she'd assumed all little girls were physically scarred as she and Sis and Sweetypie were scarred.

That revelation alone had turned her subconscious away from home. Even with Dad gone.

She squatted next to the rock again and stroked its surface. If she'd come back, she would have been with Sis during the pregnancy, maybe even identified it, and perhaps been able to prepare for the labour.

How different Sis's life would have been with a son to love and raise. Would he be alive now if Helen had stayed?

But he had died, little Stewart Downing, son of Sis.

How? Why?

She had to know.

Helen found Sis sitting limply on the top step, looking out over her kingdom of cane through narrowed eyes, cigarette hanging disinterestedly from her grim mouth, her composure regained, at least superficially. A bottle of Johnny Walker stood unopened between her feet. The wall of silence around her was so intense that Helen felt any sound would be desecration. She went inside quietly, opened cupboards in the kitchen until she found what she wanted and came back out to the veranda with two glasses.

Seating herself next to Sis, she silently followed her gaze out over the top of the cane. She remembered when you could see clear down to the ocean after the front field had been cut, a view uninterrupted until it came to the little sugar shack town of two thousand people. Now, even though the cane was high, she could see new suburbs creeping up to their eastern boundary and houses crawling up the sides of the mountains to the north and south. They once had absolute privacy. Now they were surrounded on three sides with uninvited humanity, a hundred thousand of them. And yet, despite the encroaching populace, the atmosphere of isolation persisted.

After a while, Helen leaned across and took the bottle, opened it and poured two glasses. She handed one to Sis who downed it in one swig and immediately held it out for a refill. Helen obeyed. Sis swigged again and put it down.

Helen said into the silence, "What happened to him, Sis?"

"I let him die," Sis said without preamble, her eyes still focused on the distant horizon, "that's what happened to him." She took the bottle and gulped straight from it. Then the words began to tumble from her grimly set mouth. Helen leaned forward and listened intently. "There was nothing wrong with him. I just let him die. I didn't know what to do, see. Oh, it wasn't that I didn't know how to look after him, it was just that I didn't know what I would tell anyone, jeez, the men and all. When I saw him there on the bed, I went into a flat

120

panic." She took a long deep breath. "Damn, that was a bastard of a year! There was no crop that season, not after that bloody cyclone, only devastation and hardship everywhere, but I was better off than most. We had money in the bank, we could survive, but a lot didn't. I saw so many families up and leave their farms and Bill's father said, buy up Sis, you're twenty one and you own it now, you got money, buy up because it'll never be cheaper. So I did. I bought six farms that year, kept the old owners and their families on as managers and put on a lot of local men to get the properties into shape before the next planting. They were grateful for the work. I helped them out with jobs and they repaid me by working their bloody butts off. I was working hard, too, sunrise to sunset and then some."

Sis hung her head, pondering her words as she spoke them. "Yeah, I worked so hard I bloody near wore myself out, I suppose so I wouldn't have to think so much about what happened here and you being gone an' all. Seemed at the time there was no choice, but I coulda just pottered on the way we had been. We had a good farm to begin with, I knew that me and Sweetypie would never go without. But I bought up big, like some women buy hats when they get depressed, only instead of hats, I bought cane farms. And I kept buying them. Shit. I got the biggest family owned cane property in Australia, got myself more managers than I can keep track of and I don't know how many farm hands, and not because I need the money or I'm driven by ambition. Ha! Because I didn't know how to buy bloody hats!"

She glanced up at Helen, saw the sympathy there and looked away quickly. "After he was born, like I said, I panicked, I didn't know what to do. He was making a lot of noise and I had Mr Stewart and some of the men coming up to the house for a meeting, so I wrapped him up and took him up into the rainforest and just left him there. Thought he'd be alright, thought it'd be no time at all before I got back to him, but I didn't have the place to myself again until well after dark. I couldn't find him at first, kept going around in circles before I almost tripped over him. He was still alive, but sort of limp and quiet. I brought him down here, but christalmighty, I just didn't know what to do. My breasts were filling up, but he was too weak to suck. I was useless. All those years of caring for you and Sweetypie, and I let my own son die."

Sis contemplated that, lighting a fresh cigarette off the end of the old one and exhaling the smoke slowly until it hung in a heavy cloud around her face. "Yeah, maybe I wanted him to die. I coulda done more. I coulda got some help, but I was so ashamed. How was I gunna explain his sudden appearance? No one woulda believed me, anyway, they all thought Dad was such a bloody saint. So I just sat and held him and when he stopped breathing through the night, I took him back up into the rainforest and buried him. I put that rock over him so the animals couldn't dig him up and I carved his name into it. Problem solved." She gave Helen a sudden piercing look. "You believe in God, Helen?"

Helen shook her head, unable to find words that might ease the eternal pain of a mother who had lost her child.

"Well, I reckon I still did then and I hated the sonofabitch for a long time after that. I reckon the bastard never gave me an even break. Then one morning I woke up and wondered why I hated someone who didn't exist. All those years listening to that damn priest tell us about our loving God and all that ... crap." She spat the word out. "How he watched over us and cared for us. Some God, hey? A God who looks down on a man that rapes his little girls and just..." she shrugged her shoulders, "...lets it happen? What sorta love is that?" She became pensive again. "Made life a little easier, you know, when I figured out we were all on our own, that there wasn't anyone up there to keep tabs on us and make rules for us that we couldn't keep. Like love your enemies. Now, there's a doozy, hey? That's when I figured that my son wasn't gunna go to hell because there wasn't no hell. That there was no punishment because there was no punisher. He just went into the earth where he belonged, where we'll all belong one day."

Helen said, "If I'd stayed …"

"I told you before, don't worry about it. You shoulda got out. It wasn't your fault."

"But if I'd stayed," she persisted, feeling the need for self flagellation, "you'd have had some help, maybe he wouldn't have..."

"...died? Dunno about that. Thinking about it now, I reckon if you'd been here, we'd have done the same thing. When the men came, we'd have taken him into the rainforest or the cubby. I don't reckon it woulda been any different. And I reckon," she paused, looking for the right words, "I reckon there mighta been something wrong with him. He was too limp, weak like, you know? Didn't respond like Sweetypie used to, the way she'd squeal and kick her little arms and legs all over the place. Nah, he didn't do none of that. He wasn't right some how."

"But …"

Sis turned to face Helen full on. "Jeez, Helen, will you give it a rest? What do want me to say? That you're to blame? You want me to punish you? Make you feel guilty about something you didn't even know about? Don't be so bloody stupid. It wasn't your fault. It was his. His! Alright?"

Helen sighed deeply. "Alright." She felt a sense of acquittal. Even so, her grief for her sister's loss needed expression. Resting her hand on Sis's knee, she said sadly, "I'm so sorry, Sis."

Sis dropped her cigarette butt into her empty glass and unexpectedly placed her hand over Helen's. "Yeah," she said simply, and Helen felt the energy flow between them as it once had.

They sat together in deep brooding silence, giving the child buried in the rainforest his period of mourning.

After awhile, Sis took her hand from Helen's and dug deep into her overall pocket for the cigarette packet. She offered one to Helen. "No thanks." Helen smiled in an attempt to lift the melancholy. "I gave it up just before the first face lift."

Welcoming the change of mood, Sis put her hand under Helen's chin and turned her face this way and that to examine it. "How many you had?" she asked.

"Three. No more skin left to stretch, this is it until the grave."

"Can't see no scars. Where are they?" Helen pulled back her hair and let Sis feel the concealed ridge of scar tissue behind the ears and under her hairline. "I hear about plastic surgery all the time. Seems like you ain't anybody these days if you haven't had it all nipped and tucked. You had anything else done?" Helen nodded and pointed to her breasts, belly and hips. Then she indicated lower down.

Sis's eyes opened wide. "You're kidding. What do they call that? A cunt lift?" She meant it as a joke, but Helen nodded in all seriousness.

"I had the damage repaired. That was the first surgery I had, didn't have my first face lift for another ten years." She grinned. "So you can see what my priorities were."

"Huh! Well, you ain't the only one to have that done. Sweetypie had repairs done too, eleven years ago. And what a bloody circus that was."

Helen was stunned. The first thing she could think of saying was, "How on earth did you get her into hospital?"

"Didn't. Had the hospital come here. Cost an arm and a leg, but it was worth it. She don't collapse on me suddenly like she used to."

Helen waited for the story, but Sis swigged from the almost empty bottle instead, wiped her mouth with the back of her hand and said, "I'm thinking."

Helen was still sipping her way through her first glass. She could see she would have to wait for the rest of the story. Sis was changing direction once again. "Yes?"

"That letter Mum wrote. Mum said Dad didn't know and the priest didn't know. You know, about who my ... real father was. Well, maybe that sodomising little bastard of a priest didn't know, but Dad did. I reckon he knew from the time I was born."

"How so, Sis?"

"Because of what he wrote to Mum's brothers, you know, about what a dirty trick they played on him. But more because he always treated me differently. Sure, he did the same things to me what he done to you, but he was never nice to me. He was nice to you and Sweetypie. He always treated you like you mattered. I didn't matter. Don't you remember all those times he'd come back from town with something pretty for you and Sweetypie, but there was never anything for me? Not a damn thing. I remember the day he brought back the new curtains and bedspreads for you both, but he acted like I wasn't even in the room."

"It hurt me when he did that, Sis. I was embarrassed for you. I remember hiding some of them away because I didn't want to have them if you couldn't have them, too. I remember looking over at you when he gave me those things and seeing your face. You were very good at concealing the hurt, but I could always see it."

"Yeah, I knew that. I knew it wasn't your fault. It was his intention to hurt me, not you. Because he knew. Shit. Think about it. It must have been awhile before Mum's mother knew she was pregnant, and then those brothers got hold of him and set him up. I was born way before the nine months since he married Mum and he could count. But he was a dyed-in-the-wool Catholic and once you were married, you were stuck with each other. I remember him saying so on more than one

125

occasion. Divorce was worse than death, he used to say." She shook her head slowly back and forth. "It's like all the pieces of the puzzle are finally falling into place. He always called me a wog bitch, but he never called you or Sweetypie that. And he never beat you or Sweetypie. Never. He knew alright, and he took it out on me every bloody chance he could."

"I never really thought about it before, but I believe you are right, Sis. Of course, he had to know."

Sis rose suddenly, paced up and down the veranda and hit the banister next to Helen hard with her fist, her other hand gripping the whisky bottle tightly. "Jeez!" Helen stood quickly and seated herself in the chair, watching Sis work through this part of their past. "It didn't matter how hard I tried, I couldn't please the bastard. And I did try to please him, not because I loved him or nothing, but because I thought it would keep me outa trouble. I learned everything he taught me real well – reading and writing and numbers, how to run the farm, how to build bridges and sheds, how to fix machinery, how to walk, talk and think like him – hell, I learned how to be a good son like no other son ever learned, 'cos that's what I always thought the problem was. It was because I was a girl, see, and he wanted a boy. I used to think he hit me all the time because I wasn't a bloody boy."

She touched the mangled bridge of her nose and shook her head from side to side. "Shit. Broke this bloody thing so many times I lost count, and do you remember when he ran over my foot, broke every toe, he was laughing for chrissake! And those other times he broke my hand, my collarbone, my ankle, jeez, I was the original walking wounded. It's a bloody wonder I still got any working parts left. And did I get any time off to heal? Nah, not with him. I was back working the next day every time. What a bloody monster he was."

Sis drained the last drops of whisky. "I'm remembering something," she said, a faraway look in her eyes. "Something I ain't thought about in sixty years."

"Tell me, darling."

Sis turned away so that Helen couldn't see the struggle going on in her face and stared out across the cane fields. She began with contained anger. "I'm in the bottom field with Dad. I reckon I'm about ten. It was after a big storm and one of the culverts across the road was blocked. Dad loaded me up with shovels and picks and I followed him down the road til we came to the culvert. Christ those things were heavy. They kept slipping outa my hands and I'd have to pick them up and balance them – I was such a runt of a kid. Well, Dad hacked away at the rubbish in the culvert with the pick and I followed him with the shovel. Took us the better part of a couple of hours. I was bloody buggered when we finished. We were sitting down, catching our breath. Dad was whistling – you know how he used to whistle when he was out in the cane fields, sorta like a happy whistle, no tune, just happy. He picked up a lump of dirt and started rubbing it between his hands. I say, what are you doing Dad? He says, checking the soil Sis. How do you do that, I asks. So he shows me. Rub it between your hands like this, he says, and if it breaks apart real easy like this, it's good soil. Then he sniffed it and put it close to my face. Sniff it, he says, tell me what you smell. Sorta rotten but sweet, I says. That's right, he says, that's right clever of you. He smiles at me and I get all excited because I think I'm pleasing him. I want to please him some more. And I want to know more. How do you tell when it's not good soil, I ask. I'll show you, he says, follow me. So I up and follow him and we walk all the way down to the flats. Stop at Taylor's top field. Pick up some soil, he says, and rub it like I showed you. So I do, but it doesn't come apart, it sticks to my hands like glue. Now smell it, he says. I smell it and it smells sour. What

127

does that mean, I ask. Poor drainage to start with, he says, and Taylor's such a greedy bastard he doesn't rest his soil. Expects a crop every year, but doesn't put anything back into the soil. You gotta rest the soil, like I do, every few years, just let it lie and let the cane mulch rot down into it. And you gotta have good drainage. He went on talking like this for a long time. I hung on his every word and for awhile I felt sorta … sorta …" She struggled for the right word.

"Important?"

"Yeah. Important. You know, like I counted. I thought he liked me in those few moments when he was teaching me about the soil. And then we heard a noise. It was a group of Italian canecutters going to their campfire for a smoko. About a dozen of them, filthy, smelly, unshaven, toothless – a rough looking lot. They saluted Dad and he tipped his hat to them. And then …." The words caught in her throat and her body tensed as she allowed the memory to flow.

"Go on, Sis, I'm listening."

"… and then he looks down at me with this strange look on his face, a look of pure disgust, and says, you look like one of them wog canecutters, Sis, shit you're an ugly bitch. And he sorta laughs, cruel like, and says, if you didn't have a neck, we'd think you were a bloody frog. And he goes off laughing, just walks away laughing, leaving me behind to find my own way home."

"And you, Sis, how did you feel?"

Sis paused, then said bitterly, "Crushed. I couldn't move. I didn't understand what had happened. I didn't understand what I had done wrong."

"And now you do."

"Yeah." Her face darkened as she turned back to face Helen. "Yeah, now I do. I didn't do nothing wrong. He was a cruel, mad bastard. How could you do that to a little kid and get a kick out of it?" She shook her head in disgust. "You know what else?"

"What, Sissy?" Helen asked kindly, deeply sorry for her sister's pain, but not wanting to stop the conversation. Keep her talking, she thought, let the years close between us.

Sis sat down, heavy from the effects of alcohol and memories. "I reckon … yeah, I reckon Mum planned to take me to Sydney with her. You know, in that letter, when she said I was dead. I reckon she was just telling them what she thought they wanted to hear and then they woulda sent her the money. Then I reckon she woulda packed us all up and taken us south. She wouldn't have taken you two and left me here with Dad. She wouldn't have," she turned towards Helen, "would she?" The question had an edge of desperation to it. She reached quickly for a cigarette.

Helen shook her head vehemently. "Never. Not in a million years. You're right, she was just playing it safe so she could get home. She would have counted on her mother loving you in the flesh when she arrived. And Nonna would have loved you on sight." Suddenly, she knew what Sis needed to hear. "You know why?"

"Why?"

"Because you are the image of her. Of our grandmother. In features, in size, in colouring. When I saw you come out onto the veranda earlier, my heart jumped, you look so much like her."

Sis's eyes opened wide in drunken surprise. "No shit?"

"No shit."

"Even with this mashed nose and the crew cut?"

"Even so, and she was always a most elegant woman. She had long grey hair that she wore in a chignon high on her head, always wore the most beautifully tailored clothes and had a sort of regal bearing that caught everyone's attention as soon as she entered a room, despite the fact that she only came up to my shoulder."

"Don't sound much like me except for the being short bit."

"You are more like her than you could possibly know, Sis. I bet that you command attention whenever you are with anyone."

"Well, I'm the bloody boss, so why wouldn't I? But I sure ain't elegant." She plucked at her mannish attire.

"Ah, but you love beautiful clothes, even if you've never worn them. You have a wardrobe full of them. You also have her regal bearing. And the deep, gravelly smoker's voice."

"She smoked?"

"She did. Three packs a day. And she loved a good wine or two, but I never saw her drunk. Your features are her features, your smile is her smile, and when you growl, you sound just like her telling off one of her grandchildren."

"Well, bugger me." Sis took several deep draws on her cigarette and let some of the tension go. Then she nodded as if convincing herself of what she now said. "So there's no way Mum woulda left me behind, is there, especially not if I looked just like her mother?"

"I'm certain of it. Mum had no favourites with us, she loved us all."

"Yeah." Sis gave that some thought. "Yeah. She did, didn't she? I reckon you're right about that. She never picked on me. Jeez, she never picked on any of us. I don't remember an angry word ever coming out of her fat little face." She lifted her head suddenly. "No, that's not true. I remember her losing it once. Just once." She stopped, not willing to face that memory just yet, and shook her head slowly. "And you reckon she was just twelve when she had me? Christ, she was just a kid, a poor helpless little kid."

Helen sensed Sis sinking into a maudlin state of mind. Where Mum was concerned, there was much to be sad about.

She offered her unfinished glass of whisky to Sis and said, "Let's talk about something else for awhile."

"Like what?"

"Well, I was thinking about the day we discovered the cubby. That was a good day, wasn't it?"

"Yeah. Maybe that was one day in our miserable lives that was good. Yeah. Do you remember …?"

"Like it was yesterday."

CHAPTER EIGHT

Mum slumbered uneasily in the stiflingly hot bedroom. Sweetypie was having her afternoon nap in the covered cot in Sis's room. Dad had gone across the river to see someone about buying a new pony. The girls had the afternoon to themselves.

Sis shoved bread and fruit into a cotton drawstring dillybag, tied it around her waist, and said, "Come on, let's go."

They ran into the rainforest behind the house and headed straight up towards the climbing tree. Scrambling up the steepest part of the slope behind the tree where the branches grew into the side of the mountain, they ran along the thickest branch and climbed like little monkeys to the next branch, where Sis had built a little tree house from pieces of scrap timber. Here they had views over the trees below them, right down to the flats and the Inlet.

At eight years of age, Sis was already something of an accomplished carpenter. Tools and timber stowed away in the *cleft of the branch were brought out and she began nailing an extension to their tree house.*

A noise below distracted her.

They looked down and saw Sweetypie, a naked two year old escapee from the cot they'd forgotten to lock, pointing up and giggling, "I can seeeeee you!"

"Sweetypie! What are you doing here? Wait there, we'll be right down." Sis and Helen began clambering down, but before they could reach the ground Sweetypie had disappeared with a loud giggle and a challenge, "I hide. Find me."

They leapt after her, but she was gone. Her giggles alerted them to the direction she was going in, which seemed to be straight up, and they pursued her as fast as their young legs would allow them, but where Sweetypie slipped beneath the ferns and bushes with ease, they had to push them aside and fight their way through. Her giggles became softer and more distant until they could no longer hear her.

Panicked, Sis and Helen stopped and circled slowly, trying to pick up any sound from Sweetypie, but hearing only the muffled silence of the rainforest. They called out to her, ran this way and that, called some more, then stopped.

"She'll come back down when she's hungry," Sis tried to reassure herself, but she was becoming alarmed. She and Helen knew their way around within their limited boundaries, but even so she was always pulling Helen back when she thought they were getting too far from the house. Sweetypie was too young to know about boundaries.

Exhausted, Sis sat down to think. A white face with a cheeky grin that almost split it in two poked out from under the bush in front of her. "Sweetypie!" she cried, rushing towards her with relief, but the toddler was gone and the game recommenced.

This time, they managed to keep her giggles just in front of them until they became louder and louder – and then suddenly the giggles stopped. Sis and Helen burst through the bush and nearly tumbled headlong into water. "Look." Sweetypie stood at the edge of a waterhole rimmed with black rocks, fed by a waterfall that seemed to come straight out of the ground somewhere above them. "Pretty pretty."

Sis pulled her back from the water's edge. She and Helen could swim, having been brought up next to a river, but Sweetypie had not yet learned.

They stood in a group and looked around them.

Sweetypie was right, it was pretty. Surrounded by large trees and closed in with dense undergrowth, the falling water bubbled then stilled as it flowed toward the lower edge of the waterhole and gently rolled over the rocks into a permanent stream. Sis thought it might run down into the river below, the river that ran past their own house. Even at the height of the Dry Season, the river never ran dry like some of the other streams. Maybe this spring-fed waterhole was the reason why.

With a sense of wonder, they felt the soft silence surround them, broken only by the muted sound of birds high up in the canopy and the gentle burble of the waterfall.

It was irresistible. Without a word, the two older girls doffed their dresses and panties and waded into the water. It was cool and sweet. As they immersed themselves, they were filled with the joy that comes from being the first to discover something special, something wonderful, something that belonged to them exclusively. Splashing around with much squealing and laughter, they dived into the deeper part, grabbed each other by the hands and came up together, laughing.

"Look at meeeeeeeee!" they heard and turned just as Sweetypie launched herself belly first into the water. She sank like a rock. Sis went down after her before there was time to think. And there she was, gliding through the water like a fish, eyes wide open, grinning mouth sealed against drowning, little arms and legs going like turbines. Sis reached her, yanked her by the hair and pulled her up. Spurting out a mouthful of water, Sweetypie cried ecstatically, "More, Sissy, more!"

The girls laughed with delight. "You're a real little terror, Sweetypie. Time you learned to swim. Come on, get over here. Good girl. Yes yes, on your back like that. Now look at Helen. See how she floats? I'm gunna let you go – yes yes, that's it! Hey, Helen, Sweetypie can float."

Flat on their backs with arms and legs spread like upturned starfishes, the three of them floated in the stillness, staring up through the canopy of trees, hearing the silence and not daring to breach it.

Sis felt something strange happening inside her. She let it shape and waited for understanding. It came to her tenderly.

"This can be our place," she whispered, and Helen understood immediately what she meant.

"Our safe place," she affirmed.

"Yeah. Our safe place. He'd never find it, not in a million years. Anyway, he hates it up here, reckons the rainforest makes his toes turn green." They giggled at the thought of Dad with green toes. Dad was a dill.

Pulling Sweetypie to the edge, they hauled themselves up onto a big round, flat rock and let the warm air dry them. Sis was still sore from Dad's last nocturnal visit, but she noted how the water soothed the inflammation and her body felt cool and comfortable. They shared the bread and fruit and dipped their faces into the water to drink. Sweetypie pulled back, giggling, and said, "I did wee-wees."

"In the water? Oh, Sweetypie, that's yucky. Now we're drinking it. Let's make a rule – no wee-wees in the water. Wee-wees only in the bushes. Alright?"

Chastened, Sweetypie nodded, then, never glum for longer than two seconds, she skipped over the rocks towards the waterfall. Standing directly under the shower of water, she turned and turned and turned again, then suddenly she was gone. It was a full minute of silence before Sis and Helen realised she really was gone. Jumping up, they ran to the edge of the waterfall to scan the water below, but it was crystal clear and there was no sign of Sweetypie. They called and looked around, but she was nowhere to be seen. Then came the distinctive giggle, but it was muffled and distant. Bamboozled, they waited until it came again. It didn't, but instead a small hand appeared through the centre of the waterfall and waved at them.

"She's hiding behind the waterfall," Sis said and stepped through the deluge, dragging Helen with her.

They stood in silvery darkness, the curtain of water behind them, the black rock face before them. As their eyes adjusted to the darkness, they saw a round, pink bottom dissolve into the rock. Sis lunged forward to grab it, but was too late. Her head collided with rock but her hand found an empty space. Rubbing her forehead, she sank to her knees and felt rather than saw the gap in the rock. "Sweetypie!" she called loudly. Her voice echoed back. Sis felt the thrill of discovery course through her for the second time that day. But this was even more exciting.

The gap was about six feet across and three feet high. Feeling her way with both hands, she ducked under and came up on damp sand, sensing a big space opening around her. Helen followed her in on hands and knees. It was almost pitch black, but they could see a light patch coming towards them. A small cool hand found Sis's and the voice commanded, "Come see." They followed her blindly, she with her cat's eyesight leading with absolute confidence.

The darkness gave way to shadows, they went to the right and then to the left and found themselves standing in the centre of a dimly lit cave of huge proportions, the walls curving up to a ceiling so high above them that they could not see its apex clearly. But there was light coming in from somewhere and the air was still, but fresh and cool. Sis turned on the spot, looking up until she saw a patch of wall lighter than the rest. It was a small tunnel running sideways out of the cave through the side of the mountain, letting in the air and light, but keeping out the wind and water.

Excitement rose in their breasts and they squealed and clapped. Realising what they had discovered, they began to run around the perimeter of the cave, their cave, uncaring when their naked bodies scraped against the rough walls, delighted at the feel of the cool dry white sand reflecting the poor light back at them, digging their toes deep into it and kicking it at each other. They pulled away the cobwebs draping the walls, unafraid as spiders scuttled away. Meeting in the centre, Sis and Helen flopped down in a giggling huddle and made plans.

"This is the best cubby house ever," Sis declared.

"We can bring things here. We can bring some tucker," Helen offered, "and candles so we can come at night."

"Yeah, that's a good idea, and pillows so we can lie down and ..."

"... and something to sit on and ..."

"... some plates and knives and forks ..."

"... and cups and billy tea. We can have a party."

"We can do whatever we want here. It's our cubby, our secret cubby."

Their excitement gathered momentum as they plotted and planned. They weren't paying attention to their baby sister until they heard her call out and ran to join her at the back of the cave. Her two little hands, pressed up against the cave wall, were surrounded by a spray of faded red. Sis pulled her hands away from the wall and they saw two small handprints outlined against the rock. Above them were more hand prints, and then they looked around them and saw many hand prints. Small hands, all of them. Children's hands. And they felt the presence of those who had come before, of the many dark skinned children who had found the cave just as they had and left their mark in the only way they knew how – a mouthful of powdered rock and water sprayed around their hands in a declaration, "I was here."

And when next the girls climbed the mountain to the cubby, provisions wrapped in pillow cases slung over their shoulders, they included a tin of white paint from the shed which they poured into the pump-action kerosene fly-sprayer and sprayed around their hands to join the many others on the cubby wall and announce "I was here, too."

Sweetypie at the bottom, Helen just above her and Sis at the top.

CHAPTER NINE

"Yeah," Sis said, her eyes heavy lidded, "bloody good day, that one. Jeez," she yawned and stretched, "I'm getting corners on me bum. Not used to all this sitting around." She heaved herself up and leaned against the veranda post, the cigarette hanging loosely from the corner of her mouth. Not quite drunk, but well on the way.

Helen caught the yawn and continued it. The change in conversation had relaxed them both. She said, "I need coffee." Sis nodded toward the kitchen and Helen went inside to make it.

She heard Sis outside on her mobile, following up on her voicemail messages. She didn't hurry, taking her time to find what she needed and waiting until she heard the clatter of the mobile phone on the veranda table before taking a tray laden with coffee, cake and biscuits out to Sis. They poured and sipped, poured again and sipped in silence, both of them needing a break from the intensity of the day.

Then, without realising it, they drifted into polite conversation about neighbours, sugar prices, changes in the town, Helen's daughters, Bill's cancer, climatic changes and the cost of living. Sis talked easily, as if the fifty years and all it meant had never existed. Helen wondered if that would change as the alcohol wore off. She hoped not, but suspected it might. You don't wipe fifty years of repressed pain away so easily.

The shadow from the mountain had crossed the river. "Shit," Sis exclaimed suddenly, "Sweetypie'll be home soon and I ain't defrosted the bloody cake."

"Defrost? Do you bake them in advance now?" Helen asked, remembering the daily ritual of the small baking tin coming out of the oven, filling the old kitchen with sweet aromas. As she spoke, they heard the distant murmuring of the motorbike.

"Don't be bloody silly. I buy them in bulk and freeze the bastards. Come on, I'll show you."

Helen stood back while Sis opened the upright freezer to reveal it packed solidly with cake boxes. Taking one, she removed the cardboard, sat the cake on a corkboard in the centre of the table, dug small holes into it with a metal skewer and jammed six coloured candles in around its frozen perimeter. As she leaned across to light them, the screen door banged.

"Oooooh. A birthday cake. It's my birthday, it's my birthday, it's my birthday!" Sweetypie sang as she had every day for fifty eight years, skipping around the table with pure delight, her wrinkled features twisting into a joyful grimace.

"Blow out the candles, little one," Sis said, as she had also said every day for fifty eight years, "and we'll sing you happy birthday."

Sweetypie took a noisy deep breath as Sis and Helen, united by the ritual, launched into a discordant rendition of Happy Birthday To You. Then she leaned right over the cake and blew, spittle landing in droplets on the table. She squealed as the flames became tiny puffs of smoke, then wailed, "Where's my present?"

"Here, darling," Sis said, taking a small wrapped parcel from the kitchen drawer. Sweetypie tore into the pink paper and held the silver and pink bracelet up to the light. "Pretty pretty," she declared, well pleased, and pulled it onto her wrist. Sis cut a piece of the still-frozen cake and said, "I'll bring it to you in the bath. Now hop to it."

Sis followed Sweetypie and Helen followed Sis into the bathroom, Sis carrying the piece of cake like a religious relic on a pink plate. Sweetypie filled the bath, added bath salts and bath toys, and undressed. Once she was immersed, Sis bent down to hand her the cake and Sweetypie wrinkled her nose disapprovingly. "What's wrong, little one?"

"You smell like that Johnny medicine, Sissy, and your eyes are all red and you're talking funny, all slow and shooshy. I don't like it when you talk like that. You got a headache again?"

Sis glanced up at Helen's wry smile. "Yep. Got a headache again. But it's better now. Come on, eat up." Sweetypie scoffed the cake in two bites, leaving a ring of frozen chocolate around her mouth. "Now, under you go." Holding her nose, Sweetypie fell backwards into the water while Sis quickly scrubbed her hair and scalp.

She came up sputtering. "Helly do the rest."

Sis stepped back. "Yeah, why the hell not." She tossed the sponge to Helen. "Your turn, Helly, away you go." Helen did not miss the vengeful glint in Sis's eyes.

Sweetypie splashed and swooshed the water while Helen struggled to apply the soapy sponge, getting soaked in the process. Thinking she was finished, Helen pulled away, but Sweetypie cried, "Don't forget the other bit!" and lifted her bum out of the water to expose her genitals. Helen applied the sponge again, wondering as she did so how she could have forgotten this. It had once been part of her daily life. She held the saturated sponge high and squeezed, watching the water ooze down the exposed flesh, noting with surprise how normal everything appeared and remembering with a shock of adrenalin how torn and angry the perpetually seeping wounds had once been.

Turning to make a remark to Sis, she realised her sister had slipped out of the room and left her to it. Well, so be it. It wasn't as if she had never done this before. It was simply that she had not done it for fifty years. She turned back to the task.

Towelled, powdered and nightied, Sweetypie led the way back to the kitchen. Sis had prepared the meal while they were in the bathroom. Chops, mash potato and peas with gravy. They took trays outside and watched the evening become night, Sweetypie once again chattering on relentlessly, Sis hanging on every word and giving the appropriate responses. Mosquito coils under each chair wafted their inoffensive fumes into the evening air.

Tinned fruit salad and ice-cream followed for dessert.

Sweetypie yawned loudly. "Teeth, toilet and into bed, little one," Sis ordered and they followed her inside to continue the ritual.

The pink air conditioner was turned on, then a bedtime story in the form of a Thomas Tank Engine DVD which they all sat through, and which Helen had the impression had been sat through countless times before, many hugs and kisses and lights out.

Sweetypie's day was over.

Helen went into the kitchen, but before she could offer to help clean up, Sis had it done by rote. Cake into bin, dishes into dishwasher, bracelet retrieved, rewrapped and back into drawer, everything wiped over and spotless, kitchen and passage floors quickly mopped and the ritual was complete.

Until tomorrow.

Sis went into the bathroom and Helen heard the shower running. Not sure what she should do next, she went out on to the veranda and waited.

It was no surprise when the pot of strong black tea appeared, its bearer wearing fresh shorts and a dark t-shirt. Helen gratefully poured herself a cup. She'd seen enough alcohol for one day.

Not so Sis. She produced another bottle of Johnny Walker and proceeded to put a sizable dent in it. Helen wondered if this was part of the ritual, or whether the day was simply taking its toll. Her instincts told her that the teapot was the ritual and the whisky a survival tool. She poured herself a second cup of tea and leaned back. Fatigue was about to have its way.

They watched the shadows across the cane fields darken and become night.

Sis took a long drink from the bottle, belched loudly and relaxed back into the mellow darkness. As tough as she was, even she couldn't deny that she was well and truly drunk. At least, Helen thought, she's less hostile, almost friendly, so perhaps I should be grateful. She watched Sis down the booze with the ease of a practiced drinker.

"So," Sis drawled after awhile, having had time to think about the direction in which she wanted the conversation to continue, "so you got two daughters. I was surprised when Bill told me you'd married Carrots, but I nearly fell off my chair when he told me you'd had a kid. And then another one two years later. Shit, you were almost an old lady by then. How long between getting married and having your kids – fifteen, twenty years?"

"Twenty three years."

"Seems like a bloody long time to wait before starting a family. Was it deliberate?"

Helen thought the question oddly personal, but then, she owed it to Sis after the revelation about the dead baby under the rock. "No."

"Come on, you came here to talk. So talk. Tell me about Carrots."

"Raymond."

"Alright. Raymond. But he'll always be Carrots to me."

Helen opened her mouth to begin, but her throat caught with a gulp instead. It had been two years since his death, but this still happened whenever she needed to speak of him. It was not lost on Sis who leaned forward unsteadily with unexpected sympathy and patted her knee just like any normal sister consoling the bereaved widow. "Shit, Helen," she slurred, "I'm sorry. He was your husband for … how long?"

"Forty five years."

"… forty five years and now he's gone. You still feeling it, hey?" she asked with drunken tenderness in her voice. This was the old Sis, the gentle, kind Sis she remembered as a girl. Nodding, Helen looked for evidence of the tenderness in Sis's face and found it, ever so slightly, in the softening of the jowl line, the almost imperceptible relaxation of the muscles below the eyes.

If it took alcohol to bring out this old familiar Sis, then Helen would just have to keep her drunk.

"You cried yet, Helly?"

"No. I can't. I wish I could."

"Yeah." The simple affirmation carried a wealth of understanding that bonded the two women as nothing else could.

Helen suddenly realised that Sis was the only person in the world she didn't have to explain herself to, who understood why she couldn't cry, why neither of them could cry. Not even Raymond had really understood, although he had tried.

144

A sense of relief washed through her, the sort of feeling that comes when you discover that, after a long absence amongst strangers, you are finally with your own kind again.

"You wanna talk about something else?" Sis asked.

"No, Sis, I want to tell you about Raymond. It's just that ..."

"You don't want to remember the end. So why not start at the beginning?" she said genially, flinging her hand out and almost knocking the bottle of whisky off the table. She recovered it quickly and swigged from it until it was empty. Stowing it safely on the floor next to the chair, she added, suddenly remorseful, "But I don't reckon the beginning was much better, at least not for him, poor little bastard." She sighed heavily, the smell of whisky wafting across to Helen in the still night air. "But at least I was there with you that time. Remember?"

"Oh, Sis, how could I forget. He was only a skinny little boy, barely six years old, same age as me. I wasn't sure that you would remember, though, after all, you slept through most of it."

CHAPTER TEN

Sundays were church days. Dad bathed every Saturday night and dressed in a clean shirt and trousers every Sunday morning. Even when they were rained in and the trip into town was out of the question, he remained in his church clothes all day, because it was the Sabbath and that's what you did on the Sabbath. Dad always said God would forgive them if they couldn't get across the river into town because God sent the rain which flooded the river and therefore it was his fault they couldn't go, but he wouldn't forgive them if they forgot to mark the day in some way. So every Sunday, they dressed in their Sunday best, no matter what.

It was the one day of the week when the girls could be sure that Mum would get herself out of bed, dress and get them breakfast, although she didn't follow her husband's Saturday night bath ritual. Bathing was a very erratic event for Mum and when she did, it seemed like a huge effort for her to get into and out of the bath. She complained about there being no hot water and that a bath wasn't a bath without hot water. When she asked Dad to buy a chip heater, he called her a fool and told her that this was the tropics where you didn't need hot water. She didn't ask him again.

But mass on Sundays was something she and Dad agreed on. In fact, being staunch Catholics seemed to be the only thing Dad and Mum ever had in common, although Mum's terror of her God couldn't be compared to Dad's arrogance about his.

In the beginning, the trip into town was a long, slow, bumpy ride with the two ponies hitched to the buggy, three hours there and three hours back, with three hours in between of mass and the fellowship lunch.

The girls hated it. They had to endure their Sunday clothes, which wasn't too bad during the cooler weather, but their waisted dresses and ill-fitting shoes and socks were unbearable during the Wet Season. The trip there and back was tiresome at the best of times, but was to be dreaded when the weather was bad, and more than once they hoped that the rain on the roof would bring a flood and they could stay home. If the water was over the bridge, they could play in the rainforest or go up to the cubby on the ponies or play under the house in their cotton knickers, loose smocks and bare feet.

Then Dad bought a car and the trip shortened to an hour, weather permitting. That meant a later start and less panic to get them all ready on time, although Dad would still sit behind the wheel and yell at them to hurry up.

On this Sunday, the previous evening's rain had settled the dust and a warm breeze kept the flies at bay. Dad sat at the wheel with his hat pushed back, cigarette drooping from the corner of his mouth and the usual look of impatience on his face. Nine year old Sis sprinted down the steps, jumped onto the running board, pulled six year old Helen up with her and together they squeezed into the seat next to Dad. Dad tooted the horn irritably until Mum appeared with three year old

Sweetypie in her Sunday bonnet. Balancing Sweetypie on an ample hip with one hand and the Sunday lunch platter with her other hand, Mum waddled carefully down the steps. Dad looked away. He did not get out to open the back door for her. She puffed as she leaned forward to rest the platter on the running board, opened the door, plonked Sweetypie down on the seat, retrieved the platter, put it on the floor at Sweetypie's feet, climbed in and pushed Sweetypie across to the other side.

Dad waited until she was settled behind him before starting the motor. Mum placed her hand firmly on Sweetypie to brace her as Dad took off with a lurch. The sandwiches slid around under their waxed paper cover until Mum steadied the platter with a foot on either side. She leaned forward to pat the tops of the two dark heads next to Dad, then settled back for the trip, her face turned towards the open window.

Just past Stewart's gate, Mum's hat blew off in the breeze. Dad wouldn't stop to go back and get it, he said it was her tough luck and they'd look for it on the trip home.

Mass was always boring. The girls didn't like Father O'Keefe because he either droned on in a monotone of strange sounding words or he yelled a lot, and when he yelled he sprayed spittle all over the place. So they knelt backwards on their seats and stared at the people behind them, they tickled each other until they giggled, they dragged Sweetypie off Mum's lap and tickled her, swung their legs too hard until they slipped off the pew and fell against the pew in front of them, all the time with one eye on Dad to see how much he would take. When he told them off in a whispered growl, they sat with arms folded and eyes downcast.

Sweetypie fell asleep in Mum's arms while Mum looked up at the priest with an intense hopeful gaze.

She'd been very upset the night before when she'd come into six year old Helen's room just as Dad rolled off her. She'd cried

148

and he'd hit her a lot. Sis could see a bruise coming up at the base of Mum's neck.

One good thing about church days was that Dad never hit Mum, he was even nice to her. He would take her arm after church like the other Dads did with the other Mums and escort her to the church hall where lunch was laid out on long trestle tables covered in white damask and the adults stood around in groups to eat and chat. All the kids had to stand back and wait until the adults had helped themselves before they could raid what was left over and take their spoils outside to eat.

Sis and Helen sat a little apart from the other children under the shade of a big tree, tucking into sandwiches and cake. Dad was talking with a group of men and Mum was standing by herself with Sweetypie still asleep in her arms.

Mum never talked much with the other Mums, with the exception of Mrs Stewart who always made a point of chatting with her. But the other Mums did not include her in their little groups. In fact, they seemed to take measures to avoid her. Mum sometimes looked lonely and sad, and today was no exception, although she had a distracted air about her as if she was waiting for someone to join her under the mango tree at the side of the hall.

Lunch drew to a close and the hall emptied out as people left for home. Father O'Keefe farewelled each one, but he too seemed distracted as the last family but one piled into their car and drove away.

The Downing's car remained, as Dad was talking to someone across the road and appeared in no hurry to leave. Sis and Helen were sitting on the top step at the front of the hall, finishing off the last of the home made biscuits that they'd been able to scrounge just before the women had descended on the tables to clean up.

Mum was still standing under the mango tree, Sweetypie heavily asleep in her arms.

Father O'Keefe walked past her and she beckoned him. He saw her out of the corner of his eye, but pretended he hadn't and walked faster. He had an appointment to keep and, anyway, he did not like this fat slothful woman with the lank black hair and perpetually miserable countenance. He believed, as did others, that Harry Downing could have done a lot better for himself. Still, she'd given him three fine daughters which must count as some compensation.

Mum followed him and called out his name. This time, he could not ignore her. He turned impatiently, smiled tightly and said, "Mrs Downing."

"Please, Father, I ... I ..."

"Yes?"

"I ... must speak with you ..."

"Very well. Go ahead."

"Oh, not here," she said uncertainly, looking past his shoulder to where her husband stood across the road with his hat in his hand, laughing in that loud confident way of his with a man she did not know. "Can we talk there?" she asked, pointing to the priest's house.

"It will have to be quick, then," he snapped, "I have much to do."

"Of course, Father."

She took a step towards him and he caught the first whiff of her pungent body odour. He'd been aware of it before, but had always ensured there was enough distance between them not to receive its full impact. He walked away from her quickly and she followed him breathlessly.

Helen saw Mum struggling to keep up with Father O'Keefe and gave Sis a nudge. "Where's Mum going?"

Sis looked up and watched them going up the steps of the priest's house. "What's she going there for?" she said curiously. "Come on, let's go see."

150

They left their treasure trove of biscuits on the step and ran to the house. The priest had opened the door and walked straight in, leaving Mum to follow. She did not close the door behind her.

The girls reached the bottom of the steps and looked up.

They had never been inside the priest's house before, a highset Queenslander standing a hundred yards from the church.

"Do you think he sleeps on ashes?" Helen asked, remembering something about sackcloth and ashes from the morning's sermon. She had always thought people slept on beds and it seemed strange that anyone would want to clean out their stove and spread the ashes on the floor to sleep on.

"Dunno," Sis answered, wondering herself.

Mum's voice floated out to them through the front window.

"Come on, Helly," Sis said quietly, "let's go see."

Putting her finger to her lips to make a silent "sshh", Sis led Helen up the steps and through the open door on tiptoes. Mum and Father O'Keefe were in the front room on the right, their backs turned towards the door. The door of the front room to the left was ajar and the room was in darkness. Sis pulled Helen inside.

It smelled stale and musty, the closed heavy velvet curtains letting in a sliver of light where they didn't quite meet in the centre. The narrow beam of light illuminated a large crucified Christ on the wall. A carved Madonna on a pedestal stood next to the cross, the edge of light revealing a vein of darker wood through the face and down the body like a bloodied slash. It gave Sis the creeps.

A table stood in the middle of the room, draped in heavy red velvet with stains around the skirt and black dirt where it dragged on the floor. Some books and candles were arranged on the centre of the table, the candelabra pitted with age and neglect, candle wax built up on the velvet cloth around their bases.

There was no bed in the room and no sign of ashes on the floor. Sis thought the priest's bedroom must be one of the back rooms. She moved towards the door to find it just as the priest turned towards them. He was talking to Mum with a look on his face that reminded Sis of the time she had first tasted a lemon.

He would see them if they left now. They would have to stay hidden for a while. She pushed Helen to one side of the door and took up a position on the other side.

Their black hair and tanned faces faded into the shadows around them.

Peeking out, Sis saw Father O'Keefe take a seat on one side of a desk, indicating that Mum should sit opposite. Sweetypie slumbered on in the midday heat.

Mum adjusted her daughter until she was lying comfortably across her lap. "It's about Harry, Father," she whispered shyly.

"Yes?" He leaned away from her strange foreign odour and wished that the desk was wider.

"It's the girls. It's just that, well, sometimes he ... hurts them ... in a ... sinful way."

"Mrs Downing, children need discipline, and perhaps he has to wield the rod because you do not?" A strange cheesy smell.

"Oh no, Father, it's not like that ..."

"Children must be loved, but love must be tempered with discipline. Spare the rod and spoil the child. Perhaps if you made more effort?" Was bathing unknown to this woman? How could Harry bear to go near her?

"But Father ..." Luisa looked down, sensing the priest's distaste for her, unsure of how to continue.

Needing to speed this up, for he had more important things on his mind, he said curtly, "Tell me, Mrs Downing, are you looking after your husband's conjugal needs?" The very thought was enough to make him feel ill, but the lecture was standard in such situations. "You know, a man can get irritable if his wife ignores his natural needs and he might be inclined to lash out at her or his children a little more than he should. So you must look to his needs and ensure that you keep him happy." He glanced unwillingly at the rolls of fat under her chin and bursting out of her sleeves, the sweat pooling in her cleavage, the wet patches under her arms. She was disgusting. And that smell. He couldn't escape it. What was it? More than unwashed. Acrid. Animal. Such a pity, he thought with contempt, for someone so young to let themselves go so much. Even the middle aged women of his parish looked more appealing than this pathetic creature. No, she would get no sympathy from him. He wrinkled his nose in disgust. He wanted her out of his house.

"Oh Father, he gets so angry with me ..."

"I'm not surprised. You appear to me to make no effort at all. Not even a hat for mass. A hat denotes respect before God and a recognition of your place in his service." He leaned forward instinctively to emphasise his next words, but reeled back quickly, making no attempt to hide his abhorrence. "Any man would find himself becoming impatient with a wife who gave no thought at all to her personal appearance and to the comforts of her husband."

He caught a flash of red through the window as a soft tapping was heard at the front door. He'd had enough of Mrs Downing. If she couldn't manage her children, then Harry must. It was not his problem. "Go home and do your duty, Mrs Downing. A marriage takes effort from both parties and must include the love of God if it is to succeed." She was stinking out the whole room. He couldn't stand it another moment. He rose quickly and moved to the open door. She followed him. " God bless you and keep you," he parroted as she left, his eyes on the visitor waiting for him on the veranda. She walked away with tears *rolling freely down her chubby cheeks. He did not care. She was not important.*

He beckoned to the visitor.

Sis and Helen wanted to follow their mother out. They had not understood the conversation and could see that Mum was crying, but the priest was coming back inside with a boy about Helen's age. A skinny red headed boy with a heavy splash of freckles across his pale face and blue veins showing through the fair skin on the back of his hands. They both knew him from church. He was one of the school boarders, Carrots Connor.

If he had another name, they didn't know it. He was Carrots to one and all.

Sis knew that his family were dairy farmers from the Tablelands, that he boarded at the school, and that on the rare occasions when his parents came to mass, they were notable in that their other children were all in their twenties and thirties, that the father was elderly and always grumpy, and the mother thin and dried up with weariness and lovelessness. Sis had never seen them show Carrots any affection or, for that matter, even bother to talk to him. He would just sit there with them in the pew with his red-headed brothers and sisters, his scowling father and withered mother, and when mass was over, they left without even a backward glance for their youngest son and sibling. Sis had seen him standing at the gate watching his family disappear up the road with something like relief in his face.

Now he stood shyly in the middle of the passage, his hands clasped uneasily in front of him while the priest closed and locked the front door. Then Father O'Keefe turned to the boy and laid his hand gently on the red hair.

The priest was smiling. The business of the day was over. He had the house to himself for a couple of hours before he would be required again. He had plenty of time.

Sis waited for them to go into the room where the priest had taken Mum, but instead he indicated for Carrots to go into the room where the girls were crouched behind the door. In a flash, Sis pulled Helen silently to the middle of the room and they both dove for cover under the velvet drapes of the table. Dropping the drapes to seal themselves in, they sat in the stifling, dank darkness, their knees drawn up to their sweating faces, and waited for their opportunity to escape.

Father O'Keefe's footsteps moved to the window. A softer footfall stopped next to the table. Helen's curiosity overcame her fear. She lay flat on the floor and lifted the velvet just enough to see what was happening. The room was full of soft shadows, her eyes adjusting quickly to find the priest's sandalled feet across the room and the boy's shoed feet a few inches from her.

The priest was fussing with the curtains until the sliver of light disappeared and the room was plunged into daytime gloom. There was a moment's silence, then Father O'Keefe moved to the other side of the room and opened a cupboard.

Sis lay down on her side next to Helen and yawned, sweat dripping from her nose onto the bare floorboards. She was hot, bored and full of food. She couldn't keep her eyes open any longer. She knew Helen would wake her when the priest had gone and it was safe for them to leave.

Father O'Keefe was a dark, stockily built man with a balding head set on a short thick neck and grey forgettable eyes above an ordinary nose and unremarkable mouth. His long black vestments smelled of stale sweat and cigarette smoke. As Helen watched, he discarded his outer garment by the cupboard and went to the boy. Then a pair of baggy grey shorts and large y-fronts fell into a pile next to the table and the sandals were dropped on top. The priest's feet were blackened underneath and the toe nails broken and grubby.

Helen twisted her head to see further up. Father O'Keefe had something in his hand, something he'd taken from the cupboard. It was a long piece of purple cloth with gold stitching on it. And something in a small glass jar. He placed the jar on the table.

His soldier was standing up like Dad's did, his balls tight up against its base and a lot more black hair around it than Dad had. Helen thought it was bigger than Dad's soldier. He stroked it a couple of times.

Wordlessly, he pulled Carrots towards him and wrapped the cloth around his face, pushing it into the little mouth with two fingers until the boy gagged. Then he pulled it tight and tied it across the back of the head, tangling the red hair and making Carrots flinch. The small freckled nose barely cleared the fabric. Helen heard him snuffling for breath. Even though she could not see the priest's face, she could see Carrot's, and a look of confusion was apparent in the clear blue eyes.

The priest pulled Carrots' shorts down and kicked them away. Then he leaned forward and Helen heard something moving on the table above her. When he leaned back again, the fingers of one hand were coated in something greasy. He stroked his soldier again until it look wet and shiny. Then he pushed the boy around to face the table and appeared to wipe the grease up and down the small bottom. Lifting Carrots off the ground by his hips so that his feet dangled in the air, he began to rub himself up and down against the small, bare backside. And then he lunged in.

Even with the gag, the muffled scream and sudden jerking of freckled limbs shocked Helen. She dropped the drape and wriggled backwards. Pulling her knees up, she huddled fearfully as the table above rocked and moved across the floor a few inches, the velvet drapes swaying with the violent rhythm of the rape. It lasted only a few moments, but it seemed like a long time to Helen, a long time to hear those cries above her, a long time to feel the floor vibrate under her.

Sis did not stir.

Then the priest made a soft yowl and the movement stopped. There was a pause, followed by a thud as Carrot's body hit the floor, his foot shooting under the drapes to hit her own foot. She pulled hers back. His did not move. She could hear his breath coming in desperate snuffling gasps.

Footsteps told her that the priest was moving around the room, getting dressed, putting on sandals, closing the cupboard door. Then he was standing next to Carrots. Helen heard him whisper harshly, "You are a contemptible little creature. You must be punished and punished often." He removed the gag. Carrots whimpered pathetically as the priest continued. "You are wicked and God has ordained this as your punishment. You must endure your punishment in silence. This is between you and God. If you tell anyone, he will strike you down with fire and brimstone. He will strike down your mother and your father and your brothers and sisters. If any harm comes to them, it will be because you told someone. Do you understand?"

Carrots' whimpers became sobs.

"I will leave you to calm yourself and contemplate your wickedness. When I return, I expect to find you dressed and ready to go back to the dormitory. Do you understand?" There was a silent pause. "Good. Do not leave this room until I return to fetch you."

Helen heard the door open and close, then the front door as it was opened and slammed shut. The priest was gone.

She lifted the drapes. Carrots lay on his back at her feet, his arms spread out limply, his face turned heavenward, tears running freely down the sides of his face to soak his red hair and turn it the colour of blood. His breath came in short gasps, as if each one caused pain. A foul smell came from him. Shit *and urine and blood and semen. Helen wrinkled her nose against it.*

She didn't know what to do.

She slapped Sis. "Wake up," she whispered urgently. She slapped her again and Sis opened her eyes. She sat up, groggy with afternoon sleep.

"Has he gone?" Sis asked into the darkness.

"Yes. Look, Sissy, look what he did to Carrots."

At first, Sis saw only the shape of Carrots in the gloom. She felt like she was suffocating in the still dark air.

Crawling out from under the table, she went to the curtains and pulled them open enough to let in some light. The louvres were shut. She reached forward and opened them. A warm breeze washed over her. She breathed deeply and thought how thirsty she was.

Then she turned and saw Carrots on the floor in the shaft of sunlight. At first she stared at Carrots' naked genitals, for she had never seen a boy before and wondered at how small his soldier was. Then she saw the smear of body fluids across the floor. "What's wrong with him?" she asked Helen in a whisper.

"Father O'Keefe put his soldier in him, like Dad does."

"Yeah? Smells real bad. Did he mess himself?"

"Don't know. What should we do, Sissy? He won't stop crying." Helen was almost moved to tears herself. She needed to do something, anything, for poor Carrots. So she wriggled around and lifted his head into her lap. With the same maternal instinct that she felt when she held Sweetypie, she stroked his wet face and looked down at him with kind eyes.

Sis squatted next to him and looked at his weak helpless face. She said to him comfortingly, with the wisdom of experience, "It's alright, Carrots. It'll stop hurting soon." He turned his eyes towards her. They had a strange kind of emptiness about them that frightened her. She said to Helen, "Maybe he's hurt worse than usual. Let's have a look."

Carrots made no effort to stop her as she lifted his leg and peered closely. "Cripes, Father O'Keefe got him in the bum hole. Look, it's all bloody and yucky."

"What should we do?" Helen repeated.

"Dunno. Where's his pants?"

Helen pointed to where they had been left. The purple cloth was lying on top of them. Sis took it and wiped away some of the soiling. When she pressed too hard, Carrots flinched and squealed.

Helen saw his pain and tears and finally her own tears came. She wrapped her thin arms around his thin body and pulled him close to her, then lifted him up a little so that he was cradled in her arms and rocked him to and fro. After a moment, the sobs settled into a gentle weep.

Sis waited another moment until she heard his breathing become rhythmic and even, then she finished cleaning him up with soft strokes across his buttocks and legs. She pulled his underpants and shorts up his legs, buttoned the fly and sat back, observing the calming effect Helen was having on him. Even so, that emptiness in the eyes still bothered her, that far away look. She wondered if it was the first time the priest had put his soldier in the boy. Her thoughts became words and she said reassuringly, "You'll get used to it."

He looked at her blankly.

Dad's distant voice came to them through the open louvres. "Sis, Helen, where are you? We're leaving!"

Sis and Helen looked at each other in dismay. They didn't want Dad finding them, not here in the priest's house with Carrots lying in Helen's arms and the stained purple cloth at Sis's feet.

"We gotta go," Sis said to the boy. "You'll be right now."

Helen disentangled herself after a final hug and the two of them left the room with a quick backward look of concern. He did not move from where he lay, but his eyes followed them out.

159

Dad was standing by the gate with his back turned as they ran down the veranda steps and over to where the car was parked next to him. Mum was sitting in the back, stony faced, tearless, staring straight ahead. Sweetypie, wide awake now with cakes and sandwiches in both her hands, was jumping up and down on the seat next to Mum. Crumbs and sandwich contents spilled out of the corners of her mouth onto the seat around her. Dad snapped, "Don't let her do that, Luisa!" but Mum ignored him. He glared at her for a second, then turned away as he muttered under his breath, "Bloody useless bitch."

The man he had been speaking to was coming across the road. Dad lifted his head and smiled warmly. Sis was always amazed at how Dad could talk so harshly to Mum one second, then be nice to someone else, even a complete stranger, the next. It didn't seem right.

The two men exchanged a few words, shook hands and parted. Dad got behind the wheel. He started the motor, then looked down at his two eldest daughters. "Cripes, what have you two been playing in? You smell like a bloody pig pen."

Only then did Sis realise that her hands and Helen's Sunday dress were stained with the stinking mixture of Carrots' body fluids. Dad hadn't noticed the stains, only the smell.

"Musta stepped in something, Dad," she said quickly.

"Well, hop in the back with your mother. She won't even notice," he snapped with a sarcasm that was lost on the girls. They scrambled into the back seat. Sis squashed in next to Mum while Helen pulled Sweetypie onto her lap and began to blow bubbles on the back of her neck until the toddler was squealing with laughter.

With her eyes fixed on the back of Dad's head, Mum suddenly reached across and dragged Sis into a fierce embrace. Sis could feel something desperate in the strangle hold of the soft arms around her. She was smothering in her mother's bosom and pulled away, wriggling back onto the seat as Mum reluctantly released her. Sis saw that she had left imprints of her stained hands on Mum's dress. Mum didn't seem to notice.

Sis lifted her hands and sniffed. Yuck. She needed a wash. "Hey, Helly, swim when we get home?"

"Oh, yes."

"Down by the big tree?"

"Yes."

"We'll take our fishing rods, alright? Hey, Sweetypie, wanna come fishing with me and Helly?"

"Fishing fishing catch a fishy fishy," Sweetypie squealed.

Sis took Mum's and Dad's silence as permission.

She glanced up at her mother's face, now turned towards the open window. She had never seen her look like this. It reminded her of something. She thought hard but it wouldn't come to her straight away. Then it fell into place. It was the same look that she had seen on Carrots' face just a short time ago.

Sis didn't understand. The priest hadn't done anything to Mum, so why should she look like that? Sort of far away, sort of lost, sort of sad, sort of ... defeated. She felt the need to comfort her mother and wriggled closer to her so that she could slip a hand into hers.

For a brief second, she wished her Mum was like the other Mums at church, with pretty hair and lipstick and bright dresses with waists you could wrap a belt around and shiny shoes with heels. They brought nicer sandwiches to the Sunday lunch than Mum did, and cakes and slices and biscuits and brightly coloured fruit and delicious things the girls didn't even have names for. And the other Mums smelled nice, like flowers, and they talked and laughed with the Dads and sang in the choir and knew all the children's names.

Then Mum squeezed her hand and looked down at her with sad brown eyes and a smile so tender and loving that Sis suddenly didn't want any other Mum except her Mum. "Sistina," Mum said softly and Sis's heart almost burst with love. She wriggled closer and snuggled in. The heat and sweat and smell didn't matter. Her Mum was the best.

CHAPTER ELEVEN

Helen leaned forward and rested her elbows on her knees. She was visibly shaken by the memory. Wearily, she said, "You know, these memories never really leave you, do they? They bounce around quietly in the back of your mind and if they come too far forward, you can toss them back where they belong, and you keep tossing them back year after year. But when you let them finally come forward for inspection, it's … hard. It's really hard."

"Course it's hard – what did you expect?" Sis snapped as if Helen had said something foolish. Another empty packet of cigarettes lay on the table between them. Helen had never seen anyone smoke like Sis, lighting one cigarette off the butt of another. She looked across at the hard face and wondered again how different Sis might have been now if she had stayed. Sis continued, "I'm buggered. Let's call it a night, hey?"

But there was something else, and Helen didn't want to take it to bed with her. "Not yet," she finally answered.

"Mum," Sis responded instantly, as if sharing the thought. "Yes. Mum."

"Damn. I knew you were getting around to that." Sis stared at the empty bottle for a moment, then stood and slurred matter-of-factly, "You're a bitch, Helen, you know that?"

Helen felt as if she had been hit.

"You turn up here without any warning and rip open old wounds and you think it's alright to do that." She made her way unsteadily towards the door. "Well, it's not alright." She paused at the door. "But you're not gunna stop til you've purged yourself 'cos that's what you came here to do. Don't matter what it does to me or Sweetypie, Helen will feel better and then she'll go home. You make me sick." She went inside, muttering angrily to herself.

Helen sat immobilised by the outburst. Sis was right. She was a bitch. She had come to purge herself. And she didn't want to stop. She wished she could just let it be. But she couldn't. She needed to finish it. And she needed to know Sis's secret. She couldn't leave without knowing, whatever it cost Sis.

Sis returned with another Johnny Walker tucked under her arm. Helen eyed the bottle apprehensively, her mind boggling that anyone could drink like this and still be upright.

They looked out toward the lights of the town in silence. Helen had a sudden vision of Sis here on the veranda alone, night after night. Fifty years of solitary nights, with only her lonely thoughts and dark memories to keep her company. She remembered the computer, sound system, television and DVDs inside and hoped that those machines had provided some diversion. Then she tried to picture herself by Sis's side for those fifty years, building the property together, sharing the workload and growing old together, but still solitary. Cocooned here on the farm with Sweetypie. Three eccentric old ladies with a bleak past and a colourless life.

Her own life had been full of colour and love and experiences. Loneliness was something she only experienced for the first time after Raymond died, despite the girls' efforts to comfort her. It was her own solitary nights without him that had prompted her return, not Sis's loneliness. She had never given much thought to how lonely Sis might be. Until now.

Bitch. Selfish, thoughtless, stupid bitch. She hated herself.

Sis interrupted her thoughts. "Do you reckon O'Keefe did it again?" The words were slurred and slow.

Helen brought her focus back to Sis and understood that she wasn't finished with Raymond yet. "Regularly. Until Raymond was twelve."

"Found another pretty little boy then, did he?"

"Yes. Actually, there were several, and sometimes he had them in a group."

"His own little harem." Sis snorted contemptuously. "Like Dad had here."

"Exactly."

"Poor little red haired bastard. And then he ran away. How old was he - thirteen, fourteen?"

"Fourteen."

"I remember," Sis said, her words running together. "We used to look at him all the time during mass, remember that? We wanted him to look up, but he didn't much, and if he did it was usually at you. Never could tell what he was thinking, he'd just sorta … look."

"I remember well."

"Tall skinny streak he grew into, but always frail looking, like no one fed him enough. Then he just disappeared. Wasn't much of a fuss made about it. He was there one week, staring at the floor like he always did, not saying nothing to nobody, not even his family, then next week he wasn't there. I didn't even know he'd run away until I heard someone telling Dad."

"Then you told me."

"That's right."

"And then the priest left shortly after."

"Yeah. Someone got him in the end, though. Did you know about that? Yeah! They found him in his bed at some school down south, strangled or smothered or something. Never found the culprit, but jeez when I heard, I said a silent thank you to whoever it was."

Helen was oddly silent. Sis felt a charge in the silence. She looked across and said, "What?" And then, "You know what happened to him, don't you?"

Helen nodded with a heavy head. She was getting a fatigue headache.

"So tell me."

"I will, but first I should tell you how I found Raymond in Sydney. And the family. I haven't told you much about them yet."

"I wanna hear about them, don't get me wrong, and maybe I wanna talk about Mum, but I need a bit of bracing first. Wanna join me?"

"In what?"

"A little more of the Johnny medicine." She grinned awkwardly, a fan of lines appearing around her eyes to crease the drooping mask.

"Oh, Sis, haven't you had …"

"… enough?" Suddenly, the good humour and easy manner were gone. Sis picked up the bottle and slammed it dangerously onto the glass topped table. "Don't you go telling me," she began, trying to lift herself out of the chair, but stopping as her knees began to give way under her. She lifted the bottle instead and pointed it at Helen. "Don't you go telling me what's enough. Fifty bloody years you're gone and you wanna start telling me what to damn well do? Who the hell do you think you are?" She dropped the bottle and

165

it rolled towards the edge of the veranda, whisky splashing across the tiles.

Helen raised her hands defensively. "Alright, Sis, alright." She reached forward just in time to grab the bottle before it disappeared down the steps, amazed it hadn't shattered on the table or the tiles. She turned and placed it carefully on the table. "I didn't mean to nag, alright? I'm sorry. If you need another Johnny, have another Johnny."

Sis, suddenly forgiving in the manner of a drunk, said jovially, "Have one with me."

Helen sighed, wanting nothing more than to lower her head onto a cool pillow and sleep off the headache and fatigue, yet knowing that sleep would probably elude her and the heat would make the headache worse. Well, maybe a drink wasn't such a bad idea, maybe it would relax her, maybe it was just what she needed. What the hell. "I wasn't going to but maybe it would help. Dull the senses a bit."

"Yeah. Dull the senses. Or maybe wipe them out. That's even better."

"But I want a glass. OK?"

"Ooh aah the lady wants a glass," Sis sneered mockingly. "What the lady wants, the lady gets." She swayed her way inside and returned with two glasses. After pouring, she downed hers quickly. Helen sipped, then decided on impulse that sipping was not going to help. She took a large swallow and gagged. "Argh."

Sis laughed loosely. "Jeez, you're just a bloody beginner. You gotta get it down quick, like this," and she threw a mouthful back in one swallow. "Quick like, see, then take another, and then another, and by then you won't even feel it go down."

Helen obeyed. Sis was right. She felt it course through her with an unfamiliarity that frightened her a little and knew that if she kept it up, she'd be legless within a very short space of time.

Sis watched her in amusement. "Bloody pathetic." She stretched her legs out in front of her and yawned idly. "So. Tell me. This family you reckon we got. You turned up at this relative's house …"

"Uncle Gino and Aunt Gino."

"Yeah, them with the funny names. So tell me about … the family."

Helen closed her eyes against the spinning darkness and let herself relax. After awhile, she opened her eyes to find Sis watching and waiting with hooded eyes, her body slumped deeply into the chair.

Helen sensed that what she said now and how she said it were of great importance to Sis, so she spoke slowly and carefully, trying to remember what it was like in the beginning. "They are quite a bunch, Sis. I'd never met people like them before. So noisy and free and so many of them. It was a few weeks after falling into Uncle Gino's arms before I recovered enough to meet them all, but they welcomed me with open arms. In fact, I think they believed that if they looked after me well enough, it would in some way compensate for what happened to Mum.

"I stayed with Uncle Gino to begin with. It was a very busy house, so much coming and going. Eleven cousins between Uncle Gino's family and Uncle Sonny's at that stage, but eighteen by the time they were finished. Aunt Maria and Uncle Tony couldn't have children and after awhile, Uncle Tony said I should live with them because they had a big house and no one to share it with.

"So I did, and it was wonderful. They treated me like a daughter, got me a private tutor to make up for the education I never had, let me work in the restaurant with them, gave me everything I needed and more. Aunt Maria was the physical opposite of Mum, so slender and elegant, one of those women with a feline grace about them, but whenever I looked into her eyes I saw Mum's eyes looking back. You know, soft and warm, incapable of harshness in any shape or form. Do you remember Mum's eyes, Sis?"

"Yeah. I remember. So where was the grandmother?"

"Nonna Sistina had gone back to Italy shortly before my arrival to make peace with her father before he died. While I was still at Uncle Gino's, a letter came from her, saying she had found sanctuary in the home of her childhood and would not be returning to Australia. The family was upset at first, but they tried to understand. They told me that Nonna had never adjusted to living in a new country, had never even bothered to learn English. And life here had been very hard for her.

"Anyway, I settled into life with the Benotti family. It's a well known name in Sydney now, with construction companies and restaurants and businesses. They've made their mark, but back then they were still building things up. Aunt Maria and Uncle Tony ran an Italian restaurant in Sydney. It was very popular and that's where I learned the hospitality business.

"When I wasn't studying with my tutor, I waited tables, helped out in the kitchen, watched and learned all I could. Uncle Tony's cooking and Aunt Maria's elegance and charm was what the restaurant was famous for and they took great pleasure in teaching me everything they knew."

"These uncles … .did they ever ..."

"Never, Sis. It wasn't in them to begin with. They were loving, but very careful with me. Even so, it was years before I stopped tensing every time one of them hugged me or touched me. But they were patient and seemed to understand. After all, they knew, didn't they? Or at least some of it."

Sis nodded slowly, pondering the mystery of men without sinister intentions. "So, you was having a lovely life and then what happened? How'd you find Carrots?"

Helen sighed deeply and let herself slide back into the memory of that day.

"It was just after my twentieth birthday. I remember it was a cold windy day, I'd been working in the restaurant and we hadn't had much of a lunch crowd, but some of my cousins dropped by. I took a break and joined them for coffee at one of the front tables which overlooked the street. There was a bus stop outside the restaurant and a man, a young man, was waiting for a bus. He was terribly dirty and his clothes were in rags. I remember thinking his unkempt red hair reminded me of someone, but I couldn't think who, and how cold he must be in that freezing wind in just torn shirt sleeves and trousers with holes, no socks, his shoes so worn that you could see his feet where the seams had frayed. He was hunched over with the cold and I felt sorry for him. My cousins saw me looking at him and they started to make fun of him. He couldn't hear, of course, but it hurt me that they should mock him. I thought he deserved sympathy, not derision. Then the bus came. He got on, but then he got straight off. He obviously didn't have the bus fare. He looked so pitiable. He turned his face to the restaurant - he told me later he could smell the food and the coffee and it was nearly killing him, he was so hungry. He turned and I saw that it was Carrots from home. He was pale and terribly thin. He turned away again and sat heavily in the gutter, as if he couldn't go on.

"Without thinking, I ran outside and stood behind him. I said his name and he turned with a shocked look on his face. I thought he didn't know me, so I started to tell him who I was, but he said my name before I did. Helen Downing, he said, and then he stood up and we both just stared at each other.

"My cousins followed me out into the street. They thought I was crackers. Then I told them that I knew him and suddenly they couldn't do enough for him. One of them offered him a jacket and another offered some money for bus fare. He let them drape the jacket across his shoulders and push a pound note into his hand. He was still staring at me. He told me much later that he thought I was the most beautiful sight he had ever seen."

Helen suddenly laughed, the whisky warming the memory.

"His first words to me in fourteen years, after saying my name, were 'I'm hungry.' It was such a shock to us all, the thought that he was starving. I wondered when he'd last eaten and offered him a meal in the restaurant.

"The cousins sat him down and I went out the back to cook up a huge serve of pasta. I remember we fed him bread and cake while the pasta was cooking, we were so worried he might collapse on us any minute. When I brought the pasta out, I thought there was enough for the six of us, but he finished off the lot. Oh, how he could eat! And as he ate, he seemed to get stronger before our very eyes.

"Soon he was talking, slowly at first as if he hadn't done it for a long time and had lost the knack, then faster as the food and the coffee warmed him. He told us how he'd come to Sydney to look for a job after working out in the country for a long time, but no one would give him a chance because he looked shabby and had no fixed address. He'd been living like a beggar in the park. It was so sad and he moved us all profoundly, not just with his story but because it was obvious to one and all that he was intelligent, well spoken and decent. And then he stopped talking. He looked exhausted. We didn't know what to do next. Finally, he thanked us for the meal and got up to go. As he walked out the door, he turned to wave goodbye, looking so sad and lost I couldn't bear it. I called out to him not to go, to wait. He did. I ran into the kitchen and told Uncle Tony that a childhood friend of mine was down on his luck and needed a job. He came out, looked him over and said 'What is your name and what can you do.' I'll never forget his answer. The shy boy we had always known as Carrots straightened up, looked Uncle Tony in the eye and said firmly,

170

'My name is Raymond Connor and I can do whatever you ask of me.' That made quite an impression on Uncle Tony.

"He started Raymond on washing dishes, paying him at the end of each day. With his first day's wage, he got a bath and a haircut. The next day, Uncle Tony brought in some of his old clothes for Raymond and Aunt Maria said he could sleep in the store room out back until he found somewhere to live. Within a fortnight, Raymond had found a room in a guesthouse and bought himself some new clothes.

"So," Sis interjected, "was it love at first sight?"

"No, Sis, we were too afraid of each other for that."

"Afraid? Of what?"

"I was afraid of boys, all boys. I didn't want them paying me any attention because that would lead to romance and that was the last thing I wanted."

"Understood. But what was he afraid of?"

"Sis, he had been so physically damaged by what Father O'Keefe did to him that – well, he was impotent." Helen was amazed at how easily it came out. Perhaps it was the whisky. She took another mouthful.

"Couldn't get it up?"

"Now that you've put it so delicately, yes. An erection caused him pain. And the psychological damage didn't help, either. Couldn't bear to be touched there, made him sweat and shake with fear. Of course, I didn't know about that straight away."

"But you had two kids. How'd that happen?"

"Patience, Sissy dear, I'm getting there. You wouldn't like me to leave anything out, would you?"

"Shit no. I wanna hear it all. Go on."

"Where was I? Oh, yes, the restaurant. Well, I saw him almost every day at the restaurant and we became good friends. We talked constantly. Aunt Maria once said that when Raymond and I talked, it was like we had our own language, we finished each other's sentences, we knew what each other was thinking. I guess to some degree we unintentionally excluded others from our conversation."

"Yeah," Sis nodded knowingly. "We used to be like that."

"Yes, we did, and maybe because of that I didn't really know how to conduct a close friendship any other way. Oh, I was great friends with my cousins and their crowd, but never on an intimate level. They were ... different from me. Or I was different from them."

"Yeah, I know what you mean. Felt it myself all my life when I'm around other people. So. Carrots knew about me and Sweetypie. What did you tell him about that?"

"I told him that I didn't want the family knowing in case they made fun of you. He seemed to understand. We both had secrets. It was a strange sort of bond."

"Did you ever talk about the priest?"

"Not in the beginning, although I was always conscious of that shared memory between us. No, in the beginning we talked about small things, like the food being prepared that day or the people coming and going in the restaurant. Then one day he said he'd saved up enough money to go the pictures and would I like to come? I did, and after that there were many movies and then concerts and dances. We began to explore our youth together, often in a group with my cousins, sometimes just the two of us. We discovered a love of music and dancing and had some wonderful times together. And it's odd, but right from the beginning we sensed we were safe with each other."

"Safe? As in safe from all that touchy feely stuff?"

"Exactly. Not even a good night kiss. We were perfect for each other. And even better, everyone thought we were an item. Other boys left me alone and girls didn't bother him. We were each other's cover."

172

"Then one night – we'd been keeping company for about a year – we'd been to a concert in the city and missed the last train home. He said he would walk me home and then walk back to the guest house. It was such a beautiful clear spring evening with a sleeping city around us. We felt like we were the only people on earth. And for the first time, we talked about home. He told me about the priest and about his family. He remembered living in a perpetual state of terror and confusion at boarding school. Consequently, he didn't do well and his parents were often angry with him, thinking him lazy and rebellious. When he was twelve, he told his mother about what had been happening. She beat him for being a wicked liar and blaspheming a man of God. She told his father and Raymond got another beating. Then his father told the priest about what a wicked liar his son was and that the priest should also beat him. He did, brutally and often.

"Raymond rarely went home after that. He was at the priest's mercy day and night, and he suffered terribly. But he was growing up and one day, he turned on the priest during a beating and hit him, hit him hard. Father O'Keefe screamed that he would kill Raymond and that's when he ran away. He hitched a ride out of town and just kept going. He lived as an itinerant farmhand for a few years, sleeping under the stars with nothing more than a swag and a few shillings in his pocket. It was hard, but he kept out of trouble and after awhile the fear of Father O'Keefe finding him and killing him faded. And then one day he ran into someone from home, someone he'd known at boarding school. Another victim, who told Raymond that Father O'Keefe had been transferred to a boys' school in Sydney.

"When Raymond heard that, all he could think about was what Father O'Keefe would be doing to other small boys and how he would keep on doing it." Helen paused and gave Sis a knowing look. "Unless someone stopped him."

Sis's eyes opened wide. "You're not gunna tell me ..."

"Patience, Sis. I remember we were almost home by then and I asked him if that was why he was in Sydney. He said yes, he'd found where the priest was living and he knew what he wanted to do, but he didn't know how to go about it. Then he apologised, saying I must think him an evil brute. So I told him about Dad."

"Everything? Even ..."

"Yes."

"Christalmighty. And you offered to help him?"

"Of course."

Sis pondered that for a moment. "So then what happened?"

"He told me he loved me."

"Ha! What a romance. You offer to help him kill a priest and he declares his love for you." The concept seemed to please Sis. She finished off her glass and poured another. "And then?"

"And then he told me about his – problem."

"Not getting it up and all?"

"Yes. I told him I didn't care."

"Did you tell him about you? About being afraid of being touched? About ... you know ... the scarring?"

"Yes. He said he didn't care either."

"And then I suppose he proposed?"

"No, not right then, but I believe that it crossed both our minds that night."

"Jeez, bloody Romeo and Juliet had nothin' on you two." Sis gave Helen a heavy penetrating look, as if assessing her capabilities as a murderess. Then she suddenly remembered, she already knew those capabilities. It had frightened her once, and would probably have frightened her again, had she been around for this part of her sister's life. "So," she asked, "how'd you do it? The priest, that is?"

"I'm getting to that."

The bottle of Johnny Walker was almost empty. Helen could only account for two glasses, but it was enough. Her headache was slipping away and the alcohol was lulling her into the belief that she might actually sleep tonight. She would worry about the hangover tomorrow.

"The next day, Raymond asked Aunt Maria to teach him about bookkeeping. She agreed, although the first lesson was a bit of a disaster because he couldn't see the numbers. She packed him off to get glasses. A month later, she handed the books over to him, saying he had a natural instinct for figures and should study accounting. He got a pay rise and started saving and so did I. When we had enough, he proposed. The family was very happy for us and started planning a big Italian wedding. And all the while, we were planning a murder.

"We started out by watching the school and Father O'Keefe's room. It backed on to a service alley and we had no trouble finding a spot where we could observe him. We went there on our days off and some evenings after the restaurant closed. We'd just watch him. He had a routine. Dinner with the other priests at seven, then his room by eight thirty, a glass of wine from the bottle of plonk under the bed, a cigar and lights out by nine thirty. We never saw him take any boys to his room. I don't think he had the control or the privacy there that he'd had up here. If you didn't know it, you'd have thought he was a model of propriety from what we observed. Until the night we saw him take a pair of boys blood stained underpants to his room and lie with them under his pillow. It was all I could do to stop Raymond from jumping the fence and killing him then and there. No, we had to plan it carefully. I didn't want either of us to get caught and we both wanted to make sure the job got done properly.

"It was a another few weeks before we were ready. We chose a clear, dry moonless night. We opened his window just a crack and waited outside. He came in, drank his wine,

175

smoked his cigar and turned out the lights. He was asleep after ten minutes. When we could hear him breathing heavily, we slipped in through the window, closed the curtains and took up our positions on either side of the bed. Raymond had a scarf with him, a long purple scarf that I had made just for the occasion. I'd taken some bright yellow thread and stitched Father O'Keefe's name in large letters along the full length of the scarf. We didn't know words like paedophile or molester or child abuser back then, so I'd stitched 'Defiler of Innocent Children' under his name. Seems rather melodramatic now, but we wanted someone to know."

She looked across at Sis who was nodding slowly, horrified approval in her eyes.

"We'd brought three lengths of rope. I wrapped the first across his legs and under the bed, not too tight, didn't want to wake him, but tight enough so that he was trapped. Raymond wrapped the second length around his neck, pinning him down. The third length went around his wrists, gently at first. Then we pulled the rope tight and secured it to the top of the bed. The priest woke up. Raymond balled up the middle of the scarf and jammed it into Father O'Keefe's mouth before he could make a sound. He pushed it in so hard that he dislodged some teeth and when I turned the light on, there was blood on Raymond's hand. I suddenly remembered the blood and shit on your hands, Sis, that day in the priest's house. I remembered and I was filled with rage towards this cruel man. I looked at Raymond and his face was twisted with loathing. There was no turning back for either of us.

"We worked as a team in total silence. The priest struggled at first. We tightened the ropes around the bed until he couldn't move. He looked at Raymond, then at me, then back at Raymond and it was like seeing a light go on in his head when he recognised him. Then he looked afraid, really afraid. It gave us both enormous satisfaction, seeing that fear in his face. He recognised me, too, after a moment, and looked at me with pleading eyes. He didn't understand why I should be involved, I could see it in his face. We gave him no explanations. He deserved none.

"We tied the scarf around his head so tight it puckered the skin on his face. Raymond pushed it up so that his nose was partly covered. He started to struggle for breath."

Helen stopped.

"What's wrong? Not regretting it, are you?" Sis's hands were clenched in her lap, a cigarette lying unlit on the table next to her.

"No. But what we did next – well, I'm not sure I can tell even you. You might think it too much."

"Come on, ain't nothing I'm hearing here he didn't deserve."

The honesty of Sis's response prompted Helen to continue. "We'd brought something else with us. Something to make him understand what sort of pain he'd inflicted on the little boys he'd raped." Helen paused.

"What? Tell me!"

"We'd made up a stick with something wrapped around it."

"What, like barbed wire or something?"

Helen nodded silently.

Sis sucked her breath in and shook her head, trying not to show her shock, but doing a poor job of it. She picked up the cigarette and lit it with shaking fingers. "We didn't know about that bit up here. Or the scarf or the ropes. I thought he'd been smothered with a pillow or something." She thought back to the day in the priest's house and the mutilated little boy on the floor. "Did he die slow and painful?"

"We made him suffer, Sis. We punished him for what he did to Raymond and all those other little boys."

"Did you or Car ... Raymond say anything to him while you were doing it?"

"Not a word. We didn't need to. Our actions were our words."

"Tell me you left the … the thing in him. For someone to find."

"We did. Then as soon as he stopped breathing, we slipped out as quietly as we'd slipped in. We went back to Raymond's guesthouse and cleaned up, then he escorted me home on the train, just as if we'd been on a normal date. And three days later, we were married."

"Godalmighty." Sis looked away, puffing quickly on her cigarette.

Then, unexpectedly, Helen added, "We were completely screwed up, Sis. Took us years to realise that. We never felt any guilt or remorse about what we'd done, but we abhorred violence in every other way. It wasn't until we'd had our children that we realised how messed up our heads really were. And then we didn't know what to do about it. It was too late. But he deserved it, the priest, we never had any doubts about that. If we hadn't done it, someone else would have. Or should have. The church sure wasn't going to stop him or punish him, and he had to be stopped."

"Yeah," Sis slurred her agreement. "I reckon you and Raymond did good. Real bloody good. You're right, see, someone had to stop him."

And then they were silent, the business of the priest dealt with. There was nothing more to say on the matter. They allowed the silent darkness to settle around them.

After awhile, Sis said, "I gotta pee," and went inside. When she came back, she carried a jug of iced water with her. She seemed steadier on her feet and Helen was amazed at her recovery period, then dismayed when she saw another bottle of whisky tucked into the pocket of the shorts.

"Get some water into you or you'll wake up with a headache," Sis said, as if reading Helen's mind. Helen helped

178

herself to the jug and took her turn in the bathroom, feeling a little sick after the two glasses of water on top of the whisky. When she came back outside, she was ready to say goodnight to Sis and go to bed, but Sis seemed to have revived and was ready to continue. The unopened bottle of whisky sat between them on the table.

Sis picked up the conversation, again steering its course to the satisfaction of her own curiosity. "So you and Raymond got married. Where'd you live? Did you, you know, get over your problems?"

Not willing to end this tenuous affability just yet, Helen answered wearily, "We found a flat in the city near the restaurant. I still worked, Raymond took a year off to study accounting full time, then we both worked. And no, we did not get over our problems, not like you are suggesting. For a start, we never saw it as a problem, it was just the way we were – mutually impotent. We slept together in the same bed every night like any normal married couple, pyjamas from top to toe, we cuddled, but there was nothing more. It was what we wanted. Of course, the family were expecting an offspring sooner or later. We just pretended that we were trying, but a baby wasn't happening."

Sis was studying her cigarette thoughtfully. "I reckon it was about then that Bill came out here with those papers to sign. You know, the ones giving me total authority over the farm."

"That was Raymond's idea. I hadn't really thought about it, but he said it would make things easier for you and safer for us. You weren't answering any of my letters and I'd turned twenty-one, I guess it …"

"You don't have to explain, I got the picture. But it helped, it did make things easier for me." She looked up at Helen. "I also remember instructing Bill to offer to buy you out. Why didn't you accept?"

Helen paused, then answered, "For the same reason you kept all my unopened letters. It was all I had of you."

"Yeah." They were silent for a moment. Then, "If I remember right, it's about then that your letters started having an Italian post office address on the back of them. How'd you get there? Italy?"

Helen rested her head wearily against the back of the chair and yawned. "A letter came from Nonna Sistina, saying she was ill and wanted to see her family before she died. So the whole family packed up and went to Italy. She lived in a part of Tuscany that is so beautiful, Sis, it will take your breath away. Her villa, now my home, looks out over a long valley with vines and olive trees and a clear warm light that lifts your spirits and makes you want to dance. And we did. Raymond and I and the uncles and aunts and all the cousins and their families. We ate and drank and danced and laughed and surrounded Nonna with so much life that she couldn't possibly die. So she got better, in fact, she lived to a grand old age. Oh, and didn't she adore me and Raymond! At times when she clung to me I knew she was trying to bring her Luisa back. But people outside the family thought I was Aunt Maria's daughter because I was so like her, even sounded like her and we let them believe that. Hence the press's assumption in later years that I was Italian. And Raymond looked like every Italian's idea of an Englishman with his red hair and pale skin, so we didn't bother correcting them on that point either. The one thing we feared all those years was the press discovering where we really came from. We both had a past to protect.

"Anyway, when it was time to return, Nonna said stay, and some of us did. Three of the cousins and Raymond and I. Oh, we thought it would only be for a short time, but after awhile I came to love Nonna so much that I knew we could never leave her alone again. So we learned how to manage a vineyard and make wine and endure the freezing winters. But it was about three years before we found our true calling. Or at least the one we are publicly known for."

"You mean all them restaurants and night clubs?"

"Yes. We never set out to achieve an empire. In fact, it really started by accident." Helen stopped. "Oh god I'm tired. Can't we do this tomorrow?"

"Nah. I wanna hear this now. Tomorrow, who knows, I might be shitty with you and wannna throw you out." Helen looked across at her to see if Sis was joking. She wasn't.

Helen straightened up and took a deep breath. "Alright, but poke me if I nod off. So. We were shopping in the nearby village one bright blue and white summer's day when we heard wailing coming from the piazza – the village square. We ran to see what had happened. The village baker had dropped dead in his shop. His elderly wife was very distraught, but not, as we first thought, about her husband dying at her feet. Oh no, she wasn't too fond of him, used to spend most of the day yelling at the poor man, no love lost there. No, she was wailing about who would bake the bread for the next day. Who would make the money if there was no one to bake the bread?

"The villagers took the baker away and left her alone in the shop. I don't think any of them liked her much by the way they turned their backs on her. We were the last to get there and the last to leave. She grabbed us on the way out and insisted that we help her. She said we should come and bake her bread. Well, her husband had just died and we felt sorry for her, so we said we would. After all, baking bread was something I knew how to do after all those years in that hellhole kitchen out the back here and then in the restaurant. We returned in the wee hours of the morning and baked her bread and filled her shabby little shop, but no one came in to buy. The same thing happened the next day. Then she understood what the village was doing to her. She began to wail and carry on about her worthless bakery and the hateful village and how much she wanted to leave. Out of the blue, she offered to sell us the bakery, sell it for a song I might add. Well, Raymond was always an astute investor and knew a good bargain when he saw one. We bought it on the spot, had it notarised the same day and it was done. No one came to wave the widow off, I think they were glad to see the back of her.

"So we cleaned up the shop and we baked the bread again and as the sun rose, Raymond went outside and spread cinnamon oil on the warm pavement bricks so that the aroma would fill the piazza, and then he set up a trestle table outside with the hot fresh loaves out in the open. We were sold out before breakfast. Then I said, why don't we serve coffee as well. So the next day, we did it all again with fresh coffee standing by. By the end of the week, most of the village was sitting around the piazza with hot bread and coffee for breakfast, enjoying the morning and the gossip. We started to make fancy breads and rolls and buns and pastries and different sorts of coffee and before long, we were making money. When it became too cold for the villagers to eat outside, we borrowed a little money from Nonna, extended the front of the bakery, put in a fireplace and bingo! We had a successful patisserie on our hands.

"Nonna was enormously proud of us both. She said to Raymond, why don't you do this in other villages? So we found someone to manage our bakery and started looking around. By the end of the year, we had four more patisseries in villages all over Tuscany. And we learned two things. People want good food in comfortable surroundings and they want nice people to serve it to them and make them feel welcome. Those two principles are what made us millionaires. Oh, don't get me wrong, it wasn't easy. In fact, it was damn hard work and we made a few mistakes along the way, but Raymond made sure we consolidated as we went so that, when we did go wrong, the whole lot didn't collapse under us.

"From the villages we went into the bigger towns, and from there, into the cities. We travelled a lot and looked for the right places at the right times, we watched the trends and gave the people what they wanted. Our patisseries for the ordinary man in the street, our restaurants for the middle classes and our nightclubs for the rich and famous. And we had a ball."

"So you had a ball. And then you had two babies. Not bad for a couple who didn't do nothing but cuddle, hey? So what changed?"

"I had an accident. A car accident. In Nice. I was in my early forties. I was taken unconscious to a nearby hospital and when I woke up, there was a doctor with me. He told me I was fine, just concussion, and then asked me about the damage to my genitals. He said he had seen it before in women who had been mutilated by circumcision or injury. I told him I had never been circumcised or injured. He said, well, that only leaves child rape. He watched my face when he said it. I said nothing to begin with, after all, I'd put that so far behind me and I certainly wasn't going to talk to a complete stranger about it, even if he was a doctor. He then asked about my sex life with my husband. I said nothing. Then he said he knew a doctor who specialised in fixing my sort of damage. Still I said nothing. He left.

"When Raymond arrived, he said the doctor had spoken with him and could hardly believe it when my own husband told him he didn't know what injuries the doctor was talking about. We were both highly embarrassed.

"I had to stay in hospital overnight for observation and they made up a bed for Raymond next to me. We had never spent a single night of our marriage apart and a car accident was not going to change that. In the morning, the doctor came back with another doctor, a surgeon who sat with us for over

183

an hour, talking about some of the women he had helped. He didn't ask us about anything, in fact, I don't recall saying anything more than hello. He just talked about women who had been genitally mutilated for one reason or another, how their lives were affected by it and how their lives changed after surgical repair. I had never considered such a thing. I had learned to live with myself the way I was. But after we went home, I started to think about what he had said. I talked it over with Raymond, and eventually I had it done. Hurt like hell, but after six months, you wouldn't know I'd ever been anything other than perfectly normal. Then one day Raymond said, do you think he could fix me? We went back to the doctor and Raymond went into hospital. But even after he had healed, we still lived as we had before, like brother and sister.

"Then something happened. I woke up one morning and found Raymond crying because he had an erection and there was no pain. Well, we just didn't know what to do. We were worse than virgins. At least virgins start off with a clean slate. So we went back to our doctor. He was very understanding, made us both feel as if our confusion were perfectly normal, told us that for all intents and purposes we were virgins and that all virgins are fumblers in the beginning. He sent us home to let nature take its course."

Helen paused for a moment. "Sounds like it should have been fun, doesn't it? It wasn't. We were scared, clumsy, inadequate lovers, but we kept trying. It was a humiliating experience for both of us. After all, we'd spent all our years together carefully avoiding each other's nakedness, ensuring we never looked at or touched each other's private parts. Our intimacy consisted of mutually agreeing to never be sexually intimate and changing that was more difficult than we could have imagined. But gradually, oh so gradually, feelings most people take for granted began to happen to us. And then I got sick. I went to the doctor again and he laughed at my shocked face when he told me I was pregnant. I was forty-five years old and expecting my first baby."

"And what was it like for you, giving birth?" The question came unexpectedly and Helen suddenly realised they were sharing their first real sisterly experience in fifty years.

"Hardest day's work I ever put in, and the second one was as hard as the first." She laughed. "Raymond fainted when Ria's head appeared, but with Tina he made sure he was sitting down first."

Sis said despondently, "It made me think about Mum, you know, when I was going through it. Made me think about what it must have been like for her, on her own, no one there to help or care. Yeah. Made me think about Mum a lot. Guess I wished she was there with me."

So they were back to Mum. She was there between them, as real as if she were still alive, her absence more powerful than her presence had ever been.

"I thought about her a lot, too, Sis, when the girls were babies and I had Raymond there and relatives and friends to help and support me. I thought about how lonely and hard it must have been for her here. And I wondered sometimes, especially during those quiet hours during the night when I was breastfeeding, I wondered how she felt and what she thought. She was just a girl."

"I reckon she grew up fast, though."

"Yes, especially towards the end. She must have been so desperate. And she was about that age when she was really only beginning to take adult responsibility. She knew she had to get us away from Dad, knew she couldn't keep taking the beatings. That's what that letter was all about. She wrote it not long after she spoke to Father O'Keefe."

"Poor bloody kid, I reckon she saw the priest as her last hope." Sis lit a fresh cigarette off the old one. Helen counted three empty packs on the table. "I reckon," she continued, "thinking about it now, that she had made up her mind that day to escape, one way or another."

"Yes. And what she saw that last night, well, she must have known before, but maybe that night was the first time she really confronted it. She was so scared of him, it must have taken a lot of courage for her to go for him like she did. And it sent her over the edge."

"Yeah. I reckon it did."

CHAPTER TWELVE

Mum came up behind Dad just as his eyes glazed over. He had nine year old Sis pinned down, the full weight of his body crushing her below him.

He felt something slap across his back. He ignored the first one, but the second one was stronger and unbalanced him. He turned his head to see his wife behind him, her hand raised high, ready to hit him again. Her eyes bulged with horror and fury, spittle flew from her mouth as she tried to form the screaming words that could not quite escape. But the sound she made, wild, unformed, was enough to make Dad turn to face her full on.

He caught her hand in mid-swing and held it fast for a moment, the two of them frozen in confrontation.

Forcing her arm down, he pushed his face into hers and growled menacingly, "What the hell do you think you're doing?"

She gagged, sputtered and brought her other fist up to collect him pathetically under the chin. He barely flinched from the blow, raised his own huge fist and brought it down across her cheek. She reeled back, but did not fall. Recovering with unexpected agility, she sprang across the gap between them, released a banshee scream and belted him with all her might across the face. Rough fingernails left streaks of bloody scratches down one side of his face. He was so stunned by the sheer ferocity of her attack that he took a step back, his injured face cupped in one hand.

Momentarily out of breath, for the attack had cost the obese young woman dearly in effort and energy, Mum reached out for Sis who leapt from the bed and flew into her arms. Sis felt heat and sweat and, for the first and only time in her life, rescue in the arms of her usually apathetic mother. And then she heard the words she never believed possible. She heard Mum cry, "Leave her alone!"

Dad took a step forward, looking puzzled. "What are you on about, Luisa?"

"What you do to the babies. It is sin. You do it no more!" She drew herself up and looked him full in the eye, repeating, "It is sin!"

"Bloody hell, girl, you're crazy. It's no sin. They're mine. I can do what I like."

"No! It is sin! You must stop!" she screamed back, consumed by her rage, feeling her maternal strength surge through her as she tightened her grip around Sis.

He glared at her again, then pushed past her so roughly that both mother and daughter almost fell. Then he paused in the passage, turned back to give her a malicious grin, said again, "They're mine. I can do what I like," and went into Helen's room. He pulled the sheet back, dragged her sleeping body up onto her knees and pulled her cotton panties down. Helen woke

188

suddenly, felt his hands on her and cried weakly, "No, Daddy, please don't. I'm tired."

Mum released Sis suddenly and flung herself across the passage after Dad. As he reached down for Helen, she threw herself at him, knocked him back and placed herself on the bed between him and Helen. She looked up and hissed, "I kill you if you ever touch my girls again! I bloody kill you!"

Sweetypie woke in the cot next to Helen's bed and began to cry miserably.

A strange expression crossed Dad's face, something sinister, something deadly. He reached down and heaved Mum off the bed, held her in front of him, then swung his fist. Her face crunched sickeningly, the impact knocking her back against the wall. Before she could recover, he hit her again. And again. Blood poured from her nose and from a deep cut above her left eye.

Sis screamed. Helen wriggled backwards against the bedhead, jammed her fists into her mouth and watched in terror as Dad pounded into Mum. He'd hit her before, but never like this. Sis screamed again for him to stop, but he was beyond all reason. Finally, she picked up the nearest object and threw it at him. The empty glass vase bounced off his back and shattered on the floor, arresting his next strike. He looked back at her, at Helen, at Luisa lying crumpled and bleeding at his feet, cursed them all and walked out of the room.

In the void his absence left, Sis and Helen watched their bleeding mother for a second, then as one they cried, "Mummy! Mummy!" and went to her. They squatted by her, waiting for some sign of life, shaking and prodding her until they heard a sharp intake of breath. One bloodied, swollen eye opened.

The anguish in her battered face shook both of them to the core of their souls.

Helping her to her feet, they led her shakily outside where Dad was standing on the veranda in the moonlight, a cigarette clenched between his lips. He watched them silently as they staggered down the steps and under the house to the washhouse.

They tried to apply wet flannels to her swelling face, but she recoiled at their touch. Her left cheekbone was deeply dented and her nose broken. But it was her eyes that frightened them. Red, deranged, they vibrated insanely inside their sockets, unfocused, unseeing. She breathed in short shallow gasps. Suddenly, she bellowed, sending the girls flying backwards in fear. Then she was up and running. Away from the house, across the slope and down towards the river.

Sis took off after her first, followed by Helen, down to the river and across the bridge into the tall cane. Blocked by the thick growth, Mum kept running blindly until she buried herself deep in the long stalks, pushing down the cane around her into a nest where she finally collapsed. And all the time screaming, screaming with a banshee shrill that shredded the night around them.

The girls cried out for her to Stop! Stop Mum! Don't Mum! But she didn't see them, didn't feel their small hands pulling at her, didn't see their tears or hear their desperate sobs.

And then she did stop, out of breath and out of energy. She rolled onto her back and looked up at the stars. "Ahhhhh, bella," she said softy, "bella bella." She opened her arms and the girls fell into them.

They lay like that, huddled together in sobbing silence, Sis and Helen buried in the wings of her soft flesh, watching her upturned face gaze rapturously at the sky above them. After a few minutes, she slowly pulled herself up to a sitting position, her eyes still turned upwards, then she stood unsteadily. The girls fell away from her like fledglings toppling from their nest.

Mum staggered towards the house, her head swinging heavily back and forth in rhythm with her steps, a strange choking sound coming from deep inside her chest with each laboured breath. Sis could see the glow of Dad's cigarette on

190

the veranda, unmoving, unmoved. Mum paused in the centre of the bridge and stood at the edge, once again turning her face upwards. And then she spread her arms, softly breathed, "aahhhhh," and fell forward into the water.

The girls screamed. Sis leapt in after her mother, but the current was already carrying her downstream fast. Mum rolled and floated face up, her gaze still on the stars above, her arms spread wide, crucified on the current. They heard her sigh again, she rolled face down and floated away into the darkness.

Helen looked up towards the house and screamed to Dad for help. The cigarette became a red light as he took a deep drag, then settled into a small, distant unmoving glow again. She looked back for Mum, but she had dissolved into the night. Sis flailed around in the water, calling "Mum! Mum!" and finally swam to shore where she lay in a sodden, defeated heap on the riverbank.

Mum was gone.

Helen ran down to Sis. Weeping, they stumbled back to the house. Dad was sitting naked on the edge of his bed, lighting another cigarette. "Get to bed, you two," he said.

"But Dad ..."

"Get to bed!" he yelled.

Not knowing what to do, they went inside, slipped into Helen's bed and clung to each other, shaking with shock and horror and disbelief. After awhile, they heard the creak of Dad's bed on the veranda as he settled for the night. Soon, he was snoring.

In the morning, he went into town and told Sarge that Luisa had tripped crossing the bridge early that morning and fallen into the river. She had gone under and not come up again. He told Sarge that he'd spent the morning searching for her, that his daughters were distraught, that he was afraid his beloved wife had come to a bad end. His tears were very convincing.

A search party took two days to find her body tangled in the mangroves at the entrance to the Inlet. Sarge said she'd been badly knocked around by the strong current and kept a sympathetic arm around Dad's shoulders at the formal identification, then took him to the pub and bought him a beer.

Dad sat with Sweetypie on his lap at the service, Helen and Sis rigid on either side of him. The coffin in front of them had been custom made because Mum's bloated body was too wide to fit into a normal one. It took eight men to carry it to the grave site and it bumped awkwardly against the sides of the grave as it was lowered.

When the ceremony was over, weeping women surrounded the tall handsome widower, touching and stroking his little darlings, offering condolences, reassuring them how lucky they were to have their Daddy to look after them. With hopeful faces, they promised food, housekeeping and comfort to the stony faced man.

He was attractive, affluent - and available.

Sis heard one woman comment on his strength in the face of a future without a mother for his children. Another woman answered that it probably wouldn't be long before he found a mother for his girls as he was now the best catch in the district and perhaps he would do better for himself second time around. After all, Luisa had been a funny sort of girl, what with her woggy accent and slovenly ways. No, Harry was a fine man and it was only a matter of time before a local lass worthy of him would catch his eye.

He responded to none of their advances, not then, not ever.

A few weeks later, the truancy officer came on a tired black horse. He was a pasty faced young man with wire rimmed spectacles wearing a too-big hat and a wrinkled suit. It had been brought to his attention that Mr Downing's two school-age daughters had never been enrolled at or attended the local school. Sis and Helen were called outside to speak to him, but Dad seemed to do all the talking. He told the young man how well the girls were doing with their reading, writing and numbers because he gave them lessons every day. This was true and he proved it by making the girls read something and do some simple arithmetic. He didn't mention the other things the girls were required to do during their lessons, sitting on his naked lap in the warm evenings.

The young man was not impressed. He said it was against the law for the girls not to go to school and that all children needed an education. Dad laughed at him and asked him what good an education was for farm girls, beyond reading the latest sugar prices and making sure they didn't get diddled with the accounts. The young man became belligerent and suddenly, the tone of the conversation changed. Dad's mouth tightened and he took a step closer, towering over the younger man.

He asked him how Mr Sutton's wife was these days, said he'd heard the truancy officer was getting to know her rather well and wouldn't Mr Sutton like to know about that when Dad saw him in town next week? The young man blushed and stuttered, but Dad said he'd make a deal with him. Put in the report that the girls had a private tutor, don't come out bothering them again, and maybe he'd say nothing to his mate, Mr Sutton. After all, his girls were getting all the education they needed. Hadn't he taught them to read and write and count himself? What better teacher could they have than their own Daddy?

The young man left with trembling hands at the reins and they never saw him again.

And every Sunday after mass, the girls suffered the ministerings of hopeful future Mrs Downings and sat through the endless praise of how wonderful their father was, how lucky they were to have such a fine home and farm, what a credit to the community Dad was, but oh how he must get lonely and *wouldn't you girls like some company, someone to help you, someone to look after you?*

And when Dad repeatedly discouraged such advances, the blame was gradually placed squarely on his little darlings, for they were growing into such sullen little wenches, so unwilling to participate with the other children, sticking to themselves in their solitary little group, so selfish, so jealous of their father's attention. Such an odd bunch. The eldest so hard and ... well, ugly, she doesn't seem to try at all, she'll never catch a husband the way she's going. And the youngest, such a pity, mentally retarded you know, wouldn't have picked it when she was little, why I remember a party at her house where she seemed just like all the other little girls.

As for the middle one, well, she's too pretty for her own good, that one, cold and uppity, thinks she's better than everyone else, won't talk to you even if you stand in front of her face and yell at her, snotty little thing she is.

Yes indeed, it would be a brave woman to take that lot on. Poor Harry Downing.

CHAPTER THIRTEEN

Sis rose in agitation and paced the veranda unsteadily. She was very drunk. "It wasn't suicide, it was murder, same as if he'd put a gun to her head," she said bitterly. "Never mentioned her name again, like she was some rotten bit of rubbish you just tossed out and forgot. Jeez. He just shut her bedroom door and never went in again."

"He was a happy man after that," Helen remembered, her own bitterness rising up inside her. "His unwanted wife was out of the way and he had the three of us to himself. His world was perfect. I can still hear him singing and laughing around the house after her funeral, and it cuts my heart in two as painfully now as it did then. I believe that was when I consciously began to hate him."

"I was way ahead of you there."

Sis stopped pacing and stood with her back to Helen. Her torment was palpable. A sombre silence fell between them.

She finally said darkly, "Anything else you wanna get off your chest tonight?"

"No, darling, I've had enough for one day."

"Thank bloody christ for that." Sis turned and loomed over Helen. "Well, I've had enough, too – for a bloody lifetime!" She balled her fists. "I want you outa here, Helen. I want you gone for good. I spent a lifetime trying to forget Dad and Mum and that priest and all that shit. I spent a lifetime trying to make things good for my Sweetypie and maybe have some peace of mind in my old age, and I reckon I was doing alright til you showed up and now it's all unravelled. Gone! Just like that! In one lousy day! When you showed up, you brought all the bad stuff back with you and I don't want it. You hear! I don't want it!" She suddenly grabbed the whisky bottle and took off down the steps. She stopped at the bottom step and yelled back. "I don't ever wanna see your face here again! Make sure you're gone before daylight tomorrow. Alright?"

Helen was stunned. She opened her mouth to answer, but nothing came out. She didn't know what to say.

"Didn't you hear me, bitch?" Sis screamed. "Get outa here! Leave us alone! We don't need you! We was doing alright before you came and we'll do alright after you've gone. Just go!" In the glow of the veranda light, her face twisted and contorted with anger and grief and bitterness. Then she lurched into the darkness and was gone.

In the sudden silence, Helen began to shake and feel sick. The sound of something clanking against the bridge made her jump. She heard something screamed into the distant darkness and realised Sis was across the river. She waited for awhile, nausea finally forcing her inside to the pills in her handbag. She sat heavily on the bed and swallowed several, then several more and tried to think about what to do next.

It had backfired. Her dreams of being welcomed as the long lost sister, the reunion between once loving siblings, the resumption of a once cherished companionship – it had all gone horribly wrong. She had to go. Staying was impossible now.

She tried to rise but her legs gave way under her and she fell back onto the bed. Oh god, she thought suddenly, pills and alcohol. I won't be going anywhere until it wears off. OK, I'll sleep for a little while and wake early. I'll be gone before first light. I have to be gone. I can't face Sis again.

Even as she thought it, the drugs seeped into her veins and she sank into a deep sleep, ceiling fan rotating slowly above her, mosquitoes settling for a feed on her smooth legs and the light drawing a host of winged insects into a cloud above her.

She jerked awake to the sound of something moving on the veranda. It was first light. She heard a scuff of boots. Sis! Her heart began to beat fast as the fear of confrontation gripped her. Then the footsteps retreated down the steps and she breathed again.

She felt wretched, her body lethargic, sticky and itchy. Her head pounded and she closed her eyes, turned on to her side a little to ease it and felt something cold and hard under her cheek. She opened her eyes slowly.

Pink light coming through the window. Hot. Humid. Birdsong in the rainforest. Clean cotton under her. Pillow too soft and flat. Sweat. Slightest of breezes. Cool spot at back of neck. And that cold hard thing under her cheek.

Lifting herself off the pillow, she looked down at a crown of black hair surrounding a large pair of rusty dressmaker's scissors. She clamped a hand to her head and felt the tufts of unevenly cut hair, one side of her scalp almost bare, the other side, where she had lain, long and sweat soaked.

She shrieked and stared at the scissors uncomprehendingly. Was Sis mad? Was this some sort of sick revenge? She shrieked again and heard footsteps coming up the path and the front steps at a run. The screen door banged as it was flung open and

Sis was in the passage, looking at her lying on the bed with the scissors by her side. It took a second before she understood what she was looking at. And then she did something that took Helen completely by surprise.

In two strides, she was at Helen's side, her hand outstretched. Helen flinched back and raised her arms protectively, thinking she was about to be struck, but instead, the hand went straight to the bare scalp. And then, almost tenderly, it swept across her head and down to her neck where it lingered, the fingers gently searching. The other hand pushed her gently on to her back and, with a swift glance, Sis saw that there were no injuries. She sucked in a sudden noisy breath, as if she was about to cry, but instead of tears, she began to shake. Then, with both hands, she picked up the scissors, her fingers trembling so much that the blades almost slipped from her grasp.

Helen was alarmed at the look on Sis's face. Terror, sheer terror. Her eyes were wide and wild as she stared at the scissors. In an instant, Helen knew it had not been Sis who had violated her bedroom through the night. But the alternative was too hard to accept. And then Sis began to shake so badly that her knees gave out from under her and she sank to the floor, the scissors hitting the floorboards with a clunk. She looked up at Helen and the terror became sound as a cry escaped her. She covered her mouth to silence herself, her face white behind the trembling sun-browned hand, and Helen realised Sis was going in to shock.

Helen sat up and slipped onto the floor, her arms going around Sis in a tight embrace. It was only then that she noticed Sis was still in the clothes she'd worn the previous night and that they were covered in dirt and greenery. "Shhh," she said as she might have to Tina or Ria when they had woken from a nightmare. "Shhh, it's alright. It's alright. Shhh." Sis smelled of stale tobacco, alcohol and musty soil. "Didn't you come home last night?" she asked, trying to bring some sense to the moment. Sis, her eyes glazed and unable to speak, shook her head. "What did you do – sleep out in the cane fields?" Sis nodded.

Helen, one arm around Sis, reached across to the water jug and poured a glass. "Here," she said gently, "drink this." She held it to Sis's lips and kept it there until it was empty. The shaking eased a little. She rose, her hangover in full force, pulled Sis to her feet and led her to the kitchen where she quickly made sweet coffee for both of them. They sat in silence, Sis's eyes fixed, oddly enough, not on Helen's mutilated hair ,but on her neck.

Helen struggled with her own thoughts.

Sweetypie. Incomprehensible.

Finally, Sis's breathing steadied and the shaking settled.

When Helen was sure that Sis was recovered enough, she quietly broke the silence with one word. "Why?"

" Because …" Sis began, taking a last gulp of the coffee, "… because when she's asleep, her mind sometimes forgets to stay six years old." There was no trace of the previous night's anger, but rather a struggle to believe what she saw before her now.

Helen poured them both a second coffee. "I don't understand." The Sweetypie she had known and adored would not have been capable of such a thing. What had changed?

"She … has nightmares and sometimes … she walks in her sleep." Sis looked away as if reluctant to go on.

"Walking in your sleep is one thing, Sis." Helen touched her bare scalp, "This is another. This is vindictive. Cruel." The word seemed to touch a chord in Sis and she snapped her eyes back to Helen's.

Helen was completely confused. There wasn't a cruel bone in Sweetypie's body. What the hell was going on here?

"Her mind remembers things when she's asleep," Sis said slowly, not taking her eyes off Helen's, "And her sleeping mind remembered you left us fifty years ago and it wasn't too happy about it. This was her way of getting back at you."

Sweetypie's sleeping mind? What was Sis talking about?

"She never used to sleepwalk. When did that start?"

"Long time ago," Sis said evasively, her eyes sliding away from Helen's.

And there was the secret, right there at the kitchen table, so close Helen could feel it, but still concealed from her. She reached for the moment, leaned across to grasp Sis's hand and begged, "What happened here, Sis? What is it that torments you so?"

Sis didn't pull away. Instead, she unexpectedly gripped Helen's hand as if she were being saved from drowning and said, with a catch in her voice, "Can't."

"Yes you can. Something happened the day Sweetypie was born. Something happened after I left here fifty years ago. You can tell me anything. Tell me."

"No." Sis shook her head forlornly. "Too hard. Don't wanna go there." There was a finality to her words.

"I'll go with you, Sis, you won't be alone."

"No."

"Damn." Helen released Sis from her grasp and leaned back, defeated. She had been so close. It would drive her crazy now, the not knowing.

And then Sis brought them back to the present by nodding towards Helen's hair and saying, "What are you gunna do about that."

Helen passed her hand over her scalp. What a mess. "I don't know." She suddenly thought about Sweetypie. "Will she remember?"

"See for yourself," Sis said, rising unsteadily. They went to Sweetypie's room and stood over the sleeping womanchild. "Sweetypie, wake up," Sis called softly. Sweetypie moaned and rolled over. "Come on, wake up."

Sweetypie yawned, rubbed her eyes and looked up. Her mouth dropped open and she said with wide-eyed surprise, "Oohh, Helly, what you done to your pretty hair?"

Helen understood in an instant that Sweetypie did not have a clue that she was the culprit, even though an incriminating shower of black hair lay across the pink bed. The innocent eyes said it all.

"She cut it short 'cos of the heat," Sis said calmly, "but she ain't very good at it, is she?" Sweetypie grinned and giggled. "Come on, lazy bones, get dressed. Breakfast in fifteen minutes."

Helen turned away. "I'll clean up my bed,"

"No. Leave it. I'll fix it. You've had enough." Helen followed Sis in to the bedroom and stood over the scissors. Sis lifted them from the floor and dangled them in front of her with one finger. "I buried these," she said distractedly.

"Buried them? Whatever for? They're Mum's old dressmaking sheers, aren't they?"

"Yeah. I buried them a long time ago," Sis said, shaking her head in puzzlement, "but she musta found them."

"I don't understand."

"Leave it. It's not important."

"Sis, please ..."

"I said it's not important. You're alright. That's what's important."

But Helen could clearly see that it was important by the way Sis gingerly handled the scissors, as if afraid of them. She took them outside and dropped them into the green wheelie bin under the house, came back in to strip the bed and went into the bathroom. Helen heard the washing machine start, followed by the sound of the shower. She wondered whether she should be getting ready to leave. After all, Sis hadn't said anything to change her orders from the previous night.

But neither had she re-affirmed her order to leave. Perhaps she had been too drunk to remember it this morning. Or perhaps the shock of the morning's event had diverted her for awhile. Helen sat in the kitchen and decided to see what the morning would bring. What she needed right now was a shower and a haircut. Sis emerged from the bathroom in clean work clothes and nodded once again towards her hair.

"I'll call Bill's daughter. She comes out here once a month to do our hair. She won't mind coming out early. Just ... don't tell her what happened, alright?"

Sweetypie bounced her way in to the kitchen and the ritual of breakfast proceeded as if nothing was wrong, except that she giggled every time she glanced at Helen.

Bill's daughter arrived straight after breakfast. The explanation offered was the same they had given to Sweetypie. It made Bill's daughter giggle too. She couldn't do anything but a number three shave which left a quarter of an inch of hair covering the scalp. When she had finished, Helen examined herself in the hairdresser's hand mirror. Oh god, she thought, I look like Sis. Well, she sighed to herself, if this was karma, then so be it, and after all, it was appropriate for the climate. It was even stylish in its own way if she wore big earrings and a darker lipstick. And a wig would take care of her public image until the hair grew back.

After they farewelled Bill's daughter, Sweetypie made her way up into the rainforest, leaving the two older sisters standing on the veranda again.

Sis's face seemed to have aged terribly overnight, probably from the drinking binge, but perhaps even more so from the morning's shock. She looked drained and at the end of her tether. Her mouth opened to speak and Helen thought, here it comes. Rather than hear it all again, she said quickly, "I'll pack my things and go. I promise you, I'll never bother you again." It made her sick to say it, but she knew it was the only way.

202

"Wait." The word came gruffly and Helen steeled herself for a confrontation. Instead, Sis moved uneasily from one foot to another, as if unsure how to proceed. "How's the head?" she asked tentatively. "You sorta tied one on last night." She indicated the newly mown skull, but was referring to the hangover.

"We both did," Helen replied, uncertain of what was happening here.

"Yeah. I ain't wiped myself out like that for a long time. Getting too old to handle it. I feel like shit this morning."

Helen realised Sis was trying to make some sort of amends. "Me too." Then she waited.

Sis lowered her head in a gesture of subjugation that Helen thought completely out of character. Sis was always top dog. She never bowed to anyone. Helen wished she could still read Sis like in the old days, but there were too many years of separate living between them.

"I'm sorry, Helen." The words came low and soft.

"I'm sorry too, Sis. I never thought it would end up like this." She turned to go inside. "I'll go quickly."

"No." Sis's hand was on her, restraining her gently as Helen had done to Sis the day before. She turned and looked at Sis. "I'm sorry," Sis continued, "about last night, you know, what I said an' all." She looked up, her red hung-over eyes filled with remorse. "When I saw you in there, with the scissors and your hair like that, I thought ..."

She paused. Helen thought, for godsake, tell me, tell me what troubles you so!

"... I thought you was dying. I thought, if she dies, then what will the world be like without her. No letters coming every month. Nothing to tell me that you were still out there somewhere. It don't matter that you weren't here, see? It only mattered that you were somewhere."

The profoundness of the words touched Helen deeply. "Are you saying you don't want me to leave?"

"Yeah. That's what I'm saying. I don't care how long you're gunna be here, but having you here for awhile is better'n not having you here at all. So, stay. Alright?"

Helen took a deep breath. The world was righting itself again. "Yes, darling, alright. And if you don't want to talk about the past, then we won't."

"It's not that, Helen. It's more being caught unawares. You know, like I hadn't had time to prepare, see? Maybe we can make some rules. Maybe we should say stop if it gets too hard for either of us, and come back to it later when we feel like it. Alright?"

Helen nodded. "Alright, Sis. And perhaps without the grog, or at least, not so much of it?"

Sis came close to smiling, but put her hand to her pounding head instead. "I got some aspirin. Want some?"

"Oh god yes. And then another coffee, please."

Sis nodded towards the mosquito bites on Helen's legs and face. "There's calamine lotion in the bathroom cabinet next to the aspirin. Help yourself. I'll get the coffee."

When Helen came out on to the veranda again, Sis was issuing instructions to Stubby on the mobile. There was fresh coffee and a jug of water on the table. Helen sat carefully, adjusting her sunglasses so that they didn't press on her temples too much, poured herself a coffee and sipped. Sis finished her conversation and tucked the phone into her pocket.

They sat in strained silence, both wondering where today would take them. Finally, to break the ice, Helen said, "Big day yesterday, wasn't it?"

"Yeah, sure was."

She thought of something Sis had left unexplained the day before. "So Sweetypie got the damage fixed? I didn't think she'd let a doctor near her, let alone a whole surgical team."

"Yeah," Sis said, visibly relieved Helen had made the first move. She spoke slowly, mindful of the pounding in her head. "Yeah, she was pretty rough on doctors for awhile. The old doc, remember him? He was good. He didn't mind coming out here." She paused and looked across at Helen. "Remember that time he came out after she fell on the rocks at the waterhole? By the time we got her back here and I drove into town to get him, she'd stopped bleeding. But it was kinda handy, wasn't it? Gave us an excuse for the other damage, the damage Dad done to her. Remember how kind and gentle the old doc was, showing us how to paint her with the gentian violet, telling us to keep it dry and all. How old was she …?"

Helen remembered well. "She was ten. Dad was across the river, he didn't even know. You paid the old doc out of the money pot in the kitchen. By the time Dad got home, she was in bed, sedated with a dose of that laudanum he left with us. Yes, he was good. But she didn't like him, did she, kicking and screaming. Then he told us that he had a retarded daughter and he understood. At least, having a daughter like that made him sympathetic to our situation with Sweetypie. And I do remember that gentian violet and how it stung her after her bath each night. Made her cry every time, poor thing.

"But she still got crook on us," Sis reminisced. "On me, after you left." Helen glanced across quickly, but there was no spite in the comment. "She would be fine in the morning, a bit whingey at lunch time and sick as a bloody dog by tea time. Jeez, she scared me more than once. The old doc would come out at the drop of a hat, bless him, and sit patiently outside while the sedative took effect so that he could examine her. Kept saying she should have healed a lot better than she did, but that bloody thrush could knock her off her feet so fast. It

205

got into her system and made her real sick. Then she'd have it everywhere, in her mouth and nose and ears, under her nails, down inside her thighs, under her arms, behind her knees – hell, it was awful. It was like she had no resistance to it, and every time she got sick like that, I hated Dad even more for the legacy he left her with. It was so cruel." Sis slurped her coffee noisily.

"I'm sorry to hear that. I had hoped that she'd get better as she got older."

"Well, she didn't. Then the old doc retired and next time she collapsed on me, I drove over to Stewarts and they phoned the new doc for me. He didn't want to come out. Said I should bring her in to town. Stupid bastard. I tried to explain that she couldn't leave the property, wouldn't go beyond the bridge, but, no, he knew best. Finally, Mrs Stewart talked to him and he agreed to come. I waited all day, all damn day and I'm still convinced he left us for last because he was peeved about coming all the way out here. And wasn't he an arrogant fancy-pants sonofabitch when he got here. Turned his nose up at me, thought I was some sort of farm hand, wanted to know where the owner was. Wouldn't give Sweetypie a sedative before looking at her, then got real mad when she went ballistic on him. I gave her something in the end, but he wasn't gunna stay while it took effect, was he, oh no, he had a bloody dinner party to get back to. Well, I wasn't gunna put up with that. I took the rotor arm off his car and told him he wasn't going nowhere til he'd had a look at Sweetypie 'cos she was scaring me. All limp and white and sweating that had nothing to do with the heat. So he waited, then he looked at her and all hell broke loose. Accused me of being a monster to let her get like that. I told him what the old doc used to do and he accused the old doc of being useless and out of date. Said Sweetypie needed hospital and proper care immediately and when she was better, he'd recommend that she be put into an institution.

Then before I know it, he's got her and he's dragging her out to his car, demanding I fix it for him. Well, she looked half dead and I was bloody scared stiff, so I got his car going, but when I went to get in he took off without me. I jumped in the ute and got after him real bloody quick, I can tell you.

"Ha! He got to the bridge and Sweetypie started coming round. I could see her beginning to move around in my headlights. A mile down the road and she woke up properly. Well, she took one look at the cane on either side of her and went off her bloody head, didn't she? Screaming and jumping around. Jeez, I reckon she was about thirty when this happened, real strong from working with the rocks every day and he didn't know what bloody hit him. By the time I caught up with them, he was in the ditch by the side of the road, hanging out of his car with a bloody nose and torn clothes, and there was my little Sweetypie next to him, hitting him and screaming bloody blue murder for all she was worth.

"I got her into the ute and put up with it until we got back across the bridge, then she calmed down," Sis snapped her fingers, "just like that! I got her back inside, gave her another dose of sedative and as soon as she was asleep, I went over to Stewarts and got them to ring the old doc. He came right out and treated her like he always did and got that arrogant bastard kicked out of his old practice, and right out of town.

"Next time I needed the doc - I had the phone on here by then - he sent out this young slip of a girl, promised me she was a real doctor, but she looked like a skinny school kid. She made us call her Martha and she fixed Sweetypie up better than ever with a bunch of pills. And Sweetypie just loved her. She'd come out sometimes just to visit when Sweetypie wasn't even sick and they'd sit out here on the top step and chatter away like they was old friends or something. She's the best, is Martha. She's retired now, but she still comes if we need her. Not that we do very often any more. Not since the operation."

207

Sis poured herself another cup of coffee, lit a cigarette and relaxed back into the chair. She was enjoying telling this story. Helen was simply relieved that she was talking freely again. Without the booze.

"She come out here one day a few years back, all excited, and said Sweetypie could have an operation to fix her so that she wouldn't collapse on me like she used to. Said it was because she was all open and raw down below and the thrush got into her blood too easily. Said there was an army truck with an operating theatre in the back of it down south and she could get it to come up here. What a circus that was. First, Martha came and gave Sweetypie some medicine to make her sleep really sound. Then the truck turned up and they all come inside in their army uniforms and boots and put needles in her and attached her to tubes and bottles and stuff. Then they put on green gowns and hats and things over their boots and carried her inside the truck and shut the doors. Well, I was a bloody bundle of nerves, I can tell you, but Martha, she stayed with me the whole time. Took hours but when they opened the doors, they were all smiling and saying she was fine. Then they scrubbed down her room and put a special bed in it with more tubes and machines. Martha got nurses from some agency and they took turns at staying with her for a couple of weeks, keeping her sleepy so she didn't hardly know what was going on, until they could take all the tubes out and take the machines away and put her room back the way it was."

"Sweetypie wasn't aware of what happened?" Helen asked, trying to imagine the temporary chaos it must have created in Sis's life, and remembering her own orderly experience in hospital.

"Nope. Sweetypie woke up and it was as if nothing had happened. I kept giving her the painkillers and sedatives and Martha came out every day to check. Bloody miracle, what

208

they did, fixed her up like new. No more soreness, no more gentian violet and tears at bath time, and that godawful smell got better as she healed until I couldn't even remember how bad it used to be. And she don't remember a thing about it."

Sis looked at Helen with sudden mirth in her eyes. "And you know what was best about it all? They told me that what they did to Sweetypie was what they did to blokes who wanted to be sheilas – you know, when they cut off their dongers and make a hole like a woman? Only Sweetypie didn't have a donger, did she, so they took skin from her bum instead to line the hole that was already there. Whadya think of that?"

Helen nodded. "A skin graft," she said. "That was similar to what I had, but in a much simpler way. I guess the damage I had was nowhere near as bad as Sweetypie's. At least mine had healed, hers never did. And you, Sis, what about you?"

"Ah shit," Sis dismissed with a casual wave of her hand, "I was messed up when I was little, but I got used to it and I suppose I healed, too. I don't reckon I had all that internal tearing that Sweetypie had. Hasn't bothered me for years now. But I didn't even know I was damaged until I started watching those foreign movies on SBS. And then I got real curious and sent away for some videos I seen advertised in a magazine. Well, shit, I got a shock when I saw how neat those women looked, but when it came to watching them do it with those men – well, I just up and threw the lot in the bin." She shuddered and Helen smiled. The conversation had become easy and free flowing.

"You hungry?" Sis asked suddenly.

"I could eat something. What do you have in mind?"

"Dunno. What do you fancy?"

Helen thought of the freezer inside. "How about some cake? You've got plenty."

"Cake? Haven't eaten one of those things in years. Usually just give Sweetypie a piece and chuck the rest out. They're all chocolate, only sort she'll eat of course. Alright with you?"

Helen smiled broadly. "I'd never say no to chocolate cake." They went inside together and made a fuss of getting things ready, enjoying the new found camaraderie between them. Back out on the veranda, Sis stretched her legs in front of her and contemplated her gnarled feet. "Been years since I had nothing to do for a day. Even when we're rained in, I gotta be on the ball for Sweetypie." She yawned loudly. "I could get used to this." She looked across at Helen. "So. What's next?"

"Your choice, Sis."

"Well, let me see, we could talk about the weather." She nodded towards the horizon where a wall of black clouds was building up. "Looks like it's gunna pour later today. Or we can talk some more about Dad if you really wanna, but I need to be at least a bit pissed before we do that, so let's save that for later in the day. Or we can talk about the Stewarts. Best goddamn people on the face of the earth. Especially Mrs Stewart. Shit, I still miss her and it's been over twenty years since she dropped dead in her kitchen."

"Bill sent word when she died. I grieved. She was very good to us. And to you and Sweetypie, from what Bill tells me."

"Yeah, she was. She was over here regular to see how we was doing. Only visitor apart from Martha and the old doc that Sweetypie didn't hide from. All her boys done real well, too. Bill's a good accountant and a bloody good friend. Ted has the farm now and I know I always got help there if I need it, and visa versa. Bert's in Canberra advising the Prime Minister – always was an opinionated bossy bastard, god love him. Freddy was the best town mayor we ever had for over twenty years, now he's retired up on the Tablelands. And young Ron has the Holden dealership in town, been giving me good deals and top service for forty years. Yeah, they were good boys and they're good men. And Mr Stewart always treated us like ladies, so polite, tipping his hat, giving you his arm if you met him in the street. You gotta wonder," she leaned forward and squinted against the sun, "you really gotta wonder sometimes what we would have been like if they'd been our parents."

"But they weren't," Helen responded, "and we can't change that."

"No. We can't change that." After a pause, Sis pulled herself up, sighed deeply and said, "Well, no good thinking like that, is it? We were lucky we had them as neighbours, especially her. Yeah, she never judged us, she was always kind, especially to Mum, but hell she was dumb. We practically laid it in her lap and she never got it, not even close."

Helen nodded, remembering. "I don't believe she was capable of getting it because it was so far out of her range of experience."

"Yeah. Lucky bitch."

CHAPTER FOURTEEN

Dad had been to a parish meeting in town and returned home long after the girls were in bed. He came into Sis's room with the kerosene lamp from the veranda and put it on the bedside table. Yanking the sheet back, he began to undo his fly buttons with one hand and shake Sis awake with the other. Suddenly, he pulled back and swore.

Sis roused herself and looked up through sleepy eyes to find Dad glaring down at her with disgust. She was accustomed to his disapproval, but there was something more in his face this time, something that went very deep. She followed his gaze down to her legs. Her sheet was soaked in dark blood and a sharp, acrid smell wafted upward. " Oh, I'm bleeding!"

Getting to her knees, she pulled her cotton panties down and blood flowed freely, dark and pungent, large clots sliding down her inner thighs. She had bled before, but always after Dad had been and it had never looked or smelled like this. "What's wrong with me, Dad?" she cried as she doubled over with the first cramp.

"Slut," he murmured softly, "dirty, stinking little slut." He picked up his lamp and strode across the passage to bang on Helen's locked door. She woke with a start, not expecting to be disturbed, for it was Sis's turn tonight and Helen was still recovering from her turn three nights before.

Dad had learned to accept that only the unlocked door was where he was welcome. He didn't seem to care, as long as one of them was available. He'd even accepted their fierce protection of Sweetypie, for he'd almost killed her once and been shaken to his roots by the episode. So when Helen pushed Sweetypie out of her bed and sent her to Sis's room, Dad seemed to barely notice as she scuttled sleepily past him. He had only one thing on his mind.

But he was irritable after his encounter with Sis and handled Helen roughly. When he was done, she lay limp and quiet while the bleeding and the stinging pain eased and the strength returned to her body. She heard the slam of the screen door and the creak of his bed, waited another few minutes, then made her way shakily to Sis.

Sis was sitting on the edge of the bed, doubled over and groaning, an old nappy of Sweetypie's gripped between her thighs, a blackening stain seeping into the flock mattress behind her. She'd pulled the blood soaked sheet off the bed and it lay on the floor in a heap.

Sweetypie lay asleep on the floor by the window, Sis's pillow under her head.

"Did he hurt you, too?" Helen asked, confused. Dad had never bothered them both in the same night before.

Sis shook her head, then looked up at Helen. "You alright?"

"I'm sore, Sissy, but I'll be alright. What's wrong with you?"

Sis pulled the nappy away to show Helen the black blood and lumpy clots. Helen gasped. It didn't look like the usual bleeding and it smelled pungent and strong. "Are you sick, Sissy?"

"Dunno. Ouch. My tummy hurts like buggery. You alright enough to get the basin?" Helen nodded and padded up the passage to the kitchen. She pulled the tin basin out from under the kitchen sink, filled it with water, grabbed the soap and towel and went back to Sis. Helen bathed herself first, washing away the smell of the semen and blood. Then she parted Sis's clenched legs, pulled the nappy away and wiped at the smeared blood and clots, but as fast as she wiped it away, it kept coming. Finally, she pushed another nappy up between Sis's thighs and sat by her on the bed. Sis doubled over and groaned deeply.

"I'm scared, Sissy. I reckon you're real sick. We have to get help."

"Who?"

"Mrs Stewart, I reckon. She knows about sick people. Didn't she used to be a nurse or something before she married Mr Stewart? She fixed Dad when the pony kicked him. Maybe she knows what to do."

"Yeah, maybe. Help me up, Helly. Is Dad asleep? Good. Oh jeez, ouch. Wait a minute. Urgh. Alright. Come on, let's go. We'll take the ute, but you gotta drive. I'm hurting too much."

They dressed quickly and crept outside, closing the front door gently so that it didn't bang and tiptoed down the steps. The dogs wagged their tails in anticipation but thankfully didn't bark. Dad snored loudly, flat on his back under the mosquito net. He was a heavy sleeper and for that they were grateful.

The ute was parked under the house where Dad had backed it in. Helen rolled it silently down the slope in neutral until they almost reached the bridge where she turned the key, slipped it into first gear, slowly let out the clutch until it engaged

214

and quietly puttered across the bridge. Once around the first corner, she switched on the headlights and accelerated.

It was the end of the Dry season and the track to Stewart's place powdered into bulldust around them, leaving a red tail glowing in the wake of their back lights. It took only twenty minutes before they turned into Stewart's home paddock, but in that time the front of Sis's shorts became stained red as she sat hunched forward with the pain. As they turned into Stewart's driveway, dogs set up a barking alarm.

Mr Stewart came out on to the veranda in his pyjama bottoms. "Who's that?" he called, bringing the kerosene lamp down the steps and holding it high. "Is that you, Harry? God, man, it's three in the morning! What the ..." The light of the lamp illuminated the two girls and the first thing he noticed was the blood stain between Sis's legs. "Sis Downing. Are you injured girl?" She looked up at him with a grimace. He called out to the figure coming out on to the veranda, "It's the Downing girls. You'd better take a look at this."

Mrs Stewart came quickly, took the lamp, looked at the girls' faces and the stained shorts, and understanding spread across her face. She patted her husband's arm and said, "You go back to bed. I've been wondering when this would happen. Go on, I'll take care of them." With sudden enlightenment, he nodded and left quickly.

Mrs Stewart led the girls into the house and closed the kitchen door behind them. She took three cups down from the shelf above the stove and poured simmering water from the tall cast iron fountain on the stove top into a large blackened teapot, all the while smiling a secret sort of smile.

She was a short, stout woman. Her mousy brown hair, which was normally pulled into a rough bun at the nape of her neck, hung in soft waves about her face and shoulders. An ample bosom was concealed under a frayed yellow dressing gown pulled tight over a faded cotton nightie.

215

In middle age, the beauty she had once been was replaced by a contentment that shone from her glowing chubby face, giving her features a gentleness that was a form of beauty in itself, one that would increase with the years. A mother of five strapping sons, her fondness for the Downing girls had always been evident. As she bustled about her kitchen, she created an atmosphere of safety and warmth that had nothing to do with the mild night and everything to do with her boundless generosity and unquestioning kindness.

She turned to Sis, her face all softness in the glow of the stove embers, and said, "When did it begin, my dear?"

"Tonight. I've had it before but not like this ..."

Mrs Stewart nodded knowingly and put her fingers to her lips to hush Sis to a whisper. Her husband was asleep in the next room. She bent to open a kitchen drawer and pulled out a couple of clean tea towels. Handing one of them to Sis, she said, "Pop this under you on the chair for now, we'll clean it up later." Sis did as she was told. Mrs. Stewart went back to the fountain and poured more hot water into a round china bowl. Wrapping the other tea towel around it, she sat it on Sis's lap and pushed it gently into her stomach. "Hold that for awhile until the cramps pass, dear," she said kindly. "We'll have a little talk and then, when you're feeling better, I'll get you some fresh clothes to change into. So, it's happened before? Well, I'm not surprised, my dear. How old are you now – fifteen, sixteen?"

"Sixteen next month."

"Well then, it's about the right time. And it does sort of creep up on you sometimes. A little spotting one month, a stain the next, and then, whoosh, it's all happening at once. It can be very scary if you aren't prepared, especially the flooding and the," she lowered her voice to a whisper, "the clots." She looked at their anxious, confused faces. "And you are a little frightened, aren't you, dear? I can see that. Well,

there's nothing to be afraid of. It's perfectly normal. It happens to all of us, some earlier than others. Why, I'm one of seven sisters and while one of my sisters didn't start until she was nineteen, I was just eleven. Can you imagine? Just a little girl in primary school. Oh dear, nature can be so unkind." She chuckled softly, then poured them both cups of steaming tea, added milk and sugar, opened the biscuit tin on the table and handed it around. "Hot tea helps the cramps and something warm against your tummy, like that," she indicated the bowl.

She sat opposite them. "I've been wondering when this would happen and I'm very glad you have come to me. I've been telling Harry ever since your dear mother died that I will be here for his girls, should you ever need me, but he's so fiercely independent and he does such of good job with all of you. Why, the Downing girls are the best turned out girls at mass every Sunday and you never fight or squabble, not like my lot. There are times, though," she said in a conspiratorial whisper, "when men are simply out of their depth, and this is one of those times." She patted Sis's knee again. "Does your dear father know?" she asked gently.

Sis nodded. "He called me a dirty ..."

"Oh my dear, say no more! Men can be so unintentionally cruel at times like this. Why, I remember my own dear father, bless his soul, declaring our house unsafe for a man to be in when we were all having our cycles at the same time. Poor dear man." She chuckled again. "Seven daughters born to him and Mum in just ten years, and all of us still home in our teens and early twenties before we started marrying and leaving home. I never understood why, but our cycles used to come at the same time. Mum used to say we were the sorriest bunch of wenches she'd ever seen, sitting around with sore tummies and moaning all over the place with our pale faces and dark circles under our eyes." She chuckled again at the sweet memory of it, then said sympathetically, "And it is a miserable time for

217

some girls. Now, finish your tea and biscuits and I'll show you what to do."

Thoroughly confused, Helen asked, "What's a cycle, Mrs Stewart?"

"Why, it's what is happening to your sister right now."

Helen looked down at herself and up again, the question in her eyes.

"Oh, not you too? Are you bleeding too, Helen?"

"I was, but it's stopped. It's just sort of watery stuff now ..."

"How old are you, dear?"

"Twelve. Almost thirteen"

"Well," she smiled broadly, "there you are. Two girls becoming women at the same time. No wonder Harry couldn't cope. Are you having cramps, too?"

"Well, it sort of hurts, but it usually does for awhile."

"So this is not your first time either? Well now, aren't you a pair of dark horses? You should have come to me the very first time you had a show. But you're here now, that's the main thing. Has your father told you anything?"

"About what?"

"About becoming a woman, dear, about your cycle." They looked at her stupidly. "Obviously not. Your Daddy takes care of you three so beautifully, but we'll have to forgive him for this. After all, he's just a man. Well, it will happen every month, every twenty eight days if you're lucky, although some girls are all over the place. It lasts about three to five days and then it goes. But it'll be back the next month, sure as the moon waxes and wanes. And when you marry, it will stop for awhile when you are pregnant, but it'll be back soon enough, mark my words."

Sis and Helen were completely bamboozled. They hadn't understood a word she'd said. Sis said, "Sometimes he hurts, he hurts a lot."

"Who dear, who hurts?"

"Dad."

"Oh, well, a man who has lost his wife – and your mother was such a sweet young woman – when a man goes through something like that, he's bound to suffer for a long time."

"No, I mean he hurts us."

Mrs Stewart shook her head sadly. "Yes, they do that, don't they? They don't mean to, it's just that they are a little insensitive, you know, the way they speak. They forget they're not out with the men and they just – well, they just come out with it. Even Mr Stewart, lovely man that he is, sometimes he comes home and he's all hot and bothered and the boys are being noisy and his tea might be a little late because I've had so much to do – well, he gets a little cranky and raises his voice and, yes, it does hurt. But you just have to ignore that, my dear, men are like that you see. And if you want to keep the peace, then you must turn the other cheek. They get over it. Mr Stewart's always in a much better mood after he's eaten and the boys are in bed. Then we talk and everything is alright."

Sis and Helen looked at each other. What was the woman talking about? Helen said, "But he does it all the time and he doesn't care if we bleed or if we hurt. I want him to stop."

"I'm sure he does care, but, well, it's female business and there isn't much he can do about it, is there? You'll have to look after that side of things yourself. That's what us women do, you see. We learn to handle our cycles in a quiet and dignified manner, and we certainly don't bother the men with it. Your dear father doesn't need to know when you are bleeding or cramping. He has other things to worry about, men's things, like the farm and the bills. Oh, don't look so sad. It's alright. You'll get used to it. It'll become nothing more than a nuisance after a while. Now, I'll get some nice warm water and you can wash yourselves. Pop these clean tea towels in for now to stop any more staining. I'll go get some fresh clothes for both *of you to go home in. And you can leave those stained things with me. I'll soak them in cold water overnight and wash them tomorrow. I'll give them to you when I see you on Sunday."*

She brought them two cotton nighties and underpants that were too big for them, warm water, soap and towels and left them to clean up.

After a moment, she tapped lightly on the kitchen door, waited until they had covered themselves, took the stained clothes from the kitchen and returned with half an old sheet. She proceeded to show them how to tear it into strips and place the strips inside their panties, how to take a piece of elastic and safety pins to make a belt that held the strips in place, told them how to soak the stained cloths in cold water and then boil them in the copper and blue them before hanging them out to dry, explained how often they would need to change them and that they must not bathe or wash their hair whilst they were bleeding for fear of catching a chill.

Tutored, washed, padded with cotton strips and completely confused, Sis and Helen thanked Mrs Stewart and made their way home, a pile of cotton strips on the seat between them. Daylight was only half an hour away.

As they pulled in under the house, Dad stirred on the veranda. Helen was about to turn the motor off when he leaned over the banister and demanded to know where they thought they were going at this ungodly hour of the morning. When they realised he hadn't heard them coming back and had only been woken by the dogs as they pulled in, they leaned out of the ute window and told him they were going downstream to fish, backed out and drove away again.

The fishing tackle was always kept in the back of the ute. They got it out, dug up worms and threw their lines in. It would look better if they could take something back with them.

They sat in silence. Then Sis said, "She didn't get it, did she?"

"About Dad? No, I don't think she did. Did you understand what she was on about?"

"Yeah. No. I think she was on about bleeding without Dad making it happen. All that stuff about every twenty eight days or whatever. Shit, I dunno. Bloody hell, when is it gunna stop, Helly? When is it gunna stop?"

"You mean the bleeding? Mine has stopped."

"No, I mean Dad. When's he gunna stop? You know, while I was listening to her talk, I got the feeling that she never had it happen to her. When she was talking about her Dad and all. Like all her Dad ever did to hurt her was get cranky. I don't get it."

"What don't you get?"

"Well, I always thought all dad's were like Dad, you know, and the ones with little girls could do what they liked with them, like Dad always says about us. But I don't reckon her Dad ever did it to her. Bloody hell, she called him a dear man. Would you ever call our Dad that? So whadya reckon? Maybe Dad isn't like other dads. Maybe other dads don't do to their girls what our Dad does to us." She stared into the sluggish river as the sky slowly paled, turning the water into a silvery grey-pink mirror, and pondered.

Helen didn't answer. Instead of thinking about Dad being unlike other dads, she was thinking about Sis's off the cuff question: when is it going to stop? It had sparked a new thought in her mind.

Maybe, just maybe, there was something they could do to make him stop. Stop forever.

A seed was planted. Her mind germinated it and kept it alive, but it would be a long time before it flowered and even longer before it bore fruit.

CHAPTER FIFTEEN

"When did they start for you?" Sis asked, squinting through the cigarette smoke with curious eyes.

"I was twenty when they started and forty eight when they stopped. What about you?"

"Fifty. So you just got your kids in by the skin of your teeth?"

"They were the scraping of the pot. And Sweetypie?"

"She never started and she was in her twenties before she began to develop. I reckon she was all demolished inside and nothing worked properly. Not surprising, when you think about it."

"No," Helen replied quietly, "it's not surprising at all."

"I suppose that's next on the menu, is it? Sweetypie's birthday?" Sis blew smoke from her mouth in a rush and watched it dissolve into the air. "Well, I gotta tell you, I ain't quite ready for that one yet. Been a long time since I had a conversation about anything other than the farm or what

Sweetypie did up in the rainforest. I'm outa practice, but I'm trying, Helen, I'm trying real hard."

"I know you are, darling. It's hard for us both. But you're doing extremely well."

Sis stared at her cigarette, the corners of her mouth turning up a little. Helen didn't see the wicked glint her eye. "Yeah, it is hard. Maybe too hard. I reckon I need a bit more courage," she raised her empty coffee cup, "and this ain't gunna do it at all. A little Johnny Walker's the bloke for that job. How's the hangover coming along? Hair of the dog help?" She was watching Helen out of the corner of her eye.

"No, thank you! I think I feel bad enough without adding to it. I don't know how you can ..."

Sis suddenly threw her head back and roared with laughter. The sound frightened a pair of cockatoos in the old mango tree and they scattered noisily. She laughed harder and slapped her knee with the palm of her hand, the coffee cup dangling precariously from the other. "Jeez," she gasped, the laughter settling into a chuckle, "you're bloody easy. I could always get you like that when we were kids, remember?"

Helen did remember. The practical jokes, the pranks, the friendly teasing, always out of earshot of Dad, where they could be themselves and always ending with the three of them rolling with laughter. And suddenly, for the first time in her life, she understood why.

She turned to Sis, a wry grin on her face. "That's how you kept us going, wasn't it, Sis? When you saw us becoming afraid or worn down with it all. You jollied us along."

"Yeah," the laughter settled into a long sigh, "I guess that's how it was. Could never stand seeing you both miserable for long, and you were always a sucker for it." She looked at Helen with amused pleasure. "You ain't no different now in that respect. Christ, you didn't really think I'd hit the booze again today, did you?"

"Well, I wasn't sure, I must admit. I don't know how you kept down what you drank yesterday. It would have killed me."

"Comes from years of practice, Helen, years of bloody practice." She saw the look on Helen's face and quickly added, "But I never drink through the day, I wait until my girl is asleep. She don't like it at all when I get the Johnny medicine or the stubbies out. But yesterday was an exception. Not every day my sister comes home, is it?" and she suddenly reached across and gripped Helen warmly by the hand, an impulsive act reminiscent of the girl she once was, the girl she had spent her adult life denying.

They smiled at each other, felt the gap close and inwardly rejoiced. They smiled for a long time, liking what they saw in each other, needing what they felt, allowing it to course unchecked through them.

When Sis let go to lean back in her chair, she said, "Closest I come to crying in over sixty years when I saw you coming up the steps yesterday. I reckon I can die happy now."

"Oh, no, don't do that. Not today, anyway." And they laughed together, easing the intensity of the moment, Helen's light airy laugh underscored by Sis's deep throatiness.

"Nah. I reckon I'll be around for awhile. I'm strong as a bloody ox and twice as dumb. Although I'm feeling a bit stiff in the joints today. Too much sitting around yesterday. How's about a stroll around the farm? Been more changes than you can poke a stick at."

"What a good idea. I'd like that very much."

Sis found a hat of Sweetypie's for Helen, donned her Akubra and took Helen on a guided tour. When Helen asked a question, Sis answered with knowledge and pride. In her boots, work clobber and hat, she seemed as tall and strong as any man, and Helen wondered at the illusion. Sis didn't quite top five feet, but there was a strength and power about her that made you feel it would be a mistake to cross her. Raymond would have called her a tough cookie.

Although Helen understood little about the machinery in the shed, she knew enough about cane farming to appreciate what Sis had achieved here. She asked question after question which seemed to please Sis. They talked about the properties acquired over the years and who managed them. Helen knew some of this from Bill, but was surprised to hear some familiar names, sons and grandsons of people she remembered from her childhood. She remarked that Sis must employ about half of the locals, and Sis chuckled her agreement, then went on to tell her about the history of each family. Some had suffered losses during bad seasons or after a cyclone and been forced to sell, and sell cheap. Wherever possible, Sis had kept the family on in their own home and proudly boasted of fifth and sixth generations running properties their families had started over a hundred years ago. When she talked about the sound economic benefits of employing tried and trusted people rather than bringing in new people with unproven backgrounds, Helen remarked that it sounded more like an act of compassion than business. Sis retorted by asking her why one couldn't be implemented without the other.

"You're a softie at heart, Sis. You don't like to see people suffer."

"Ain't nothing wrong with that, hey?"

"Nothing at all. And it seems to have worked well for you."

"I only bought properties with good histories and I didn't take on any ratbags. Like them Hogans up near the Daintree – remember them? He had to sell because he was a lazy drunk and he'd let the place run right down. Never looked after the soil, lotta drainage problems, shit, woulda taken more money than it was worth to get that place up and running. And he had the gall to come begging for me to buy it off him and keep him on to manage it. Not bloody likely. Still and all, felt sorry

225

for his missus, wasn't her fault. And his kids turned out to be right ratbags. No, I reckon I can spot a good deal when I see one. And a good working family. Although some of the kids these days are a bit of a disappointment. They all wanna go to university or go on the dole. Not interested in the family farm any more. Seems like kids nowadays don't wanna work, not like we did."

"Oh, Sis, it's not the kids. They are the same as always, they just have different ways of expressing themselves now. It's us. We're different. We're getting old."

"Getting old is a luxury I ain't been able to afford."

Helen looked at the nuggety body that walked next to her with powerful strides and thought about some of her contemporaries taking it easy in retirement homes next to golf courses and swimming pools, of friends who had succumbed to illness or, like Raymond, death. She couldn't imagine Sis fitting into any of those scenarios. "Would you like that luxury, Sis?"

"What, growing old? Sitting on my veranda and staring into space? Dunno. Reckon I'd be bored shitless."

"Wouldn't you like to indulge in some other things though?"

"Like what? I don't know nothing else but cane farming."

"Like … travel?"

"With Sweetypie? Get real."

"But if you had the chance."

"You mean if Sweetypie goes before me? I'd be outa here faster'n you could say ready set go. But that ain't gunna happen. She's as strong as an ox, like me. It'll be a competition to see who outlasts who. Nah, she'll be around for quite awhile yet. Anyway, I reckon I seen more of the world on the television than I ever could travelling. Best thing that ever happened to me, television. Felt like the world was coming to me. Next best thing was getting a VCR and then the DVD recorder last year. Now I don't miss nothing. Best thing after that was learning about computers and getting on the internet. Shit, I can talk to cane farmers all over the world on the internet. And guess what, some of them even heard about me. On the other side of the planet. Can you beat that?"

"Wouldn't you like to meet some of them in person?"

"Nah. They think I'm clever and classy 'cos I wrote a bit about cane farming and I own the biggest privately owned cane property in Australia . Do you think they'd think I was clever and classy if they met me? Nah, let them think I'm educated and good looking and drive a bloody Rolls Royce. Tickles my fancy, that does."

"But you'd travel if you got the chance?"

Sis thought about that. "Yeah. I'd travel if I got the chance. Why do you keep asking? Got something in mind?"

"No. Just wondering."

"Well, stop wondering and keep up. You always were a slow coach." She grinned broadly, remembering how often she'd called her younger sister that in their childhood. "Come on, I wanna show you the bridge. Had the bloody government build it for me. Took them to court and proved that my bit of road begins on my side of the river, and their bit of road includes the bridge. Paid enough taxes to the bastards, made them seal the road from town and build me a bloody humdinger of a bridge."

She pointed out its dimensions and strengths, then declared they'd had enough exercise and she needed a drink.

They returned to the veranda and Sis brought out cold water and cold beer.

She saw Helen glance at the beer. "I know, I know. Jeez, between you and Sweetypie, a gal don't get to have any fun."

"Oh, I'm not casting aspersions on your drinking habits, Sis, it's just that the very thought turns my own stomach. You go right ahead."

"Well, thank you for your blessing," Sis mocked with a grin. She stretched her legs out before her, sighed and belched. "You know what I've never had, not in my whole miserable life?"

"Tell me."

"A holiday. So I'm declaring today a holiday. I'm gunna sit here and have another bloody day off and get a bit pissed. But just a bit, til you tell me I've had enough." She grinned again.

Helen laughed, remarking inwardly at the complete lack of tension between them compared to yesterday.

She sipped her water and remembered the many times they had sat here on the veranda waiting for Dad to come home. They would talk and laugh until they heard hooves or tyres on the bridge, and then their stomachs would knot and Sweetypie would be hurried along to run into the rainforest or locked in Sis's or Helen's bedroom. Would he be in a good mood? Would he be angry with Sis and beat her? Would he pull one or the other onto his lap and demand what he always demanded? Or make them undress and sit on the swing …

"Why is the swing still there?" Helen asked suddenly.

"I took the bloody thing down and tried to burn it after the cyclone. Damn thing was too wet, shit, everything was too wet. Then Sweetypie found it on top of the pile and created havoc. Christ, so many tears over a bloody swing. So I put it back up." The grin had gone and the mask was back. Helen regretted asking the question.

"She didn't understand?"

"Course not. Doesn't remember, does she? Except in her sleep. I tried to get rid of it several times, even replaced it with a new one, but she wanted the old one back. Used to make me sick in the gut to see her on it. In the end, I threw a paddy and broke it while she was up at the cubby. Couldn't get rid of it, but at least I could stop her from using it."

A sudden wave of grief washed through Helen as she thought about Sis dealing with Sweetypie's madness on her own. She had been more than a handful when there had been two of them.

"Oh, Sis, I'm so sorry. So very, very sorry."

"Yeah," Sis said with absolute understanding of why she was sorry, "I know you are. But it's alright. We done alright here. Anyway. Enough of that. I'm gunna get pissed," she grinned playfully, "but just a little bit, alright?"

It came to Helen with a jolt that she could never convey to Sis how much she had missed her over the past half a century, how much a part of her was Sis. Her words, her attitude, her way of seeing people and the world. So often she had heard herself speak and realised it was Sis coming out of her mouth, especially when the girls were little. "A clean girl is a good girl, Ria." "If you eat your crusts, Tina, it will make your hair curly." Silly things, things a parent repeats parrot fashion after their parents. Only for Helen, Sis had been that parent.

She had spent her entire childhood absorbing Sis's influence. It had only been in the end that Sis had succumbed to her influence.

"You do that, Sis, you sit here and get pissed. I think you've earned it, don't you?"

"Hell, I have, I bloody well have!" Sis slapped her knee energetically. "I haven't had a single day off in fifty years. How many people can say that, hey? Shit, it's good to have you back, Helen, so damn good. I'd forgotten what it was like to talk to someone, you know, really talk, even if all we got to talk about is this crap."

Helen grinned back at her. "At least we don't have to explain ourselves to each other, Sis. And this shit, as you so succinctly put it, has been festering inside us like an abscess for five decades. So let's lance the boil and let the poison out. Let's do it this once and agree to never have to bring it up again."

"Done!"

They heard the bike coming down the mountain. "Your turn to do the sangers today," Sis announced. "I'm just gunna sit here like Lady Muck and do nothing. I'm on holiday."

"Must it be Vegemite?"

"She won't eat nothing else."

"Then Vegemite sangers it is." Helen was enjoying herself. It had been more than two years since she had felt any sense of fun. She waved to Sweetypie who was filling the dogs' water bowls and went inside.

Sweetypie came up the steps declaring, "Rain coming, rain coming, smell rain coming!"

Helen looked out through the kitchen window, Vegemite pot in hand, and peered towards the build up of black clouds. The front was coming in over the ocean like something out of a science fiction movie, as high as a mountain and squared off at the front as if someone had scraped a ruler across it. It wasn't hard to see that the monsoon season was well and truly upon them, but she had forgotten Sweetypie's sixth sense with weather. As a child she could predict rain long before the first cloud appeared in the sky.

She called out, "When will it arrive, Sweetypie?"

"Tonight. After tea," Sweetypie answered with the confidence of a meteorologist. "Where's my sangers?"

"Coming, darling."

The sandwiches and cordial were consumed with the accompanying chatter. Now that she was feeling more relaxed, Helen tried to take part in Sweetypie's detailed description of her morning. She watched Sweetypie's face, her innocent aged face, and her heart wept for what might have been.

Sweetypie told them she'd seen a big black rainbird on a low branch near the cubby and would they like to come and see it, it was sooooo pretty.

Sis slapped the table and said, "Yep, I reckon that's a good idea, little one. I reckon a swim is in order, too. Whadya say, Helen?"

"I say: I don't believe I could make it up to the cubby without help. I'm not a young woman any more."

"Hell, who is? Can you ride a motor bike? No? Well, aren't you the useless one. What happened to the farm girl who could ride bareback all over the mountain? Never mind. You can ride in the trailer. Sweetypie," she ordered, "take the rocks out of the trailer and put a blanket in it. You're taking Helly for a ride."

Helen gripped the low sides of the trailer as it rattled up the stone path. She was amazed at the neatness of each stone diligently concreted into place, at the carefully pruned undergrowth on either side of the track that made her feel as if she was travelling along an English village lane. A very hot and steep English village lane. The last time she had made this journey, the track had been a muddy mess.

Facing backwards for better balance, she watched Sis following her on the other three wheeler, grinning and showing off as she pulled up onto the back wheels and yahooed loudly. Prince and Lady barked and cavorted around her, picking up on her excitement. Sweetypie giggled constantly as she manoeuvred the bike expertly up the mountainside.

The lushness of the rainforest wrapped itself around Helen with its intoxicating smells and low dappled light and she was a kid again. She caught the excitement and grinned at her silly billy sisters.

The waterhole was exactly as she remembered it. Sitting there on the flat black rock, looking up through the leaves to the rainforest canopy, she felt the extraordinary muffled silence enfolding itself around her, the spirit of tranquillity that she had not encountered anywhere else in her half century of travels. The timeless connection with thousands of years of little dark children before them who had sat here and gazed up into the trees just as they did now.

The water was crystal clear as always, cool on her itching legs, sweet in her mouth. Sis and Sweetypie paddled around her, naked and uninhibited, their breasts floating on the surface like wrinkled pockets of lard. They laughed and squealed and belched and farted, pulling faces as they made the water bubble around them. After a few minutes, the mood caught at Helen and she flung her swimsuit onto the rocks, climbed up after it, turned and dive bombed into the water. When Sis told her to stand on the rocks again, she obeyed and looked down. Sis was peering up between her legs. "Oh, you want to check it out, do you?" she laughed, parting her labia while Sis inspected closely. Then Sweetypie climbed out and stood next to her, mimicking her pose, crying, "Look at me, too, Sissy! Aren't I pretty?" Sis threw her head back and laughed at their outrageousness.

"They turned you both into a couple of pretty little virgins," she cried and lunged forward to pull them back into the water with an almighty splash.

When they had tired of their games, they sat on the rocks and let the warm air dry them. After awhile, Sweetypie went around to the other side of the waterhole where it was shallow and sat waist deep in the water, staring around her dreamily. They observed her other-world contentment.

"Tell me, Sis, have you anything in place, any contingency plan for Sweetypie in case you die first?" Helen suddenly asked.

"Contingency plan? Yeah. Sure. Hey, Sweetypie," she yelled across the water, "tell Helen what you gotta do if I don't wake up one day, or I'm not there to get your tea for you."

"Oh, silly billy, she knows."

"Tell her anyway. She forgot."

And in the same singsong voice in which she'd repeated her mobile phone instructions, she chanted, "If you don't wake up, I come up to the cubby and eat the lollies. I must eat them fast and not stop until they are all gone. If you're not there to get my tea, I must come up to the cubby and eat all the lollies. I must eat them fast and not stop until they are all gone. Boring boring boring."

"And if it's dark?"

"Then I must get the big red torch from on top of the fridge and come up on the bike with the lights turned on."

"And who do you tell?"

"No one. I must not talk to anyone. If anyone comes, I must run into the rainforest to hide because if they find me, they will take me far away where strange people will be mean to me. There! You're a silly billy to forget, Helly."

Helen replied, "I didn't really forget, little one, I just wanted to see if you had."

"Silly billy. I never forget."

Helen turned to Sis. "Lollies?"

"Come and see." She led the way behind the waterfall into the cubby.

Helen gasped with surprise at what she beheld.

Four tall elaborate candelabra, each holding at least a dozen short fat candles, stood guard at the four corners of the cavern. Melted wax from many years of use lay deep at their bases. "Catalogues?" Helen asked, nodding towards the candelabra.

"Of course," Sis grinned.

Two iron bedsteads in the middle of the floor space were draped with white linen and frilled pillow cases. Sis and Sweetypie's old beds. There were no mosquito nets. "Still no mosquitoes in here?" Helen quizzed.

"Nup, never a one," Sis answered.

A large sideboard with a collection of crockery, cutlery and utensils dominated the space. Two chairs and a table were set as if a meal was about to be served. As indeed it might be, for a large modern gas barbecue stood to one side, and next to that, shelving with packets and cans of food, enough to feed two people for many weeks. An assortment of other household goods lay higgledy piggledy in a large box next to a wardrobe with the door open to reveal it full of clothing. And the whole arrangement sat on a huge Persian rug, royal blue, scarlet and gold.

The mother of all cyclone shelters.

"How on earth did you get it all in here?" Helen asked.

"Took it all apart, lugged it in, put it all back together again. No bloody worries. Hey, Sweetypie, show Helly where the lollies are kept."

Sweetypie rolled her eyes at them as if they were idiots and opened the sideboard door. She took out a glass jar jammed to the top with tablets of every colour and size. "Good god, Sis, what have you got in there?" Helen took the jar and turned it around and around.

"Just about every sort of sedative and tranquilliser known to mankind, I reckon. Been collecting them for years. I get a monthly prescription for Sweetypie from Martha, but I only use them when she really needs them. I save them when she doesn't." Suddenly, she drew Sweetypie towards her and held her tight to her side. "Enough there to put an entire army to sleep. Enough to make sure that if the worse comes to the worse, one little old girl just goes to sleep and no one can get to her."

"No one would ever find her here, Sis."

"That's the whole idea. Do you think I want some old fart of a priest who never knew her going through the motions at her funeral? Do you think anyone would even come to her funeral? How bloody sad would that be? No, let her go here, where she's happy, where's she's safe. What happens after I'm gone doesn't matter anyway, as long as we go at the same time. And I never figured you'd take care of her. Nothing meant by that, either, so don't get your nose out of joint. It's just that it was always me that was meant to take care of her. Do you understand? It was always my job from the moment she was born, Helen, nothing more." She looked down at Sweetypie's head resting on her shoulder and kissed her white hair. "You're still my little Sweetypie, aren't you precious?" Sweetypie nodded silently. "Come on, another dip and then back home. Rain's coming and the track gets slippery when it rains. Never stops you though, does it, Sweetypie? You're just a little rainforest rat who loves getting wet and muddy. But it bothers me. So let's go."

Back at the house, it was frozen birthday cake, candle, Happy Birthday, bath, chops and mash potato on the veranda, fruit salad and ice-cream, and bed for Sweetypie. Sis gave her a tablet as she tucked the mosquito net around her, "just to make sure she doesn't give your pubes a trim tonight, Helen." Then dishes, mop the floor, clothes in the washing machine, and a pot of tea on the veranda.

The rain arrived like thunderous applause at dusk just as Sweetypie had predicted. Heavy tropical rain that overflowed the gutters within minutes, rattling across the iron roof like a herd of cattle, making conversation impossible. With it came a cooling breeze.

They sat in companionable silence, thinking their own thoughts.

As darkness enveloped them, the rain eased, but the breeze melted away and the mosquitoes arrived in hoards. Sis lit two mosquito repellent coils and placed one under each chair. She smoked and drank in silence until finally, she said, "You know, I relive it almost every day."

"Relive what, darling?" Helen said, her thoughts momentarily on whether or not she should ring her daughters that night. She had promised she would call them as soon as she had settled in with Sis.

"The birthday party."

Helen's attention was snapped back to the present and to the past in the same instant. "I know what you mean," she said. "I can find myself back there at the drop of a hat. A certain smell or colour or sound will do it, and I'm nine years old and standing in the Front Room in that dress Dad brought back from town. White organza. Blue for you and pink for Sweetypie. I'm really there, the memory is so sharp. It still haunts me."

"Yeah. I know what you mean." They were silent, knowing they must begin, but reluctant to. Finally, Sis said, "We should have let her go, should have let her slip away then. It would have been kinder than to let her live with what happened."

"Yes," Helen replied wretchedly, "We should have let her go."

CHAPTER SIXTEEN

"They're coming, they're coming!" Sweetypie cried, jumping up and down with such unbridled excitement that the freshly pressed pink ribbons in her carefully braided blonde hair threatened to come loose. Sis and Helen ran from the Front Room where they had been setting out the food and games to join her on the veranda.

A parade of vehicles crossed the bridge in convoy. Eleven in all, polished and gleaming for the outing. As they approached, small girls in their Sunday best clutching gaily wrapped packages could be seen sitting up high in their seats in anticipation.

Birthday parties were always an event, but this was the first party to be held at the Downing property and it promised to be special. After all, the Downings weren't short of a quid and it was common knowledge that Harry spoiled his girls rotten. Private tutors, shop bought clothes, the big house. No sugar *shack party here with home made toys and making do with what they had.*

And maybe it signalled the end of Harry's period of grief. After all, his wife had been gone three years now. It was time for him to enter the mainstream of life again and cast his eye around for a new mother for his girls. He had shut himself away with his daughters for long enough, discouraging visitors, sacrificing his own needs to the needs of his motherless girls. Admirable, indeed, but you can keep up that sort of devotion for just so long.

Yes, there was as much anticipation amongst the adult guests as there was amongst their six year olds. It was time for Harry Downing to join their world again.

Harry left his seat on the veranda and waited for the guests at the bottom of the steps.

The girls waited above him, Helen and Sis on either side of the birthday girl. They couldn't stop grinning. Dad had brought new dresses for each of them, blue for Sis, white for Helen and pink for Sweetypie. Organza with bows at the waist and skirts that floated and swirled when they moved.

The incongruous bare feet below the swirling skirt of Sis's dress was only because Dad had forgotten to buy her shoes as well, although he'd brought home a pair of white court shoes for Helen and a wondrous pair of shiny pink court shoes with satin bows and matching frilly pink socks for Sweetypie. Sis felt special because he'd remembered to buy her anything at all and she'd be damned if she'd wear her work boots with the new dress. She'd scrubbed her feet almost raw to remove the grubby stains and they would have to do.

As the guests pulled up in front of the house, the girls ran down the steps to greet them. Smiling parents watched as little girls gathered in a giggling group around Sweetypie, crying "Happy Birthday!" and thrusting gifts at her until they spilled out of her arms to be collected up by Sis and Helen. Like

238

a gaggle of small geese, they went up the steps and into the Front Room, oohing and aahing at the decorations, the party food and the birthday cake. Their giggly chatter spilled out onto the veranda where the adults were gathering around Dad for afternoon tea.

One of the little girls told Sweetypie she looked like a princess. Sweetypie twirled on her pink toes so that her skirt flew out around her, crying, "Aren't I pretty! Aren't I pretty, Sissy? Look at my pretty dress, Helly!"

Squealing with delight, she stood amongst a circle of presents on the floor, each wrapped in coloured tissue paper and bright ribbons, clapped her hands joyously and called for her Sunday School friends to come and see what she had been given. Her older sisters took their positions over by the window, letting the flock of little girls take their places of honour around Sweetypie.

"Go on ..." Sis began.

"... unwrap them," Helen finished.

Sweetypie twirled on her toes once more, then clapped her hands. She flopped unceremoniously to the floor and tore into the prettily wrapped parcels with such enthusiasm that they had to step back to avoid being tangled up with them. So much laughter, until they saw him watching her from the other side of the room. The laughter died in their throats. No no, not today, not this day. It was too soon. She was still too little. Didn't he understand that?

Dad stood in the doorway, the other parents gathering in a laughing group behind him. His eyes devoured the little girls before him, devoured them as if they were a feast for his private consumption, and in that instant, Sis and Helen understood that a feast was exactly what it really was. Dad had not arranged this party for Sweetypie, he'd arranged it for himself. A banquet of tanned bare legs, soft white bodies, plump warm hands, pink rosebud mouths, bright eyes flashing

239

with excitement, responsive pretty little creatures purely for his amusement and titillation.

He inspected each little girl in turn, safe to do so in front of their own parents because they would never suspect. He was so well regarded and such a good father to give his little girl a birthday party like this without a woman to help him. A man to be admired and respected. A good man.

No one suspected, no one but Sis and Helen.

Feeling as if they'd had the wind knocked out of them, Sis and Helen cleaned up the torn paper and began the games. They went through the motions of pin the tail on the donkey, spin the bottle and other games, but all the while they watched Dad. Out on the veranda with the adults, drinking and talking, he kept looking in through the window, a half smile of smug pleasure giving his handsome face a hint of arrogance and cruelty that only the girls understood. And when the party was over, he stood on the veranda and waved the guests away, his mind already on the real business of the day.

"Daddy, Daddy, I want the swing!" Sweetypie cried, still elated and breathless with excitement. He took her hand and skipped down the steps with her, lifted her onto the swing and pushed. "Higher, Daddy, I want to go higher!" He gave the swing a hard shove. An odd sort of alertness had taken hold of him, as if his own mounting excitement needed containment. His eyes glittered as he caught the swing and pushed it again. Still Sweetypie cried, "Push me higher, Daddy, I want to go higher!"

But instead of pushing the swing again, he caught it and held it fast. Sis and Helen, watching from the top step, knew their baby sister was in peril.

"Sis, Helen, come down here and get on the swing with Sweetypie. Come on."

Reluctantly, they obeyed and sat either side of Sweetypie. He pushed the three of them back and forth. Sweetypie squealed and giggled but her sisters were deadly silent. They held onto a rope with one hand and Sweetypie with the other. They flew high up into the mango tree and down into Dad's waiting hands, back and forth until they were dizzy with it. Then he stopped and held the swing still.

"Take your clothes off," he said. They did as they were told, as they had done on other occasions, but never with Sweetypie. "Back on the swing," he commanded and lifted each of them on.

They sat with their backs to him while he removed his own clothes. Then he pushed them until they swung high, their legs swaying up and down with the motion, their hair flying out around them, the black on either side of the blonde. Each time they came back down, they felt the heat of his hands on their backsides. They knew he was watching their bums squashed together, pink and smooth, flying up and away from him, then swinging down to barely graze the top of his erection before being pushed away again. It was a game for him, they knew that, a game that gave him a lot of pleasure and which they endured, but this time they were afraid. When he moved around to the front of the swing for a different view of the girls, they gripped their baby sister tightly between them.

"Inside," he suddenly ordered, his breath coming in short shallow gasps. Sis and Helen jumped off the swing and pulled Sweetypie down after them. Sis was about to tell her to run into the rainforest but, as if reading her mind, Dad said, "None of that," and caught Sweetypie up in his arms. He trotted up the steps with her slung over his shoulder. She looked back at her sisters, waved and giggled. She had not the slightest inkling of what was to come.

Sis and Helen ran after him.

Sis cried, "Leave her, Dad, she's too little!" He didn't seem to hear her, but then, he rarely did when he was like this. He heard only the raging demands of his own flesh.

Before they could reach him, he'd taken Sweetypie into Helen's room and turned the key.

They banged on the door, then Sis ran to get the key from her own door. Even as they turned it in the keyhole, they heard Sweetypie's fretful cries coming from within. By the time they pushed the door open, she was screaming with such shrill terror that even Dad was alarmed. Her naked body thrashed around violently on the bed, small fists flying at his face and chest, feet beating a tattoo against his abdomen as she did everything within her feeble power to fight him off. Her terrified eyes bulged as the screams escalated.

Her wild display daunted him for but a second, his look of bafflement quickly replaced with a fierce determination to finish what he had begun. He had no doubt in his mind that this display was only temporary, that when she learned what he wanted, she would acquiesce as her sisters did, that the tears would quickly dry and the harmony be restored to his happy home.

He grappled with her, but her flailing made her as slippery as an eel and she slithered out of his hands again and again. Finally, in complete exasperation, he grabbed her tightly around the waist, flipped her over onto her belly, pulled her backside into the air and lunged into her, impaling her so sharply, so violently, that she stiffened, arched and flung her arms out in front of her, looking for all the world like a diver leaping into a pool.

Sis and Helen launched themselves at him, screaming to let Sweetypie go, but he was beyond hearing them. Nudging their beating fists away from him as if they were nothing more than flies, he began to thrust into the little body, every motion tearing cruelly into her soft tissues, her body stiffening and arching with each thrust, her mouth wide as her breath escaped in silent gushes, her unseeing eyes turned up to the uncaring heavens, oblivious to her sisters' desperate battle to save her.

Inflamed by the warm smooth body in his grasp and the wild screams of his other two daughters, aroused by the touch of their fists beating against his sweating body, Dad reached a height of eroticism that urged him into a thrusting frenzy until he came with a sudden stillness and a loud moan of release. He pulled his hands away, freeing Sweetypie's body so that it slipped from his own. Pushing Sis and Helen aside, he left the room.

Sweetypie lay catatonic on the bed, bleeding from the savage tears that cut her flesh from anus to vagina, blood and semen issuing from the still gaping rectum, eyes glassy, pupils dilated, her mouth agape. She didn't seem to be breathing.

Weeping with despair, Sis and Helen pulled her up onto the pillow and turned her onto her back. They shook her without response. She was dead, they were sure of it. Standing back from the bed, Sis experienced a rage that drove her outside where Dad was recovering with a beer left over from the party. "She's dead!" she screamed. "You killed her!"

"Don't be bloody silly," Dad said with a yawn. He was thinking a nap before tea might be a good idea. "It never did you no harm, it won't do her no harm."

"She's dead! She's dead!"

"For god's sake, will you leave a man alone? I said she'll be alright. Now get into the kitchen and get tea on. I'm getting hungry." He leaned back in post coital languor and closed his eyes.

Sis ran back to Helen who had dragged Sweetypie into a sitting position, the small blonde head lolling forward like a rag doll. Helen looked up. "Is she breathing, Sissy? I can't tell."

"Dunno. I don't think so. Oh, Helly, what we gunna do?"

They looked at each other, overwhelmed by despair and their own powerlessness to save her. Then Sis clenched her jaw with determination. "We gotta get her away from Dad, I know that

243

much. He mustn't touch her ever again. Ever, ever!" Then her face collapsed into despair. She looked down and stroked the blonde hair, pleading. "Oh, Sweetypie, don't be dead, please don't be dead."

"The cubby," Helen said suddenly, "let's take her to the cubby. He won't be able to get to her there."

"Yeah. The cubby. She'll be safe there." Sis suddenly felt galvanised into action. "What's he doing now?"

"He's still out on the veranda. Shall I get Ginger?"

"Yeah, but be quiet. And don't worry about the saddle, just throw a blanket over him. Bring him around the side, I'll take her out the back way. Be quick, Helly."

Panic sent Helen flying down the front steps and across the grass to the stables. Dad didn't stir. He was napping.

She brought Ginger to the side of the house where the ground rose up to meet the veranda. A gap between the veranda and the slope of the mountain provided the perfect place for Ginger to stand while Sis mounted him, drew Sweetypie across her lap and inched back as Helen jumped on in front of her, facing backward so that she could hold Sweetypie in place between them. Sis turned the pony towards the entrance to their secret track just as Dad, disturbed by the pony's whinnies, came around the corner of the veranda.

"Hey, what's going on?" he called out at the sight of his three naked daughters on the pony. "You gotta get my tea, no time for ..." The words died in his mouth as he saw Sweetypie's head hanging limply to the side, her open unseeing eyes, her face deathly white, tongue lolling from her mouth. "Oh marymotherofgod."

He reached out, his fingertips barely brushing the blonde hair as Sis violently reined Ginger away from him. She kicked the pony into a trot as Dad cried, "Where are you going? Hey! Come back! I didn't mean to ..."

"We're taking her where you'll never find her!" Sis called over her shoulder as they melted into the rainforest and disappeared from his view.

Within seconds, the rainforest closed in around them, muffling all sound. At first, they listened for Dad's footsteps behind them, but heard nothing. After a few minutes they knew they were safe. Even if he was trying to follow them, the chances of him stumbling onto the path to the waterhole were remote, and Ginger left no hoof prints in the soft leaf litter.

It was a struggle to keep Sweetypie's limp body from slipping away from them. Sis finally let the reins go, trusting Ginger to know the way, and wrapped both her arms under Sweetypie's arms to prevent her from falling. Helen wrapped her own arms around them both as they silently adjusted to the movements of the pony beneath them. They heard only the ka-plop ka-plop of Ginger's hooves and the muted birdcalls above.

Sweetypie grew cold between them. The struggle to keep her on the horse kept Sis and Helen from sinking into total despair, but fear wrapped itself around their hearts. The fear that they had lost her forever.

They reached the waterhole and lowered Sweetypie to the ground, tethering Ginger behind the big tree above the waterfall. The blanket was soaked in blood. Sis threw it into the waterhole to retrieve later. It coloured the water pink.

Still convinced Sweetypie was dead, they carried her into the sanctuary of the cubby and laid her on the rough beds they'd made up out of old blankets and towels, pulled a sheet over her and looked down at her.

"What now?" Helen asked.

"Dunno," Sis replied softly. She saw blood oozing through the sheet, evidence of Dad's atrocity. "Let's clean her up," she said, a tremor in her voice.

Helen saw the blood and nodded her understanding. It gave them something to do.

They busied themselves making a fire to heat water in the billy. Sis threw Helen old clothes from the bag next to the collection of kitchen utensils and they dressed quickly. She tore a threadbare towel into pieces and, when the billy was warm, they pulled the sheet back and began to wash Sweetypie's body.

They were adept hands at cleaning up after Dad, but even as they washed away the blood, more appeared. Sis took a clean piece of towel, rolled it into a thick wad and pushed it between Sweetypie's cold thighs. When they had done all they could, they sat back and looked at each other.

"She's so cold, Sissy. Is she really dead?" Helen's chin wobbled and her eyes filled with tears.

"Yeah. I reckon she is."

Sis looked away from Helen's distress and fought off her own tears. She saw the hands on the wall and stared until she found Sweetypie's white prints there. Baby hands. Not much smaller than the hands lying limply before her now. So small. So helpless. So very, very still.

Her own tears came. "I dunno what to do."

"Should we ... bury her or something?"

"Nah, I don't reckon. Not yet. Not till she starts to smell."

"She looks so ... far away."

"Yeah. Sort of lonely."

"I don't want her to be lonely, Sissy." They were sobbing now.

"Me neither. Come on, let's try to warm her up."

They lay down next to the cold marble-white child, one either side and hugged their bodies tight to her, their arms wrapped around her and each other. She might be dead, but she was still their little Sweetypie and they would hang on to her for as long as they could.

They wept, tears spilling from their faces onto the face of their sister. They wept until exhaustion overwhelmed them and then they drifted into a fitful sleep. During the night, Sis woke with a cold backside. She rolled over and stoked the fire, pulled more wood onto it, waited until it flared and rolled back to Sweetypie.

Although still cold and white, Sweetypie had closed her eyes sometime during the night and pulled her lolling tongue back into her mouth. Even as Sis tightened her grip around her and Helen, she felt the whisper of a breath on her face. Relief swept through her. She tried to wake Helen, without response. Exhaustion had taken its toll. It didn't matter. When Helen woke, she'd tell her then.

She pushed the blonde hair back from the sweet face, kissed it lovingly and snuggled down into her.

Weak light streaking through the tunnel high above them woke the girls. They rolled away from Sweetypie and sat up.

Helen's eyes opened wide. "She's breathing, Sissy."

"Yeah, I reckon she come good through the night 'cos we kept her warm. But look," she pointed to the wad of towelling, "she's still bleeding real bad. We gotta stop that." Sis looked around her. They had used everything they had in the cubby. She thought for a moment. "I'm going down to the house to get some more stuff. You stay here and keep the fire going so she don't get cold again."

"But Dad ..."

"Don't you worry about him. I ain't afraid of him no more." She pulled herself up to her full height and felt an empowering rage surge through her. "If he ever touches our Sweetypie again, I'll ... I'll kill him!"

Helen was not convinced. "But what if he follows you back?"

"Not a chance! He'd never keep up with me. Don't you worry, alright? You just keep the fire going and keep her warm."

"Alright, Sissy."

"Good girl. I'll be quick as I can."

Sis took Ginger to the waterhole and let him drink his fill, then rode him down to the edge of the rainforest, dismounted and surveyed the house. Dad was nowhere in sight. He would have left for the cane fields by now anyway, so it should be safe to go inside. She led Ginger to the stables and walked to the house. As she reached the veranda, Dad opened the front door. He looked as if he hadn't slept.

"Where is she?" he asked without a trace of anger.

"Somewhere where you can't get to her," she snapped with such venom that he took a step backward. He looked down at his twelve year old daughter in her old dungarees and sleeveless shirt, her bare feet damp with leaf litter and her unkempt black hair already plastered to her head with sweat. But instead of the contempt he normally conferred on her, he looked distracted and confused.

Sis felt a shift in power and let it surge through her. Taking a step towards him, she raised her voice and said angrily, "We got her safe, but she's like she's dead and it's your fault! You ain't never gunna touch her again. You hear me, Dad, you ain't never gunna touch her again!"

"I didn't mean to hurt her, Sis, I would never hurt her ..."

"Bullshit!" she shouted, "You hurt her real bad and you don't care. You never care! You don't care about her or Helly or me, you don't care about nobody but yourself and your bloody soldier!" She flung herself past him and went inside. "I gotta get some things for her." He turned to follow her into the house, shoulders slumped miserably. "Stay away from me! I'll get what I need and then I'm gone. And don't try and follow! You'd never find us. We're staying where we are until she's alright. We'll come back when we're good and bloody ready, and not a minute before."

He turned away and went back out onto the veranda.

When she had gathered up what she needed, she stormed past him on the veranda and began the trek up the mountain, wondering if she had seen what she thought she had seen.

Dad sitting on the veranda with tears running down his cheeks.

She didn't mention it to Helen. It didn't make sense. Besides, they had more important things to worry about.

As the day progressed, Sweetypie's body went from cool marble white to warm and sweaty. The bleeding eased soon after Sis changed the towelling wad, but still Sweetypie remained unconscious. Her body grew hot and dry, so they carried her outside to the waterhole and sat chest deep in the cool water with her supported between them. When her body chilled and she began to tremble violently, they carried her back inside and covered her in blankets.

And so the cycle began, hot body into cool water, cold shaking body into blankets, over and over as the day slowly dragged by.

They tried to force water between her lips, but it dribbled out uselessly. During one of their spells in the water, they let her head loll forward too far and her nose and mouth dipped into the water. With a reflex action she gulped, coughed and sputtered. Sis let it happen again, careful that they didn't let her head drop for more than a second. As soon as she gulped, they pulled her up. And so they managed to get some water into her.

For three days and three nights, the cooling and warming cycle continued. Sis and Helen didn't have a clue what they were doing, they just did what seemed sensible as each situation arose. When the wad of towelling became pink and smelly, they changed it. When she felt hot, they cooled her. When she felt cold, they warmed her. When she felt alright, they dozed. Their care was haphazard but intensive.

On the fourth morning, Sweetypie opened her eyes and screamed fit to lift the roof off the cubby. She screamed with back arched and arms and legs flung wide. Her eyes rolled around wildly inside their sockets. Nothing could be done to stop her. She screamed until her body could take no more, then

249

lapsed back into the catatonic state, eyes open and staring, breath coming in shallow gasps.

Sis and Helen wept in fear, frustration and sheer exhaustion. When they were sure that Sweetypie was calm again, they resumed their positions on either side of her, hugged her tight and slept fitfully.

During the night, Sweetypie woke up screaming again. This time, as Sis was brought abruptly awake, she said over and over, "It's only a dream, Sweetypie, it's only a dream. You're alright, nothing's going to hurt you." Her words seemed to penetrate and Sweetypie gradually calmed and slept, her eyes closing peacefully. An hour later, the scene was repeated, and after that, every so often through the night.

As early morning sunlight filtered down through the canopy above the waterfall, Sis and Helen carried the sleeping Sweetypie out to the waterhole. Her skin was hot and dry and Sis knew she needed water urgently. As they lowered her into the water, she woke with a jerk and began to scream again, thrashing her arms and legs around.

Sis understood in a lightning flash that Sweetypie thought she was still in the bedroom fighting Dad off. With mock anger in her voice, she commanded, "Sweetypie! What are you doing? Stop that, do you hear me, stop that!"

As if coming out of a long dark tunnel into bright light, Sweetypie gradually opened her eyes and looked around her, dazed and weak, her jaw hanging slackly. "That's better," Sis said quickly, "that's a good girl. What did you think you were doing, giving us all a fright like that?"

"Sissy," Sweetypie whispered so weakly that both girls leaned forward to hear her, "I had a bad dream, Sissy."

"Yeah, that's right, you had a bad dream. Yeah, you been sick, you got a fever and it made you have a bad dream."

"Had my party," Sweetypie tried to continue, but Sis jumped in and stopped her.

250

"Nah, silly billy, you ain't had no party. You ain't even had your birthday yet. It's your birthday today. You just had a bad dream, that's all."

"Oh, bad dream, very bad dream. Oooh, Sissy, I feel sick and I hurt."

"Yeah, you got a fever, that's why you feel sick, and you slipped on the rocks near the waterhole and cut yourself. That's why you hurt. Don't you remember?"

Sweetypie shook her head.

"It don't matter. You gotta have some water to drink, that'll make you feel better."

Helen, quickly picking up on Sis's words, scooped water into her cupped hands and put it under Sweetypie's mouth. Sweetypie sipped slowly, rested and sipped again.

They carried her into the cubby and patiently helped her sip from a cup. As she slipped back into sleep, they made damper and billy tea. When Sweetypie next woke up screaming, they repeated the dream story while they hand-fed her the warm damper. Without thinking, Sis stuck one of the candles in the middle of the piece of damper and they sang her Happy Birthday.

They lived in the cubby for almost three weeks while Sweetypie's fever settled, but the torn tissue refused to heal, weeping a foul smelling discharge like an open sore. They quickly discovered that sitting with her in the waterhole was the only thing to sooth the pain and pacify her.

But the nightmares continued. Each time she woke up screaming, they reassured her until she was calm, and if they were eating, they stuck a candle in the food, whatever it was, and sang her Happy Birthday, establishing a habit that was to become a ritual.

Sis made the trip down to the house every few days when she knew Dad was out in the cane fields, finding fresh food and clothing left in a pile on the veranda table for her. Every time she collected the things he'd left for her, she felt the power, the fact that Dad had accepted her terms, and she was determined not to lose an inch of that precious ground when she came home.

Finally, after sleeping most of the night through with only a couple of screaming nightmares, Sis decided it was time to go back. But before they went, she made a pact with Helen. "We gotta protect Sweetypie from him, no matter what. Alright?"

"Yes. We have to be strong."

"Yeah. Real bloody strong, because it ain't gunna be easy."

"He might try to hurt us to get to her, Sissy."

"Then we gotta promise each other that we must never be weak. We gotta do whatever it takes. We gotta be real strong. No crying. Don't ever cry. Not about nothing. 'Cos that's weak. You got that?"

"Yes, Sissy, I'm not going to cry. Ever again. I reckon we cried enough for all our lives here in the cubby."

"Yeah, I reckon so too. We gotta be tough. You know, like hard inside. We gotta make ourselves hard towards him, no matter what happens. Otherwise, if he gets to her again, he'll kill her for sure. We both know that."

"I hate him, Sissy. I'm scared of him."

"I hate him, too, but don't be scared, Helly," she said, remembering the surge of power she had felt when confronting him. "There's just so much he can do. We just gotta be stronger and tougher than him. Can you do it?"

"Yes."

"Pact?"

"Pact."

They spat in their palms and shook on it.

Sis went down the mountain, collected Ginger and rode the three of them down the track.

Dad came home from the cane fields to find his chops and mashed potato waiting for him on the veranda. He ate in silence, his two eldest daughters watching him with cold hard faces.

"Is she gunna be alright?" he finally asked.

"Yeah, as long as you leave her alone," Sis answered.

"I'll leave her alone, you got no worries about that," he replied, as if he had given it a lot of thought. "You're right, she was too little." Looking chastened, he added, "I never wanted to hurt her.

It was on the tip of Sis's tongue to tell him how much he hurt her and Helen every time he touched them, but something in Dad's face stopped her. It wasn't remorse or repentance. It was more a complete lack of comprehension. He didn't understand that he hurt them. He wasn't a stupid man, far from it, but he simply didn't have it in him to understand. Sis saw it in his face, looked away with disgust and thought, Ah hell what's the point.

She went inside to Sweetypie who was resting in her bed.

"How you doing, little one?"

"I'm sore, Sissy."

"Yeah, I know. It'll get better."

"Where's Dad? Did he remember my birthday?"

"Course he did. Do you want to see him?"

A veil dropped across Sweetypie's eyes. "I had a bad dream," she murmured.

"Yeah," Sis said vehemently, "you had a whopper of a bad dream, but that's all it was, and you fell on the rocks at the cubby and hurt yourself, but you're gunna get better real soon. And Dad ain't gunna hurt you, he ain't even gunna touch you. I promise that."

"Did he remember my birthday?" Sweetypie repeated.

"Sure did. I'm gunna go get the cake now, it's been cooling long enough and we'll put the candles on it and then you can blow them out."

"What about my party?"

"Sweetypie, Sweetypie, I keep telling you that there ain't no party. You dreamed that. There's just me and Helly and Dad. Alright?"

"Yes. But I'm so sore," she whimpered.

"Why don't I run a cold bath for you? That'll help, hey?"

"Yes. Alright."

Sis went downstairs to the washhouse. Dad followed her. Sis ignored him while she filled the bath, but he waited in the doorway until she had finished. When she turned, he took a step forward. She yelled, "No!" and pushed him away. But he was persistent and reached out for her. "No bloody way!" she cried and ran upstairs.

Joining Helen on the veranda, Sis sat fuming with her arms folded across her chest. Dad came up the steps and stood before her. She looked away from him, still feeling the power, but now uncertain how long she could maintain it. Helen looked on, frightened. Neither of them had ever challenged Dad like this before. They had never even thought to.

"A man has needs," was all Dad said. He pulled Sis up, gripped her by the arm and dragged her inside. She struggled, but even though at twelve she was a well built girl, she was no match for his size and strength. Suddenly, as though wearied by her struggles, Dad said, "If not you, then Sweetypie."

Sis froze in his grasp. She looked up at his resolute face and understood that this was the trade off. If she wanted to keep Sweetypie safe from him, this was to be her ongoing sacrifice. She understood that sometimes choices are made for you, that you have no say because there are no other options. It had to be this way, for her and for Helen.

And she also understood that this was her punishment for taking control, albeit only temporarily.

The power shifted back to Dad.

She glanced to the side and saw Sweetypie lying on the bed, rocking to and fro with the discomfort of her wounds. She stopped struggling, called out to Helen to take Sweetypie down to her bath, and gave Dad what he wanted.

CHAPTER SEVENTEEN

Sis sat forward heavily, hung her head and sighed deeply.

Helen leaned back against the chair and closed her eyes.

The remembering had wearied them. For awhile, they were content to just breathe.

The rain stopped. The low clouds before them were lit up with an orange glow from the town lights. Every few minutes, a narrow shaft of white light from the distant lighthouse cut across the softness. The air was still, heavy and quiet.

"I have something for you," Helen said gently into the poignant silence.

Sis looked at her, her face haggard and drained. She held a crushed empty cigarette packet in her hand. The ashtray was overflowing. "What?"

Helen went inside and came out with a small parcel wrapped in gold paper. She turned the veranda light on and handed it to Sis who opened it slowly and held it up to the light.

A worn gold ring with a single large diamond lay next to a plain gold band.

"What's this?" Sis's voice was heavy with fatigue.

"It was Nonna's. Your grandmother's. The one you were named for. And her mother's before her. It went to Aunt Maria after Nonna died and she had passed it on to me, but when I told her about you and Sweetypie, she was so angry with me that she took it back and told me it belonged to you. You are the eldest, the firstborn grandchild, Nonna's first granddaughter, regardless of the circumstances of your birth. It's yours Sis, and Aunt Maria ordered me to tell you that it is yours with love."

Sis examined it closely, her face unreadable. "So the old auntie was angry, was she?" she asked softly without taking her eyes off the rings.

"Furious. I weathered quite a storm when I finally told her the truth. She tried to understand why I lied in the beginning. After all, they were all guilty of a monstrous betrayal of Mum, so they weren't exactly innocents themselves, but she will never forgive me for keeping silent for so long, for leaving both of you up here alone without a family. My only saving grace has been that I did tell her while she still lives, that it is not too late."

Sis held the rings in the palm of her hand, her face stony. "Not too late for what?"

"To bring you back into the heart of the family where you belong, where you have always belonged, as she so beautifully put it. She's in her eighties now, still hale and hearty, but she told me she only has one thing left to live for and that is to hold you and Sweetypie in her arms."

"Don't be stupid. We can't leave here, you know that. I'd never get Sweetypie past the bridge, let alone to Sydney, if that's what you're thinking."

"Yes, I know that, but you have a whole family waiting for you and they all want to meet you. They can come here."

Sis closed her hand around the rings. "Nope. That's not such a good idea, either. Can you imagine Sweetypie coping with a bunch of strangers? And what would they make of her, hey? No, I been keeping her away from the cruel mockery of strangers all her life and we're both too old to change that now. Shit, you know I nearly killed someone the last time anybody had a laugh at Sweetypie's expense?"

Helen shook her head. "Oh, Sissy, I can't imagine you hurting anyone. Ever."

"Well, I did, and I don't regret it one bloody bit."

"Tell me."

"She was a hairdresser."

"She?"

"Yeah. We used to have a real good girl come out here years ago and cut our hair for us, so's Sweetypie didn't have to leave the property. I used to cut our hair before that – remember? We musta looked like shit, though, 'cos Mrs Stewart came out here one day with this young hairdresser, said she knew Sweetypie couldn't go into town, but that it was every girl's right to have a good hairdresser. She was kind and always made Sweetypie laugh, and she did exactly what I wanted." She patted her crew cut. "Although I don't think she'd have done this for me. Ha, the one we got now, Bill's daughter, is good, you saw how nice she was, but the first one, she liked to fuss and put rollers in Sweetypie's hair and coloured ribbons, you know, make her look real pretty. Anyway, she got married and had a baby and sent one of her girls from the salon out here in her place. She was OK, but she kept looking at me and Sweetypie out of the corner of her eye, like she couldn't quite believe it. And the silly bitch forgot to take her money with her when she left. So I sent Sweetypie up to the cubby and followed the girl into town. I found her in the salon taking the piss out of me and Sweetypie in a real nasty way. I saw red and laid into her. The others had to pull me off her. She was gunna have me for assault, but Sarge talked her out of it and then she got the sack. I hear she left town 'cos there was a bit of loyalty to us back then, but shit, there's no one left in town who knows us any more, 'cept the Stewart boys and their families." She clenched her fist around the rings. "So why would I expose her to that sort of thing now?"

"Yes. I understand. But a visit from Aunt Maria?"

"Dunno about that. Gotta think about it for awhile first."

"She said she wanted to talk to you on the phone after I'd cleared things with you."

"Jeez, what would I say?"

"Just let her take the lead. It'll be fine."

"Maybe." Sis was clearly anxious about the whole idea. "Dunno. Been too long."

"Well, you don't have to do it tonight, darling. Leave it for awhile. When I call her in a few days, we'll make a start then. Alright?"

Sis tightened her face around a fresh cigarette as if repressing excitement. "Yeah, in a few days. Give me time to ... you know ..."

"Prepare?"

"Yeah." She straightened up suddenly. "I dunno about you, but I've had enough. You ready for bed?"

"Oh, yes, definitely." Helen yawned noisily. "Good night, darling. Sleep tight, don't let the bed bugs bite."

Sis rose and looked down at her. "Ain't heard that for fifty years. Did you used to say that to your girls at bedtime?"

"Every night. And I thought of you every single time."

"So you bloody well should have." Sis was smiling. Helen smiled back up at her. Sis said, "You go shower first, I got some things to do in the kitchen." She paused at the door.

"Might be a good idea if you lock your door tonight. Just in case. Alright?"

"Alright, Sis. I'll probably sleep better if I do."

Helen was already in bed when she heard the sound of Sis's bare feet padding up the passage to the bathroom. The rhythm of the ceiling fan overhead eased her into sleep like a lullaby.

She was woken through the night by the sound of feet padding up and down the passage, followed by a scratching, scraping noise. She listened for a moment, wondering why Sis was up again or if she had even gone to bed yet. There was no clock in the bedroom to check the time, but the feel of the night told her it was somewhere after midnight.

The feet padded up and down the passage again. Helen suddenly realised that it was not Sis. The padding was heavier and the steps not evenly spaced, as if the padder were uncertain about the direction the feet should go in.

It was Sweetypie.

Helen rose quietly, turned on her light and checked the door. It was still locked.

The padding stopped outside her door. She tensed. Then the scratching noises came again, not from the other side of her door, but from the other side of the passage.

She heard a growl and then it was Sis's footsteps in the passage, as distinct as if she had announced herself.

Helen unlocked the door and opened it warily, just enough to peer out.

Sweetypie stood in her nightie directly across the passage, the orange glow of the town lights reflecting back from the clouds outside to filter in through the front screen door, casting her into deep, rich shadows. Her back was to Helen. The hall table was pushed to one side, the mirror propped against the wall on the floor.

259

Sweetypie raised an arm and Helen gasped silently when she saw the kitchen carving knife held with a fierce grip in one hand.

Helen opened the door a little wider and stood uncertainly in the shaft of light from her room.

Sweetypie suddenly thrust her arm down and dragged the point of the blade across the wall, cutting deep grooves into the surface that sent flakes of paint and timber floating to the floor. Her head and shoulders shuddered with the effort.

An arm reached across Helen and flicked the light switch off, making Helen jump. A hand came up and covered her mouth. Sis was standing before her, her other hand against her lips, urging her to be silent. She froze.

Sis took a step back, turned slowly and went to Sweetypie in silence. She was naked except for a pair of white cotton socks and Nonna Sistina's rings which Helen had felt scrape against her mouth.

Sis waited until Sweetypie had attacked the wall, once, twice, three times, waited until the arm finally dropped and Sweetypie's shoulders relaxed and drooped. Then she said in a soft, soothing voice, "It's just a dream, Sweetypie, just a dream. All gone now, all better." She reached across slowly, smoothly and freed the knife gently from Sweetypie's grip, then moved the knife behind her and jerked it twice towards Helen, who took it quickly. "Back to bed, little one, back to bed." Then she turned Sweetypie away from the wall.

Helen cried out silently and stepped back, the knife suddenly held in front of her as if to ward off evil.

Sweetypie's face was unrecognisable, twisted and hard, every line etched with bitterness, hatred leaping from cold glittering eyes, her mouth pulled down in a snarl, the white hair flying around her head in wild wisps. She looked straight at Helen without seeing, her vision turned inward to something so venal that her whole being was poisoned with it.

Sis turned her again and guided her back to her bed. Helen followed shakily. Sis sat Sweetypie on the edge of the bed and stood before her with both hands on Sweetypie's shoulders. She looked back at Helen's shocked face and said in a whisper, "The tablets in the bathroom cabinet, the pink ones – get four of them. Quickly."

Helen jumped to obey. Sis pushed the tablets into Sweetypie's mouth, held a glass of water to her lips until she swallowed, then lowered her back on to the pillow and waited. Helen stood at the door, staring at the ugly twisted face, waiting for Sweetypie, her Sweetypie, to come back.

After what seemed like an eternity, but was only about twenty minutes, the drug began to take effect, the sinister features melted away, Sweetypie closed her eyes and began to snore. Sis stood, indicated for Helen to go out onto the veranda and joined her after a moment. She was wearing a bathrobe.

They sat in the dark. Helen realised she was shaking. She looked across at Sis's face in the deep orange shadows and said, "What was that all about?"

Sis lit a cigarette and took a long, deep drag. She rested her head back and stared out into the night. "I told you," she said wearily, "that in the night she forgets to be six years old."

"But her face, Sis! I have never seen ..."

"What you saw tonight was what she would be if her brain hadn't decided to survive by keeping her permanently six years old. If she ever moved on, even by one day, if she ever consciously remembered what happened, then that is what she would become. That ... that creature."

"But the knife, the wall – what was that all about?"

Sis held the cigarette before her for a long minute, then said, "Who knows?"

Helen knew she was lying. She knew it instantly. She opened her mouth to say as much, but Sis, pre-empting her, said, "I'm buggered. I'm going back to bed. And don't worry, I gave her enough sedative to keep her asleep for half of tomorrow." She rose to go inside, then paused at the door and said, without turning, "Sleep with me tonight if you want, if you'd feel safer. It's cool in my room. I keep the air conditioner going all night and the bed's big enough for an army. And no bloody mozzies to bother you." She went inside.

Helen sat alone and stared into the darkness.

Something was wrong here. Something was very wrong. She sensed it in Sis's lie. Who knows? she'd said. You know, Sis, and you aren't telling me. What could be so bad that you can't tell me? We are sharing our lives again. I know it can't happen overnight, but you have already been giving up secrets to me – your son, for one. What else was there that could be worse than that, worse than Dad, worse than what they had done to Dad? You have to tell me, Sis. You won't be free until you do.

The first sounds of morning began to drift out of the rainforest. A soft birdcall. Leaf fall through the canopy. Muffled animal steps.

With the instinct of one who was born to these noises, Helen knew sunrise wasn't far away. She smelled more rain in the air.

She pulled herself up out of the chair, her body aching with fatigue and went inside.

Sis was already under the sheet.

Helen dropped her robe and nightie to the floor, her spirit rejoicing at the feel of cool air on her skin. She parted the layers of netting and slid in under the sheet with her back to Sis. She sensed Sis was awake.

After two years of sleeping alone, the warmth of another body next to her filled the cold space of loneliness that had cut its way deep into her heart after Raymond's death. She slid backwards towards her sister, felt her turn and an arm reach out and pull her close. They snuggled into each other spoon fashion, as she had with Raymond during all those twisted innocent years, as she had with Sis during all those comforting nights after Dad had visited one or the other of them.

She felt Sis's pubic hairs tickle her backside and the touch of cotton socks against the soles of her feet, the comfort of heavy breasts pressed against her back. Sis's body had always given her comfort and a sense of security when there had been nowhere else to draw it from. A strong body. A loving body. And then Sis leaned in and kissed her softly on the back of the neck. Helen sighed deeply with the deliciousness of it, leaned back to touch her sister gently on the face and stretched like a cat.

They slept.

Helen woke in an empty bed to the sound of heavy rain and the aroma of brewing coffee. She went into the passage, smelled fresh paint and saw that Sis had already sanded, filled and painted over the deep scratches on the wall. She remembered that smell when she'd first arrived and wondered just how often it happened.

Sweetypie slept through the morning, as anticipated, while Sis went out to attend to business and Helen phoned her daughters. The morning passed quietly, their mutual weariness from the disturbed night unstated but understood.

Sweetypie appeared as lunch was being made. She was bleary eyed and as sweet and innocent as ever. No trace of the previous night lingered in her face. Helen found the change hard to reconcile. She had not fully understood the seriousness of her sister's insanity or the imprisoning impact it had wrought on Sis's life until now.

She watched Sweetypie wander around the house aimlessly, heavy and slow with the after effects of the sedative. They watched a little television in the kitchen, then went out on the veranda, drank tea and stared into the mesmeric rain. Even the dogs sheltering from the rain at the end of the veranda seemed lethargic. Finally, Sweetypie curled up in the chair and dozed.

Sis returned briefly to tell Helen she needed to go into town for some extra groceries. As Helen watched her cross the bridge in the Landcruiser, the rain stopped.

Sweetypie woke with fresh energy. Rubbing her eyes, she said brightly, "I better go fix the track."

"It'll be wet, darling," Helen said, "why don't you wait until it dries off a little."

"Silly billy, you know I like it when it's wet. Wanna come?"

"No, little one. I'll wait here for Sis to come home. Do you need any help loading the rocks into the trailer?"

"Course not, I always do it myself, you know that. I gotta put my track clothes on, though."

She changed, got the bike from the shed and melted into the rainforest, the dogs at her heels.

Sis came home in the late afternoon. "Where is she?" she asked, dropping bags of groceries onto the kitchen bench.

"Fixing the track," Helen replied as she began to unpack the bags.

"Without that?" Sis pointed. Sweetypie's mobile phone lay on the table.

"Oh. I didn't realise ... is it a problem?"

"Yeah, it sure is," Sis said without accusation. "She forgets the time and stays up there til all hours sometimes, and she'll be a little out of whack today, what with all that extra stuff I gave her last night." A heavy rattle on the roof signalled the return of the rain. "And I'm always worried about her slipping and hurting herself in weather like this. Mind you, she rarely does, she's such a little rainforest rat, but I still worry about it. Well, let's get this out of the way, we'll have a cuppa and give her, oh, I reckon another half an hour."

They talked idly about the farm and about Tina and Ria, about Aunt Maria and the many cousins, but all the while

Sis kept one eye on the rainforest. Finally, she said, "I gotta go get her. Why don't you make yourself useful and get tea started? Chops in the fridge, spuds under the sink. And don't give me that look. She won't eat nothing else, you should know that. Your fancy cooking would be wasted on her." She went outside, took the bike from the shed and, like Sweetypie, melted into the rainforest.

Helen did as she was told. The chops were grilling and the potatoes mashed as Sweetypie came up the front steps. "Mmm, smells yummy, Helly."

Helen waited for Sis to follow, but she didn't show.

"Where's Sissy, darling?" she asked.

"Dunno."

"Didn't she bring you back?"

"No no. Is tea ready now?"

Helen turned towards her, serving spoon in hand. "You didn't see her at all?"

"No no. Where is she?"

"That's what I would like to know." She served the food. "We'd better wait until she gets here, don't you think? She might get cross if we eat without her." Covering the plates in plastic wrap, she went out onto the veranda to wait.

The rain intensified as the light dimmed. Helen stood looking up towards the entrance to the track, now shrouded by a wall of rain. She was becoming concerned. She went inside and pressed the button on Sweetypie's mobile phone. She heard an answering ring coming from the office. Sis had also left her mobile phone behind.

She went back outside. It was growing dark. Something was wrong, she could feel it. "Sweetypie," she said, "did you see the other bike?"

"Yes yes, it was in my way. I had to move it."

"But you didn't see Sis?"

"Silly billy. I already told you that. Where is she? When can I have my tea? I'm hungry."

"In a minute, darling, in a minute. I think I'd better go get Sis first. Where's the torch, the big one in the kitchen?"

"You know. Oh, you are a silly billy."

"Get it for me, darling. Then you wait here on the veranda while I get Sis. Alright? Good girl." Helen pulled on Sis's oilskins and, torch in hand, went out into the deluge and headed up the hill.

Grateful for the solid path under her feet, she moved slowly, shining her torch from side to side in the dripping gothic darkness. She found the bike a couple of hundred yards along, skewed sideways, the front smashed in. Sweetypie had said she'd had to move it, so it took another twenty minutes before Helen found where it had slid off the wet track and collided with the base of a large tree. It was a full half hour again before she found Sis another twenty yards down the slope, her head badly grazed and bleeding from a deep cut across her forehead. She was unconscious.

Unable to drag her up the slope, Helen gripped her under the arms and heaved. Together, they slipped and slid downhill in the mud and rain until they suddenly broke free of the undergrowth and found themselves behind the equipment shed. Sis was still unconscious, but breathing normally. Helen leaned her against the shed and went down to the house, calling to Sweetypie, but there was no answer. The house was empty. Three plates of food lay untouched in the kitchen.

Helen phoned for an ambulance and went back to Sis with clean tea towels to bind her head and an umbrella to keep the rain off.

Sis lay as she had been left. The sight of her slack-jawed, ashen face filled Helen with terror. The wound on her forehead gaped and rain mingled with blood to cover her face in rivulets of red.

Helen propped the umbrella against the shed and lay Sis down until her face was under its protection. She rolled one of the tea towels into a ball and pushed it into the ragged wound, then wrapped the other tea towels around her head, mopping up the rain-diluted blood as best she could. It was almost half an hour before she heard the ambulance crossing the bridge. She ran around to the front of the shed and waved her arms wildly until they saw her. When they had pulled up as close as they possibly could, she beckoned for them to follow.

They dealt with Sis swiftly. Helen went back to the house, changed quickly into dry clothes, found the keys to the station wagon and followed the ambulance into town. Only as she pulled up at the hospital did she remember that Sweetypie had not been in the house. She wondered where she was, then pushed it to the back of her mind. Sis was her priority for now.

Helen stayed with Sis during the examination, x-rays and treatment, but had to sit in the waiting room while Sis was taken into the operating theatre. Her heart pounded.

Surely she hadn't come this far only to lose Sis?

Sis emerged from theatre with her head completely bound in white bandages. Black bruising was already appearing around her eyes. After reassurances from the doctor that the skull fracture would heal and there was no long term damage, Helen took her place next to the bed and waited.

Sis regained consciousness a few hours later. She came around gradually, her hand resting in Helen's. "You're alright, darling. You've got a small fracture in your skull and you've got some stitches, but you'll be alright." A nurse fussed around the bed, taking blood pressure and checking pupil reactions.

"Sweetypie?" Sis asked groggily.

"She wasn't in the house when the ambulance arrived and she hasn't been answering the phone since. She'll be alright, Sis, there's nothing to harm her there. And I'll go back, once I'm sure you're comfortable."

"What time is it?"

"After midnight. But don't worry, I'm sure she's in bed by now, safe and sound."

But instead of being reassured, Sis gripped Helen's hand fiercely and hissed, "The lolly jar."

The colour drained from Helen's face. She'd not even given it a thought.

"Go now," Sis cried huskily, "and hurry!" She became distressed and the nurse fetched a doctor. As Helen left, Sis was being administered a sedative.

Helen drove out of town with a sense of urgency and turned into the road that would take her back to the farm. It was still raining heavily and the road was already under a few inches of water, the white lines and edges of the bitumen completely invisible in the headlights. She tried to determine the location of the road by keeping the tall cane equidistant on either side of the car, but it suddenly became impossible to judge as she approached a bend in the road where the field on her right was fallow. She felt the tyres of the car lose their solid grip on the bitumen and lumber sluggishly in the mud at the side of the road, and suddenly she was crashing into the field on her left.

The car came to rest fifty feet into the field, the cane casting eerie shadows around her as it loomed over the car.

She turned off the headlights, undid her seat belt and waited until the shaking stopped. The last house she had passed was almost half a mile back. She knew no one would come this way again tonight. She looked at her watch. Two thirty. She reached across the passenger seat for her bag and found her mobile phone. The battery was flat. She tossed it aside and thought about what to do next.

A packet of cigarettes and a lighter lay on the passenger seat. Helen had not smoked for many years, but she lit up now, opened the window and blew smoke out into the steady rain.

The sense of urgency had passed. She knew Sweetypie was dead. Knew it as surely as she had known anything in her whole life. Sweetypie would have sat there on the veranda like the good little girl she was, waiting for someone to give her tea, then realised no one was there to do that and would have gone to the cubby and done as she had been instructed to do.

Helen drew deeply on the cigarette and thought about Sweetypie dead in the cubby. She felt only a merciful relief. Her baby sister was finally free. Then she remembered what Sis had said about leaving her there in the cubby, undiscovered, safe from strangers, and realised that there was more to do yet before that could be ensured. It suddenly became clear to her what must be done.

For a start, she couldn't stay here all night. There was nothing for it but to get wet. She climbed over the back seat, opened the back of the station wagon and stumbled over the flattened cane until she felt the road under her feet. Tepid water sloshed around her legs, but there was no real current and, she realised, no real danger as long as she kept to the road. Even in the dark with the warm rain keeping her vision to a few yards, she knew she could do it by feel, but it was slow going. She was grateful that it wasn't cold.

By the time she reached the bridge, the river was a swirling black torrent, but still well below her. She crossed carefully, seeing the house before her lit up like a Christmas tree under water. As she came up onto the veranda, she shed her wet clothes and went straight into the bathroom to dry off and change.

Sleep was out of the question. She made strong coffee and sat in the glow of the kitchen light on the veranda. And thought.

She knew the next step was to notify the police that Sweetypie was missing. Not dead in the cubby. Missing. And their search for her must be diverted away from the rainforest. Sweetypie was gone, but she had to be protected in death as she had been in life. And Sis had to be protected, too.

There was only one way to do that.

Helen went inside, found a pair of Sweetypie's sandals, collected a torch and went downstairs to the Landcruiser. She found the fishing rod and tackle box, then in the light of the torch, made her way carefully downstream until she came to the huge Morton Bay Fig with its exposed roots already under water. She let the tackle box drop on its side, spewing its contents across the dark wet ground, then bent down to jam one of the sandals under the submerged roots and threw the other sandal into the current. She took the fishing rod and cast out into the river, cast badly so that the line caught in the lowest overhanging branch of the tree, pulled back until the hook caught fast and dropped the rod. It floated, bobbing up and down in the fast current under the tree. It would look as if Sweetypie had cast badly, tried to retrieve the snagged hook, lost her footing on the slippery tree roots and been swept away by the current.

She went back to the house, dried off, changed again and settled on the veranda with another pot of coffee.

A strange kind of peace settled over her. She had come home to make amends and perhaps plan a new life with Sis. But fate had planned it for her. There was nothing more to be done.

The rain eased as the first grey light heralded the dawn. She went inside to shower, clean the kitchen and make a phone call.

She told the police about Sis and the car accident, that when she'd reached the house she'd found Sweetypie missing, that her sister had been preparing to go fishing when she had left to go looking for Sis. She told them she'd checked under the house, in the sheds, all around the house down to the river and there was no sign of her, but that her fishing gear was scattered around the base of the Moreton Bay Fig where they normally fished. They said they would be at the farm in half an hour.

She went back into the bedroom to attach her mobile phone to its charger.

When she emerged from the bedroom, the morning sun streamed in through the screen door, casting long shadows from the hall table, and her senses were assailed with the same odd feeling of imbalance that had struck her when she had first entered the house. This time, she stopped, went back into the bedroom, closed her eyes and imagined herself back here fifty years ago. Four steps from the bed to the door, open the door, look into Mum's room across the passage…

Her eyes flew open. That was it! She stepped across the passage and ran her hands over the freshly painted wall where the door had once been. Sis had made a lot of changes, she knew that, but there was something more here. Something unexplained. She went outside and walked around the veranda. On the south side were three evenly spaced windows for the three bedrooms, as there had always been. Across the front were the two big double windows. Nothing different there. But on the northern side, where once there had been three windows mirroring the south side, there were now two windows towards the back for the bathroom and the office, and the third window, the kitchen window, almost at the corner of the house, with a large expanse of blank wall between. Sis had moved the windows. That should have explained it, but still Helen felt an imbalance.

Her curiosity aroused, and perhaps because she needed something to distract her while she waited for the police, she went inside and stepped out the three northern facing rooms. Then she stepped out the length of the northern veranda. There appeared to be a gap of seven feet between the back kitchen wall and the office wall. She stepped it out again, carefully. Same result. Back in the passage, she pushed the hall table aside and stood exactly where Sweetypie had stood the night before. She took the mirror down. Running her hands over the wall, she felt ridges under the fresh paint. Many ridges. Hundreds of ridges. She went into the kitchen and took a sharp, flat-bladed knife to use as a scraper. The paint peeled away under the blade to reveal slashes across the wall, some deep, some wide and shallow, all filled carefully with plaster in different shades relative to the age of the repair. This had been going on for many years.

Why? Why this particular spot on the wall where the door had once been?

Helen tapped her fingers against the tongue-and-groove timber. The sound came back hollow. There was a space behind the wall, a space between the new kitchen and the new office. A space where Mum's room used to be. Where she had left Dad that day fifty years ago.

Helen replaced the hall table and the mirror and went back out onto the veranda to think it through.

The police arrived. They were polite and efficient, but not overly concerned. After all, it was only the crazy old Downing woman, it was surprising she hadn't done something like this before.

Helen drove to the hospital to tell Sis. She tried not to think about what Sweetypie might have suffered before she died. Or what Sis's reaction would be.

CHAPTER EIGHTEEN

Bye Helly bye bye. Hope you find Sissy quickly 'cos I'm real hungry. Smell the choppies yummy yummy. Come on doggies, come sit here, Sissy's not here to tell you off, come sit here on my feet, ooh smelly doggies, go away, wet smelly doggies.

Mmmm choppies and mash yummy for my tummy. Long time, Helly, you're a long time. Sissy'll get cross if we don't wait. Come on Sissy, my tummy is making noises, listen, grumble grumble noises. Oh where are you, Sissy and Helly? Why aren't you here to get my tea?

They're just silly billies, bet they got lost, silly billy, silly billy. Better find them 'cos they're lost, yes yes, go find Sissy and Helly, I don't get lost.

Grass is wet, hair is wet, everything nice and wet, wet smell, wet warm track smell, mmmmmm, nice leaf smell, nice rain, wet rain, nice wet rain.

There's Sissy's bike, ohhh she's gunna get cranky 'cos her bike broke, cranky Sissy cross Sissy, there's 'nother rock come loose, rain makes them loose, bad rain wet rain, squishy wet bike in the rain.

Want my tea, Sissy, you aren't here to get my tea.

If Sissy's not here to get my tea, I gotta eat the lollies, I'm not a silly billy, I know what to do. If Sissy don't get my tea, I come up to the cubby and eat the lollies. I must eat them fast and not stop until they're all gone aha aha aha eat the lollies eat the lollies eat the lollies.

Cubby's cool, cubby's dry, sand is dry, dry sand, cool sand, squish toes in sand, squishy squishy.

Matches in the drawer, light the candles, pretty pretty pretty sooooo pretty.

Mmmmm hungry, lollies oooooh lollies lovely lollies. Don't taste real nice yucky yucky taste, awful taste, cordial make them better, raspberry cordial yummy yummy eat all the lollies eat all the lollies all the lollies.

Feel sick feel funny.

Sissy where are you Sissy?

Oh Sissy I fall down, spill the lollies, feel wobbly sick in my tummy, not hungry now feel sicky icky ooohhh Sissy where are you?

See there! See it there Sissy! On the wall near the hands no there behind the candles now over there oh it's gunna get me get me get me! Ooh the hands are moving oh hands here hands hurting hurting me Sissy too many hands big hands ooohhh big dark thing Sissy it's gunna get me oh Sissy it's gunna get me!

See it's coming to get me big big oh lots of hands oh hands everywhere oh oh hands all over me, don't like hands all over me oh big hands big hands hurting oh hurting Sissy oohh Sissy. Scary! Scary big black thing hurting me! So many hands hurting.

Ooh sick in sand sorry Sissy don't get cross don't be cranky sorry Sissy be good girl now good little girl good little Sweetypie scary scary sleepy hands sick scary Sissy Sissy Sissy Sissy Sissy Sissy sissysissysissysissysissysissy ......

CHAPTER NINETEEN

Helen waited until the nurse left the room and closed the door behind her. Sis lay propped up on pillows, the drip and blood pressure cuff immobilising both arms. She gave Helen a penetrating look. "Is she alright?"

"No."

"Did you see her?"

"No."

"Prince and Lady?"

"Nowhere to be seen." Helen wasn't sure whether Sis's contorted features were from the swathe of bandages or fear.

"Well, what then? What?"

"She wasn't at the house. Sis, you know where she went. If she was alright, she'd be back by now, but she isn't. I can feel it. So can you. Right?"

Sis sucked her breath in sharply. "Yeah," she whispered, "I can feel it. Shit." She looked away.

"I called the police."

"Oh jeez, they're not gunna go up there and find her, are they?"

"Sis, I arranged it so they would look elsewhere."

"What are you talking about?"

"I fixed it so that they thought she'd gone fishing and … well … drowned."

"Oh jeez oh jeez. Drowned. Shit. Fishing? She never went fishing without me."

"Yes, darling, we know that, but they don't. In fact, when I told the police, they didn't even seem surprised. One of the bastards actually sympathised with you for how difficult it must have been to keep her under control for so many years. They thought it was a wonder she hadn't come to grief before."

"Jeez jeez jeez Helen, what if it didn't work, what if …"

"… she's up there sick, but not dead? I'll go up as soon as the way is clear, don't you worry, but I can feel it, Sis, I can feel that she's gone."

"Yeah, yeah, I felt it too, but you gotta be sure. Christalmighty, Helen, if she's suffering …"

"You'd know it before me. Remember, darling, when we were children, remember how in tune we were, how quickly we sensed if anything was amiss with each other. But especially you and Sweetypie, from the moment she was born. Trust your feelings now. She's gone, but I promise I'll go up to the cubby as soon as the police have gone. They're searching the river now, but they think they'll find her close to the Inlet because the current is so strong. Look," she went to the window and pulled the curtain aside, "it's started to rain again. The Wet Season is upon us. The river won't go down much between now and Easter."

"Aahh shit, Helen, what if they do find her? What if they find the cubby?"

"They won't. If they do decide to look on the mountain, they'd never know to look for the cubby. You have to know

276

where it is to find it. Did you ever tell anyone, anyone at all about it?" Sis shook her head slightly. "I thought not. That was always our secret. She was the one to discover it. It always belonged to her. It was where we took her to heal, it's where she went for fun, it was always her place. Let it remain so."

Helen took Sis's hand and they watched the rain in morbid silence.

A nurse came in briefly. When she left, Sis turned her head to watch her go. "Ugh!" She flinched and closed her eyes.

"Pain, darling?"

"Yeah. Bloody stitches and one mother of a headache. How long they gunna keep me here?"

"Until you can uncross your eyes and see straight." She smiled down at Sis. "Stay here for a couple of days, Sis, stay and let me take care of things at home. Alright?"

Sis gave Helen an odd look. "You always were a cool one, weren't you? Back then and now. It comes easy to you, Helen, but it don't to me. My stomach is all in knots, in fact, the whole business makes me feel real sick. Damn, I wish I could cry."

"Yes," Helen answered thoughtfully, "it would help, wouldn't it? As for being cool, well, maybe that's the only thing I learned from Dad, the cold bloodedness. Maybe it was his legacy to me."

"Don't be bloody stupid. It was your defence against him. You sorta sealed yourself up inside so he couldn't get to you."

"You think so?"

"I know so. I used to see you doing it and I used to wish I could be like you."

"Really, Sis? I always wanted to be like you. I always thought you were so tough, that you could take anything. I wanted so much to be like that."

"I wasn't tough. I was just bloody scared."

"Me too."

They looked deep into each other's eyes. "I'm scared now," Sis whispered.

"Not me, darling, not any more. What can hurt us now?"

"Not scared for me. Scared for her."

"I'll go to the cubby. I promise."

"Alright. But go now. Not later."

"OK. I'll call you tonight before you settle and I'll be back early tomorrow."

The police were still searching within sight of the house when Helen got back. She watched them for awhile, then one of them came to her and said they were moving the search further downstream. They would contact her as soon as they found anything.

As the last police car disappeared over the bridge, Helen left the house and headed up the track. The rain had stopped, but the track was still wet and slippery. She rested several times to catch her breath, the steep slope taking it's toll in places where the track veered almost straight up before turning north and following an easier path. She took it slowly. There was no reason to hurry.

At the waterhole, Sweetypie's bike sat on the edge of the flat black rock.

The smell of death already filled the cave.

Sweetypie lay on her side, her head and neck arched and mouth agape. Eyes like frosted glass still held the terror of her black pursuer, the demon that her fragile tormented mind had never been able to completely expel. It had been there in her dreams and in her last moments of life as the surge of chemicals to her brain wiped out the barrier of protection and left her alone with the brutal memory of her attacker.

Prince and Lady lay forlornly on either side of her, barely raising their heads at Helen's entrance, the sorrow in their eyes as tangible as human grief.

Helen fell to her knees in the sand by her baby sister and wished with all her heart that she had not come, that she had not given in to Sis, that she had simply accepted what she knew to be. This was not the final picture of Sweetypie she wanted in her head. She wanted her baby back, her pretty little sister in her pink organza and her excited innocence. She wanted them all back on the swing, the pink, blue and white organza flying out behind them with the black and blonde hair mingling across their shoulders and their laughter scattering the birds in the mango tree.

A pure and happy image with no monster standing behind them planning their own private hells.

She wanted it all back, but different. She wanted Mum alive. She wanted Dad to have never existed. She wanted Sis and Sweetypie to have husbands and children and grandchildren and the three of them to grow old gently together, to talk about wonderful memories of their childhood, to share the ups and downs of a normal progression through life.

Helen, who had not cried for sixty years, had not shed a tear over the death of her beloved husband, had murdered without conscience when she believed it to be the right and necessary action, who had hidden her two sisters away in a secret past and left them to survive or not without her, now lay down next to the womanchild who had been her sister, enfolded the cold body in her arms as she had done here so many years ago, and regretted, truly regretted what it had come to.

She wept.

The sobs came hard and painful at first and then, like a floodgate being opened, they poured from her. She lifted her face to the empty heavens and wept aloud, wept for her sister who never had a chance, for the fragile life she and Sis should have let slip away but fought to keep because they loved her so desperately. For Sis who had never known anything other

279

than the small claustrophobic world she'd had to create, never known life beyond the farm in a time when the world should have been at her feet, never experienced the tender touch of a man, never known husband or children or grandchildren. For herself and Raymond, for the lost sensual years of their youth together, for the struggle to become normal when neither of them ever understood what normal meant. For the months of bedside vigil while he slowly and painfully left her and the desolation, the space in the world and in her heart he had left when he died. For the family she had lied to, the trust she had shattered with her recent confession, the grief and confusion she had caused Aunt Maria and her daughters who loved her, but could never truly know her. For the twisted bitch she was and the evidence of it lying at her feet.

And she wept for what the world believed Sis to be – hard, vulgar, severe, a bloody minded man in an ugly woman's body, while she knew her to be unstintingly loyal, generous, kind and patient.

She wept for the woman the world saw in herself – beautiful, successful, wealthy, a good woman happily married to a fine man with two lovely daughters, sought out by the rich and famous all over the world, with everything she had ever wanted. Respect. Love. Admiration.

The world saw her as a model citizen, but in private she destroyed lives, lied and betrayed without conscience.

The full realisation hit her and the weeping became a howl of despair.

She was her father.

Tilting her head back, she cried out to the cruel universe, "No! Not that!"

After awhile, the weeping ceased. She lay quietly, tenderly stroking the white hair, the cold skin, remembering the dear creature Sweetypie had been. Then she rose, took a bedspread from one of the beds and covered the body.

She went to the back of the cubby, found the white handprints she and her sisters had added to the many handprints that had been left before, knelt and placed her palms flat against the lowest set of prints. So small, Sweetypie's hands. She'd been two years old. A happy innocent child, so cute with her little fat belly, knock knees and small plump hands.

Helen pressed her palms into the handprints and let the connection with sweet innocence drain the last of the tears from her.

Yes, she was a product of her father, but the terrible things she did in the past had been done in order to protect innocence and nothing could change that, for it was as it was and could never be any other way. She had become what she had been moulded into by her childhood, the melding of what she knew and what had been latent inside her. With a different background, a normal background, a nurtured background, those latent qualities might have made her a teacher or a nurse, but because she knew the dark side of human nature, she had become the murderess in order to protect and punish, the celibate in order to have love, the betrayer in order to be free, and the liar in order to be believed.

But wasn't it strange, so strange, that in her heart she had always felt she was a good person? As if the things she had done, the things she had seen, the things she had experienced had left part of her untouched, uncorrupted.

Was that how Dad had felt? That in spite of the pain and suffering he had wreaked on his daughters, he had still thought he was a good person?

The thought caught at her mind and she felt sick.

She screamed silently, inwardly, "Are we all insane? Is there but one of us who is not?"

For had she not felt relief at Sweetypie's death? Was that not what she wanted – the death of one sister in order to free

281

the other? And fate had placed what she wanted squarely in her lap, as always.

Sis was free now. Free to be completely hers. That was why she had come back. Raymond had left her alone and she had wanted Sis to replace him. Her motives had been completely self serving.

She was loathsome.

She stood slowly and surveyed the hands on the wall. Her own were just above Sweetypie's. She saw with a shock how small they also were. And suddenly, she understood that it wasn't her fault. She was damaged goods, as were Sis and Sweetypie, and it wasn't their fault. The lies, the betrayal, the murders, the driving need to be publicly perceived as a good citizen – they were inevitable. If life was made up of choices, as she and Raymond had so carefully taught their daughters, then her choices had been made for her before she was even old enough to understand what they might have been. She'd been made incapable of being any other person than who she was, for other hands had forged her nature, warped her instincts, driven her to unnatural ambitions. Rough hands. Ugly hands. Unnatural hands.

Unnatural hands committing unnatural acts.

And unnatural acts beget unnatural consequences.

Dad, if I could kill you all over again, I'd do it, but slower, make you suffer longer, make you suffer harder. Damn you, you bastard! I ended your suffering, but you left us with ours forever!

Suddenly, she was exhausted beyond endurance. She called the dogs to heel, gave the shrouded body one last look, and left.

Turning Sweetypie's bike downhill, she slipped it into neutral and freewheeled it carefully down the track, then walked it to its place in the shed. She fed and watered the dogs and went inside.

The message she gave to the nurse for Sis was simple. It is as we thought. There is nothing more to be done.

Exhausted physically and emotionally, she slept most of the afternoon in Sis's bed. She slept deeply, peacefully, without drugs, without dreams.

The voices in the night were finally silent.

When she woke, she spoke briefly to the police on the phone, then she took the sledgehammer she found in the shed and began attacking the passage wall. The timber had been so weakened by years of gouging that it splintered easily under the impact.

When she had made a big enough hole, she picked up the torch and poked it through. What she saw sent her reeling backwards, foul air issuing from the hole to form a cloying cloud around her. She staggered outside, found Sis's cigarettes on the veranda table and smoked until the shaking ceased. Then she went back in for another look.

The space behind the wall enclosed a double bed, wardrobe and dressing table, the latter jammed up against the far side of the bed. A body lay on the bed, mummified but recognisable. A man in rotting dungarees and work boots. She knew it was a man because she knew it was Dad. But where his head should have been, there was only the remains of a disintegrating blackened flock pillow which still bore the slashes of a sharp instrument. Something long stuck out of one of the slashes. She pushed the torch in a little further to highlight it. It was an axe handle, its head buried deep in the pillow where Dad's neck had been.

The tunnel of light from her torch followed the body down until she found the head sitting neatly between spread legs. His dull hair hung limply across the skull, papery blackened skin stretched tautly across protruding cheekbones, the eye sockets empty, discoloured teeth prominent under the point of the nasal septum.

The hairy blackened, shrivelled remains of his genitals still protruded from his gaping mouth. His dungarees appeared to have been cut to pieces around his groin, as if the genitals had been cut away in a frenzy.

She fled back to the veranda and breathed deeply until she regained her composure. Then she replaced the mirror to conceal the hole, locked the house up and drove in to see Sis.

A nurse was removing the tea tray as she arrived. Helen waited patiently until she was gone. "We're going for a walk," she said. She collected a wheelchair, made Sis comfortable and took her down in the lift to the gardens. The rain had stopped and the air was filled with a fine warm mist. They found a dry seat under a flowering Poinciana tree.

"Well?" Sis asked tentatively.

Helen leaned towards her and said in a low voice, "I found her. It's over."

Sis covered her face with her hands. "Oh oh oh my Sweetypie," was all she said, but it conveyed a depth of grief that caught at Helen's newly raw emotions. "Did she look … peaceful?"

Helen remembered the anguished torment on Sweetypie's face. "Yes," she lied, and promised herself it would be the last lie she would ever tell her sister. "She just went to sleep."

"What did you do?"

"I covered her and left her as she is. She's safe there."

"What about the bike? What if the police go looking …"

"I took care of all that. The bike is back in the shed. They'll look, of course they'll look, but even if they were to find the waterhole, they'd never find the cubby. Remember, it took a tiny two year old to find it in the first place."

"But … well, the smell. You know, in a few days time …"

"It's already pretty bad, but the waterfall acts like a deodorant. On the waterhole side, you can't smell anything.

Anyway, they'd just think it was a dead animal in the bush somewhere. It's nothing to worry about."

Sis lifted her head at the tremor in Helen's voice and gave her a perceptive look. "You haven't been crying, have you? Not you, Helen, not after all these years."

Helen pulled herself up straight and took a deep breath, the emotion bubbling just beneath the surface of her composure. "It got to me, it finally got to me," she said, "what Dad did to us all, what we all became. Sixty years of hardening my heart couldn't withstand what I felt when I saw our little girl."

Sis nodded slowly, carefully, one hand bracing her bandaged head. "Yeah, well, she deserves a few tears, you gotta admit that."

"Yes," Helen answered simply.

They sat very still and quiet under the Poinciana tree for awhile, hands joined, bonded in their grief and their bitterness.

Then Helen said gently into the silence, "I knocked a hole in the wall."

"What? What are you talking about? What wall?"

"The passage wall. I found him."

Every muscle in Sis's body tensed. Her face twisted into an angry grimace. "Jeez, Helen! What the hell did you do that for?"

"What happened there, Sis? Why isn't he in the river?"

"Oh jeeeeez," Sis suddenly cried. She pulled her hand out of Helen's grasp and clenched her fist. "Why the hell couldn't you leave it bloody well alone! Why'd you even have to come back? Why now? We were doing alright without you. And now look at us. I never had a sick day in my life and now I'm in a bloody hospital. And my Sweetypie's dead! Damn you, Helen, damn you straight to hell!"

"I've been to hell and, as I remember it, you were with me during every minute of the stay," she responded evenly.

It stopped Sis in her tracks. Breathing heavily, she closed her eyes and put both hands to her head. "I'm dizzy, Helen. Get me back to bed."

Helen wheeled her back to her room in silence, made her comfortable and shut the door. Then she repeated, "What happened there?"

Sis remained silent for a moment and Helen sensed that she was gathering her courage. When she finally spoke, the anger was replaced with a sad resignation of the past. "I'm not like you," she began, "I'm not as calculating as you. Do you remember when it started, I mean when it seriously started? Not all those times we'd daydream about what we would do if he was dead. I mean that night when he said he was gunna have Sweetypie, that she was big enough and she wouldn't care anyway 'cos she was certifiably crazy. The night of the fight. Do you remember?"

"Godalmighty, Sis, how could I ever forget?"

CHAPTER TWENTY

He came into the room through the night and lifted Sweetypie
from her place next to Sis, lifted her in his arms and carried
her quietly outside. Sis woke with a jolt and ran outside just as
Dad laid the petite fifteen year old on his bed. As Sis reached
him, his hands moved down to the girl's thighs and she stirred.

Sis knocked his hands away and pushed him off the bed with
all the strength she could muster. At the same time, she yelled
out, "Helly! Out here! Get out here now! He's got Sweetypie!"
Helen was there in an instant.

He looked up from where he had fallen, his back against the
railing, and began to laugh. At first the girls thought he might
be drunk, but it wasn't Christmas, there'd been no parish party
and he never drank at home. But he laughed as if he was drunk.

Sweetypie woke and looked around her, at her Dad sitting on
the veranda laughing, at Sis and Helen standing guard over
her, and she began to titter. "Is it funny?" she giggled.

Helen, her body tensed and ready to defend Sweetypie, looked down at her sister. "Go inside, darling, quickly now. Go back to Sissy's bed. We'll be there in a minute."

Still giggling without knowing why, Sweetypie did as she was told.

Dad's laughter faded away. He rose and brushed himself off. "What the hell do you girls think you're doing?" he demanded.

"You promised, Dad," Helen snapped.

"Yeah, you promised you wouldn't ever touch her," Sis growled.

"Did I now?" he smirked. "Well, let me tell you both something. I do what I bloody well please. I run this show, not you," he poked at Helen, "or you," he gave Sis a shove. "She's mine and she's ready. Anyway, she wouldn't care. She's bloody nuts, you know that as well as I do. Certifiably crazy with her bloody cakes and candles and pink pink pink. She'd wake up tomorrow and never know a thing. So get out of my way and stay out of my way." He made for the front door.

Helen stepped into his path and put her hands up to stop him. At eighteen she was as tall as him and as slender as a sapling. He grabbed her by the arm and swung her away easily.

Sis jumped in front of him and pushed him again, but he was ready for her this time. As her two hands came up to his chest, he grabbed them, swung her around and shoved her down the veranda steps. She cried out as she toppled backward and landed with a thud on the ground. Helen ran to her, helped her up and turned to confront her father. "You didn't have to do that!" she cried. "You could have just had me like you always do. Why'd you have to hurt Sis? She hasn't done anything wrong."

Dad leapt down the steps and gripped Helen by both shoulders. "Don't you talk to me like that," he snarled. "Don't you ever bloody talk to me like that! Who the hell do you think you are, hey?"

288

Helen slapped his hands away. She demanded, "You want to do it to me, Dad? Then do it and be quick about it! I want to get some sleep." She lifted her nightie. "Come on, get it over with."

But instead of taking her up on the offer, Dad looked over Helen's shoulder and saw the merest hint of a smirk on Sis's face. "What the hell are you laughing at?" he demanded. Suddenly, he pushed Helen aside and, without warning, lunged forward and hit Sis squarely in the mouth. She dropped backwards with a grunt, but was up on her feet and flying at him before he had time to regain his balance.

At almost twenty one, she was a short, but well built young woman with a muscle strength to match any man her age and a masculine toughness to go with it. Hatred for the man before her filled her with rage and, in this moment, she saw her chance to have it out with him once and for all. She was surprisingly light and quick on her feet and when she lashed out with her fists, she collected him twice on the face before he realised what was happening. It was the trigger he had been waiting for. She might be strong and quick, but she was no match for his height and the strength his answering rage released.

He hit back and Helen heard the crunch of bone as he broke Sis's nose. Then he flayed her with his fists until she dropped, bloodied and beaten in spite of Helen's screaming efforts to stop him.

Stooping to tend to Sis, Helen felt herself lifted away and thrown to one side. She rolled onto her knees as Dad fell to his. He yanked Sis's nightie up and lunged into her. Helen was stunned, for Dad had made it plain many times that he considered Sis to be nothing more than a dirty slut since her monthly bleeding had commenced and had refused to touch her in any way other than violently. Helen got to her feet, kicked out and knocked him away. But it was too late, he'd gotten what he wanted.

White semen dribbled from Sis's scarred vagina.

Getting to his feet, he looked both his daughters over with a contemptuous sneer and went back to his bed. Lighting up, he inhaled deeply and blew the smoke out through his mouth with disdain, his vision focused on the distant cane fields, his girls already dismissed.

Helen helped Sis into the washhouse where she tenderly bathed the cuts and bruises, kissed the forlorn face and took her back to her own bed, leaving Sweetypie sprawled across the bed in the other room.

Dad's snores could be clearly heard from the veranda.

They lay in each others arms, Helen gently stroking her injured sister, speaking soft reassurances until she slept. Then Helen rolled over, snuggled in spoon fashion and thought about what had happened.

She'd had enough, she knew that much.

Sis would be twenty-one in a few weeks, legally an adult with all the freedom that implied, but Helen knew there would never be any freedom for any of them, not for Sis, not for herself and never for Sweetypie. Dad would never let any of them leave, for he needed them to work the farm, keep his house and provide him with sex whenever it suited him. His own private empire.

And it would only be a matter of time before he got Sweetypie. After tonight, there was no doubt about that.

Dad lost interest in his girls when they took on the bodies of women. His contempt for Sis had been apparent for several years and he already detested the changes in Helen, the pubic and underarm hair, the breasts, the full hips. Every day she prayed that her monthly bleeding would start, for surely he would leave her alone when that happened. But when it did, and it was imminent, she was sure of that, Sweetypie wouldn't stand a chance. For something in Sweetypie's body was all wrong. At fifteen, she still had the smooth genitals of a small girl, no armpit hair and her chest was as flat and skinny as a boy's. She'd grown in height, but some vital part of her development was not keeping up with her years.

No, there was no chance for Sweetypie now, that was clear. And next time, it might be Helen he beat to a pulp.

She reached back and caressed Sis's bare backside. Loving arms tightened around her in response.

Yes, she'd had enough. They'd all had enough.

They'd played word games in the past about what they would do if Dad died, had even half joked about putting poison in his food ...

Poison. Helen's eyes opened wide in the darkness. Yes, that was possible. There was plenty to choose from. The shed was full of tins of poisonous substances used on the farm. She had no idea what they were or how much she would need or what effect they would have, but she would do it. She bloody well would.

Sis stayed home the next morning, not emerging from her bedroom until after Dad left. Her face was swollen and discoloured, her nose broken again and her mouth split in three places. She showed Helen the two loose teeth, but quickly turned her head away as Sweetypie skipped up to them. Completely oblivious to the drama of the night before and the battered results of it standing next to her, she chattered away until Helen found her something to keep her occupied.

Then Helen took Sis out to the shed and told her what she was thinking.

"You can't," Sis said without hesitation.

"Why ever not?" Helen demanded, not expecting an argument.

"You can't ... kill him."

"Got a better idea?"

"Oh come on, Helly, you can't be serious. It's wrong. It's a sin. And if we get caught, we go to jail and then what happens to Sweetypie?"

Without hesitation, Helen replied, "We won't get caught. I've thought it all through. The Wet will start soon. We'll wait for the first big rain. We'll wait until the river's up and we're cut off. I'll put something in his food ..."

"What if he tastes it and won't eat it? What if he figures out what we're doing? We'll cop it then, won't we?"

Exasperated, Helen said, "I'll find something here that we can use. For goodness sake, Sis, if we don't, the next time he goes for one of us, he'll kill us. I thought he was going to kill you last night. And how long do you think we can keep him away from Sweetypie? He's made up his mind he's going to have her and he will. You know it. Don't you see? It's him or us now."

Sis stared with glum resignation at the containers of poison. She cast her eye over them all, then said, "They won't work, they all smell too strong. He'd know it straight away." She went to the back of the shed and pulled a packet off a high shelf. She flipped open the top to reveal a white powder. "What about this, it's rat poison and it don't stink."

Helen took the packet. "It's white," she said. "He would never see this in his mashed potato." She sniffed the white powder carefully. "Yes, this might do. How much do you think we'll need?"

"Dunno. I only put out a bit for the rats. Kills 'em quick, though."

"Quick. That's good. Alright, we'll try this." She gripped the packet fiercely in her hands. "The next big rain, Sis, the next big rain."

They waited with mounting tension over the next two months for the onset of the Wet Season, manipulating and manoeuvring to keep Dad away from Sweetypie and Sis.

A massive front of black cloud built up in the east over the ocean, but when it finally arrived, it brought a lot of lightning with only a little rain. And then, after a week of disappointment, a gift appeared in the shape of a sweeping green-black cloud mass, fanning out over the mountains and the ocean.

Sweetypie said, "Big rain coming, Daddy, big big rain."

The air was thin as if they were at high altitude and Dad said, "Cyclone's coming."

The wind sprang up during the morning and, by lunch time, Dad had sent all the farm hands home to batten down.

The girls were no strangers to cyclones, this was not their first, but they could see from the start that this one augured more than just the tail of a cyclone with its fierce winds and deluges. This one was building up around them like a top spinning ominously overhead.

The wind was already a high pitched whistle when Helen dropped half a cup of powder into Dad's mashed potato. She added extra cream and salt and sniffed it carefully. It smelled like mashed potato. She spooned copious quantities of onion gravy over the plate.

Then she made separate mashed potato for herself and her sisters. She carried Dad's out to the veranda where they joined him for the evening meal.

Sheltered as they were by the mountain behind them, they sat and watched the wind cutting wild swathes through the cane. The rain had begun, but it was still sporadic and thrown around by the wind. A solid grey wall of rain was bearing down on them from the north.

"Gunna get some damage out of this one," Dad remarked, grimacing a little as he patted his midriff. Indigestion. He belched loudly.

A few minutes later, he doubled up.

"What's the matter, Daddy?" Sweetypie asked with genuine concern.

293

"Dunno," he replied. He looked up at the girls, saw that they were fine and said, "Well, it can't be the tucker or we'd all be crook." Seconds later, he dived for the edge of the veranda and vomited over the railing. Helen silently cursed. There went the mash potato and it's poisonous contents.

But she needn't have worried.

He collapsed on the veranda and curled up in agony. Sis and Helen were not expecting this. In their ignorance, they had thought he would just lie down and die. Wasn't that what the rats did?

Sweetypie looked panicked. "What's wrong with Daddy?" she asked again.

"He's alright, little one, he just had too much to eat. Don't you worry, we'll look after him." Helen looked at Sis and saw the fear in her eyes. She had to get them both out of here. "Hey, little one, why don't we all go into the rainforest for awhile and see what it's like in a cyclone?"

Sweetypie's face lit up. "Oh, yes yes! It'll be all wet and windy! Yes yes!"

"Come on then. Let's go. Sis. I said let's go."

Sis took her horrified gaze from Dad and looked up. "Yeah," she said huskily, "let's go."

Sweetypie turned to leave, but looked back as Dad groaned loudly. "Oh, Daddy, Daddy ..."

"He's alright, darling. He's just got wind in the gut."

"Bad wind. Bad wind."

"That's right, bad wind. If we leave him for awhile, he'll be alright."

Helen took her by the arm and almost ran with her to the edge of the rainforest, Sis at her heels.

They stood under the canopy and watched the branches swaying wildly above them, but where they stood it was almost still. They slid around in the mud and let the rain drops wash it off their feet and clothes. The rain was warm and dripped heavily from the trees around them. It smelled delicious. They played hide and seek until the wind screamed so loudly that they couldn't hear each other. When Helen thought it had been long enough, they ran back to the house.

Helen led the way through the gap between the back of the veranda and the mountain and stood in the kitchen, listening. The only noise was the wind. She cleaned up Sweetypie and bedded her down with promises to wake her if the cyclone got worse, then went back to the kitchen for Sis.

"What now?" Sis asked, her face grim.

"We'll go outside and see," was all Helen could offer.

They walked slowly up the passage, listening and looking for any sign of Dad. At the screen door, they peered out. He was nowhere to be seen. They stepped out onto the veranda.

Dad was lying at the bottom of the steps, face down, his body twisted into a contorted kneeling position, his arms bent and his face resting on clawed hands.

The girls waited at the top of the steps for a few moments. He didn't move.

The screaming wind made any further talk impossible. Sis gripped Helen by the arm and begged with her eyes. Helen nodded.

She went down the steps and, with each step away from the house, the wind tugged at her more strongly. As she reached Dad, her hair whipped around her face. She pulled it back and held it there.

The wall of rain was only minutes away.

Helen poked him at first, one foot on the lowest step, ready to flee. He was still. She placed her hand on his shoulder and felt rigid muscles under her palm. She looked up at Sis, who watched with both hands up to her fearful face.

Helen gave him a little shake. He rolled onto his side and she jumped halfway up the steps.

His face was covered in mud, vomit and blood, his mouth agape in a final gag, his eyes screwed up in agony. He lay unmoving in the upside down crouching position, his hands still clawed.

After a minute, Helen went back to him and gave him a kick.

No response. She knelt close to him and looked into his face. His mouth was blue. She stood, looked up at Sis and nodded.

He was dead.

She joined Sis on the veranda and they sat on the top step. They watched him for awhile and then the rain hit. It came at them almost horizontally, fierce and stinging. They backed up until they were standing against the door.

Then Helen went down, grabbed Dad's ankles and hauled him halfway up the stairs. She was thinking about what to do next.

They should bring him inside, but he was covered in mud, so she stood with her arm around Sis and watched the cyclonic rain bathe him clean.

His body uncurled, but his hands remained clawed.

Sis screamed something at her. She couldn't hear above the wind and thundering rain. Sis pointed towards the stables.

The animals. Had Dad taken care of them?

They had been so involved in the act of murdering Dad that neither of them had noticed whether he had gone out to see to the animals. They stood uncertainly for a moment, then Sis gave Helen a nudge. I'm going to check, she mouthed. Helen grabbed her hand, mouthed I'm coming too, and went down the steps, skirting around Dad carefully.

They had to double over against the wind and rain as they left the immediate shelter of the mountain. It cut into their skin and exploded the breath out of their lungs. They held onto each other and stumbled their way to the stables.

Sis led the nervous ponies from the stables into the more sturdily built shed and tethered them at the back where it was most protected by the mountain. The milking cow was led from her stall and tied up next to the horses. The chooks had already gathered just inside the doorway. Helen herded them to the back of the shed and saw that the dogs had followed her and Sis. She tied the two German Shepherds up next to the cow.

Enough food and water for the night and possibly the next day and it was done.

For the first time, it hit them both that they were responsible for these creatures now. Dad was no longer here to take care of things. The farm. The machinery. The animals. Themselves. It would all be up to them from here on in.

They stood in the shed doorway and surveyed their work. If the shed survived, the animals would survive. They looked at each other. As if reading the other's thoughts, they grinned and joined hands in an empowered understanding.

They could do it, they knew they could. There wasn't anything on the farm that they couldn't do. After all, hadn't the bastard spent their entire lives training them?

It took everything they had to close both shed doors against the force of the wind outside and drop the massive crosspiece into place. The wind was fast increasing in strength and the heavy rain came at them parallel to the ground, cutting into them like a million needle pricks. But the wind was behind them on the way back to the house and it almost lifted them off their feet. They felt like they were flying.

They peeled off their soaking clothes on the veranda, made a pot of tea and sat naked behind the screen door while they watched Dad slowly unfold in the rain like a soggy flower until he was lying limply sprawled on the steps. Then they went down and turned him over so the rain could complete its task. When they were sure they would not cart a trail of filth inside, they carried him in and laid him on Mum's bed. They dressed, cleaned up the kitchen, mopped the passage floor and shut the house up.

About midnight the walls of the house began to shudder as the wind changed direction to come straight at them from the flats. When they heard the first louvre shatter, they woke Sweetypie and went downstairs to the washhouse.

When Dad had built the house, he had made the washhouse of solid rock, the back wall dug into the side of the mountain, a narrow open slit across the top of one wall for ventilation, thick timber beams across the roof and a solid timber door which could be secured from the inside by a heavy crosspiece. The girls now lifted the crosspiece and dropped it into place across the door. The washhouse was now a cyclone shelter.

The three huddled together, singing and telling funny stories to keep Sweetypie from feeling afraid.

As Helen had predicted, when they emerged soon after daylight, the river was up over the old bridge. Although the brunt of the cyclone had passed, the wind still buffeted the landscape and the rain would linger for at least another day. Most of the windows were intact with only a louvre missing here and there and the rest of the house looked undamaged.

They made breakfast and kept Sweetypie busy. The door to Mum's room remained closed.

Finally, Helen took Sis outside.

"You know what to do now, don't you, Sissy?"

"Wait til you've gone, get Sweetypie to bed for a nap, wrap the bastard in the bedspread and put him in the river, see to the animals and it's done. Yeah, I know what to do."

"Good. I'd better get going." She looked up at the mountain, its crown invisible in the rain. "It'll be slow going, Sis, I might be gone awhile."

"Take Ginger, he's sure footed, he'll get you through."

They surveyed the scene before them. The cyclone had left little remaining of the stables, but the house and equipment shed, tucked into the side of the mountain, remained intact. They could hear the ponies whinnying nervously inside the shed. Debris from the rainforest lay scattered across the expanse of muddy grass down to the river. The bridge had disappeared completely and the water was already halfway up the slope to the house. It flowed fast and deep and there was more to come. Even though the wind had dropped to a flapping breeze, the rain continued to pelt down and they could see little beyond the flooded river. But they could see enough to know that every cane field in the district was flattened and submerged. There would be no crop this season.

Sis helped Helen into the oilskins. "Go right up to the waterhole, that way you'll clear the river. Then across to Stewart's Ridge and follow the road in from there. You'll be safe that way. Stay clear of the flats. I reckon it'll take several days for them to drain, the way this rain is still coming." Her hands trembled.

Helen, steely eyed, took her hands and held them tight. "I know what to do," she said, "don't you worry about me. It's you that has to get it right. Can you do it?"

"Yeah, 'course I can." She didn't sound as convincing as she hoped.

Helen gripped her by the shoulders. "Sis! You have to do it just right. Everything we talked about, can you remember it all? Can you do it?"

Sis straightened her shoulders and pushed Helen away from her. "Get going," she said, "you worry about what you gotta do, I'll worry about what I gotta do. Alright?"

"Yes, alright."

Sweetypie flung open the screen door and bounced towards them. "Cyclones are fun!" she announced, her mouth smeared with biscuit crumbs. "EEEEEE!" she squealed, mimicking the scream of the wind. "EEEEE."

"Sweetypie!" Sis's nerves were on edge. "Quiet! We've had enough noise for awhile. And don't pout. Go down to the washhouse and clean your face. Go on, go."

299

Sweetypie stopped at the top of the steps. "Where you going, Helly?"

"Into town, darling."

"Oh, liquorice, liquorice! I want liquorice!"

"Sure darling, I'll bring you liquorice." She waited until Sweetypie had disappeared under the house before turning to Sis and pulling her into a fierce hug. "It'll be over soon," she said, " and then you'll see, we'll be free and happy and no one will ever hurt us again. I promise. Alright?"

"Yeah," Sis returned the hug. "Be careful and get back as soon as you can." As Helen reached the bottom step, Sis suddenly cried, "Money! You got any money on you? You gotta bring something back for Sweetypie."

Helen ran back up the steps into the house and reappeared a few minutes later with a brown handbag poking out of one of the coat pockets.

Sis watched nervously as she trudged through the mud to the shed, a pair of shoes slung over one shoulder to keep them clean for town, and waited until she emerged with Ginger saddled. He was jumpy, having been spooked by the cyclone. "Be gentle with him," she called out, "don't let him throw you!" She knew Helen had never been thrown from a horse in her life, but she needed to say it anyway, as if the saying would invoke protection for her.

Helen mounted the pony, rain pouring from her wide-brimmed hat, her wet oilskins hanging heavily down the pony's flanks, her small bare muddied feet sticking out below. She tied the shoes by their laces to the saddle horn, then turned Ginger towards the cubby track and waved to Sis. "Be careful!" Sis called, waving back. "And hurry home!"

Sis stood looking up at the mountain for a long time, her spirit with her sister, her mind picturing the wet track, the waterhole and the ridge down to Stewart's farm. She stood there until the task at hand could wait no longer.

While the river ran in flood, the door of opportunity lay open.

Sweetypie agreed to a nap without argument. It had been an exhausting night for all of them. Sis kissed her sweet face, closed the bedroom door and opened Mum's.

Bracing herself, she went to the bed, preparing to wrap Dad in the bedspread and drag his body down to the river. She knew the current would carry him swiftly to the Inlet and, with any luck, the crocodiles or the open sea would claim him before anyone found him. Even if he was found, he'd look as drowned as any drowned man, or so Helen had assured her, and in the heat and humidity, with the muddied water to help it along, decomposition would happen very fast. There would be little to find, if anything at all.

Sis leaned over the bed to grab the bedspread and, as she pulled it across his chest, felt the merest brush of air on her arm. She looked down, gasped and jumped back.

Dad's eyes were open. Bloodshot and swollen, they followed her in the shadowy room without a single movement of his facial muscles. Just the eyes, as if they were a separate being from the limp lifeless body.

She stood rooted to the spot, her hands covering her mouth against the scream which she knew must not come, for Sweetypie was only a few yards away.

He knew.

She could see it in his eyes. He knew what they had done. And what she was about to do. She stood, unable to move while Dad's eyes silently accused her, holding her imprisoned in her guilt and fear. She began to tremble so violently that she thought her legs were going to give out on her.

Finally, unable to withstand his scrutiny any longer, she fled the room and ran out into the cleansing rain. Collapsing on the bottom step, she let it pour over her, the rain, the guilt, the fear. There were no tears, she was incapable of that, but she shuddered as each wave of emotion broke over her.

Then an anger surged up inside her. Helen should have taken care of this. She would have done it, no matter whether Dad was dead or alive. She would have ignored those eyes, wrapped him up and dragged him down to the water.

Sis straightened herself up.

Yes. Helen would have done it, and if she could do it, so could Sis. And Sis must do it, for Helen would be back soon with Sarge, and Dad had to be long gone. She mustn't let Helen down!

She slumped again.

It had to be done, she knew that. But not right away. There was time. Maybe that's all it would take. He was so close to death, if she just left him there for awhile, nature would take its course. Although nature had nothing to do with it.

The memory of his torment cut into her and she flinched.

God I'm so bloody weak, she thought, why can't I be more like Helen. She's smart and strong, I'm just weak and stupid.

She heard Sweetypie padding up the passage. As the creak of the screen door came, she called out, "Get yourself some biscuits from the bickie tin, little one, while I go see if the animals are alright." She heard the footsteps go back.

She milked the cow, fed the chooks and the dogs and spent a long time with the ponies. In calming them, she calmed herself. She decided to leave them in the shed a while longer until she'd had time to check out what remained of the stables.

When she was sure she could face Sweetypie and have another go at disposing of Dad, she went back up to the house.

Sweetypie had brought the biscuit tin out onto the veranda and was consuming them in handfuls. Normally, Sis would have stopped her, told her she mustn't spoil her appetite for lunch, but today, the biscuits could be her lunch. Sis handed

302

her the milk bucket and said, "Help yourself, little one. And
wash up when you're done, your hands are all grubby."

She went inside and, as she approached Mum's room,
remembered with a jolt that she had forgotten to close the door
as she fled. She hoped Sweetypie hadn't seen anything.

Something lay on the passage floor outside Mum's room.

Sis stood over it, not understanding. It was Mum's old
dressmaking shears, but they looked muddied. She picked them
up. It wasn't mud. It was blood. She dropped them where she
had found them and went into the room.

If she thought the sight of Dad's open eyes had unsettled
her, what she saw now threw her back against the door to
slip down into a horrified crouch, unable to breath, unable to
comprehend.

The small axe from next to the wood stove in the kitchen
lay with its head buried in the pillow, the handle sticking up
and blood from the severed neck soaking into the cotton. Many
slashes on the pillow bore testament to an enraged attack.
Dad's head, so roughly separated by the sharp axe, lay in an
orderly manner between his legs which had been pulled wide
apart. The head had been pushed firmly down into the gap of
his crotch where blood soaked into his dungarees and where
once his genitals had been. His balls and penis protruded from
his mouth, stuffed in so hard that the black pubic hair formed
a fringe around his lips. His dungarees had been shredded
around the groin by the blades of the dressmaking shears as
they had cut into his genitals .

His dead eyes were open, the look of terror still palpable.

He had seen her coming.

Sis scrambled out of the room on her hands and knees, pulled
the door shut behind her and sat hunched in the passage until
she could breathe, until the full impact of what she had seen
sunk into her consciousness.

"What you doing on the floor, silly billy?" Sweetypie said with a giggle, her grinning face looking through the screen door. "Are we going to play?"

Sis looked up at her. At the sweet face, the clear eyes, the innocence, the pure unadulterated innocence. She rose unsteadily, pushed the door open and made her way with trembling legs to the chair next to Sweetypie's. Sweetypie sat down again, pulled a handful of biscuits from the tin and offered them to Sis. Only then did Sis see that what she had thought were grubby fingers were really biscuit crumbs stuck to blackening congealed blood.

Dad's blood. And the death feast was a handful of biscuits.

Sis led her to the edge of the veranda and held the bloodied hands out into the rain until they were washed clean. Sweetypie wiggled her fingers with the pleasure of it and shook them. "Are we going to play?" she asked again, giggling.

"No," Sis whispered, still weak with shock, her chest painfully tight. "No little one, we're just going to sit here for awhile and watch the rain."

"Yes yes, I like watching the rain. Look, Sissy, it makes smoke come down from the mountain."

Sweetypie watched the misty rain drift down around them with an open mouthed wonderment, watched the afternoon become evening while she hummed and swung her legs on the chair, watched the light melt away into grey darkness with an unconcerned yawn, while Sis watched her. As she observed the innocent unawareness, the total lack of comprehension about what she had done, only then did Sis begin to understand how completely and dangerously insane her sister was.

And it was all her fault, hers and Helen's. They should have let her die up there in the cubby, should never have allowed her to live with the memory of what Dad had done to her lurking somewhere in her subconscious, thinking that her shattered life could go on as if nothing had happened.

And so here they were, Sis and Sweetypie, sitting in the dark waiting for Helen to bring Sarge back, waiting to tell a simple lie when nothing was simple, not even Sweetypie's simpleness. Waiting to get it over and get on with their lives, waiting to become normal, to be like everyone else who seemed to take being normal for granted.

Waiting for what? Boyfriends, marriage, children?

Sis's head throbbed and the tightness around her chest made each breath come hard.

What a joke, she thought despairingly, her future suddenly looming before her as clear as crystal. There would never be boyfriends, marriage and children for her, there never could be. She was all messed up, she wasn't a girl at all, not like the other girls at church who wore bright lipstick and flirted and smiled at the young men with such ease and confidence. Sis's fear of men was so deep rooted that she knew she could never let one near enough to put an arm around her or, perish the thought, kiss her. The very idea made her shudder. Anyway, those young men didn't look at her like they looked at the other girls. Rather they treated her like one of the boys, talking about cane prices and the latest farm machinery instead of picnics and tennis dates. And she responded like one of the boys. Because she knew she was ugly, unfeminine, undesirable. She knew she had made herself like that, deliberately, gladly. She worked at it and she never wanted it any other way.

As for Sweetypie, there was no choice now. She must be protected at all costs, must be kept apart from the rest of the community, must be kept safe here in her little closed-in world. The farm must become Sweetypie's island and her prison. With Sis and Helen as her wardens.

Sweetypie yawned loudly and said, "I'm hungry, Sissy. When we gunna have tea?"

Sis hadn't given food a thought, and there was no way she was going back into the house, past that room to the kitchen as if nothing was wrong. She thought it through quickly.

To stay in the house overnight with Dad's dismembered body was unthinkable and she was incapable of carrying out the rest of Helen's plan right now. They would spend the night in the cubby and in the morning, Sis would leave Sweetypie at the waterhole, come down very early to dispose of Dad and go back to collect Sweetypie when it was done. And the night in the cubby would give her time to renew her courage. There was food and bedding up there. They would be safe in the cubby.

But first she must go back inside and get what she needed. She opened the door and saw the shears on the floor. Taking a tea towel from the linen cupboard, she picked them up, wrapped them and went outside. Sweetypie was still on the front veranda. Sis went around the side of the house and dug a shallow hole with her hands in the soggy soil under the mango tree. It would do for the moment. When she came down from the cubby, she'd bury them deeper, further from the house. For now, she just wanted them out of sight.

She went to the shed, milked the cow, hastily saw to the other animals, then closed the door and dropped the crosspiece in place. Tomorrow she would see to them properly.

She led the way up the track in the rain, kerosene lamp held high, blessing the cyclone and the flooded river for giving her this night to collect herself, to think, to make plans. As she reached the waterhole, she heard the wind pick up overhead in the treetops and sensed the change of direction. It didn't matter. Inside the cubby, they were devoid of all outside sensations. Even the noise of the rising wind was so muffled that they slept without disturbance. Or at least Sweetypie did. For Sis, the night was torment.

In the morning, she came out of the cubby to find the cyclone on top of them again. There would be no trip down the mountain this morning. She checked many times during the day, and the next day and the next before it was safe to go back to the house. By then, the mountain had defoliated, the bare trees giving her a spectacular view down to the ruined cane fields and across the flats to town. The endless sheet of water was a dull grey mirror all the way down to the Inlet. It would be many days before that dispersed. At least it would give her time, for no one would be getting through for quite awhile.

She left Sweetypie drinking billy tea and went down the mountain.

When she reached the house, her heart sank. The river was higher than she had ever seen before, the water all the way up to the bottom veranda step and, although the rain had eased and the wind dropped, it would takes days, maybe weeks to go down.

The roof and walls were miraculously intact, but every louvre in every window had shattered, debris from the mountain had been deposited a foot deep on the veranda and a river of mud had washed down the mountain, through the flimsy kitchen and the passage to submerge the front steps.

The stench hit her as she reached the veranda. Pulling her shirt up over her face, she climbed over the debris and waded through the deep mud in the passage. Mum's bedroom door was stuck. She went outside again and made her away around to the gaping space that had been the window. She saw that the wardrobe and dressing table had been blown against the bed by the force of the wind, hiding Dad from her view. Climbing in through the window, she peered around the wardrobe, gagged savagely and fled. She couldn't face it yet.

Sis ran from the house, splashing her way through the flood, and didn't stop until she got to the shed. Taking a moment to catch her breath, she threw the crosspiece down and went in.

The milking cow lay dead and bloated, the stink rising up to hit her as the dogs leapt to greet her. She freed them and when *they began sniffing around the cow she kicked them outside. Then she went to the ponies which were in a distressed state. Part of the shed roof was gone and the stored feed was wet and rotting. She could do nothing more than free them and let them fend for themselves. She knew they wouldn't wander far. The chooks lay dead in a pile against the far wall where they'd bashed themselves to death in their frantic attempts to escape. She grabbed them by their legs and threw them out to the dogs.*

Sis went back to the house and collapsed on the bottom step, her feet in the water, looked around her at the devastation and howled like a dingo into the soft rain.

It was too much. Too much for just her. Where was Helen? Why hadn't she stayed, why hadn't she waited? They could have told Sarge that they couldn't get through until the bridge cleared. He would have believed that. But no, Helen wanted to go up over the mountain so it would look like they were desperate about Dad falling into the river.

Yeah. They had to look like that, they had to look desperate, they had to be believed. Shit, Helen would be back in a few days with Sarge and here was Sis feeling sorry for herself. Stupid bloody Sis, that's what she was.

Sis dropped her head into her hands and tried to think, tried to capture that clarity of thought that came so easily to Helen. She struggled with it until it came to her suddenly that there was nothing here she couldn't take care of. With Sweetypie safe up at the cubby, she had the next few days without interference to do what needed doing.

And what needed doing? Piece of piss, she thought. Bury the damn cow, fix the hole in the shed roof, shovel the mud out of the house, clean up the veranda, board up the windows until they could replace them, rebuild the kitchen and ...

... and there it was. Dad. Even as she pictured what she needed to do, she knew she couldn't do it. She could do everything else, no worries, but not that.

She straightened her shoulders. Well, if she couldn't do it Helen's way, she'd do it her way. If the problem was that she could not go into that room and touch that stinking corpse, then she bloody well wouldn't. She would seal up the bedroom, seal it up so that it became a coffin and a grave in one hit. Yeah, she could do that. There was plenty of lumber and paint in the shed and she was as good a builder as anyone in the district. Dad had taught her well.

Then she laughed, loudly, insanely at the irony of it. Dad had taught her how to make his own coffin. How bloody funny was that?

Courage suddenly energised her, she went back to the shed and began.

It was weeks before Sarge and his men got through. They found Sis and Sweetypie eating their lunch on the front veranda. Everything at the Downing farm seemed in order, the shed repaired, the stables almost rebuilt and the ponies in their stalls, the boarded up windows awaiting new glass, the interior freshly painted, the floor boards polished and gleaming.

As for the smell, well that would go eventually, Sarge assured them of that. A dead cow left a strong smell, even after it was buried and he could understand why she buried it so close to the house, after all, the rest of the farm had been under water at the time and the cow had needed disposing of quickly. As for the dogs that kept digging it up, Sarge suggested a few boulders rolled down from the mountain to rest over the grave might deter them.

Then Sarge asked if Helen had got back from town alright, and the conversation took a whole new direction.

CHAPTER TWENTY-ONE

Sis looked exhausted. This particular trip down memory lane had cost her dearly.

Helen walked to the window and stared outside, taking it in. She now understood Sis's reaction to the sight of the shears on her bed and her damaged hair. She thought of the axe in the pillow and the evidence of the frenzied attack on Dad with the shears and shuddered. Sweetypie's attack on her could have been worse. Much worse.

And then she thought about Sis living with Dad's corpse in the house for fifty years. She said, as if to herself, "I could never have imagined ..." She turned back to Sis and said, "So that was the strange look I saw on your face when I said I was staying. I saw you look at the house and I knew there was something secretive going on, but I could never have imagined ..."

"Why would you?" Sis sounded like a frail old lady. "I don't think about it any more. He's been there for so long and no one ever suspected. Not even Sweetypie. And when you did turn up a couple of days ago, well, hell, it was a shock for me to have to think about him being in there again. He's just there, he's always been there, it ain't important anymore."

Helen shook her head sadly. "We both kept secrets from each other. When we were young, we kept nothing from each other. How did we get like this, Sis?"

"Jeez, I don't know. It all went wrong, didn't it? It wasn't like we planned. But don't sweat it, Helen. It's finished, isn't it? Just leave him be, patch the hole up and go on like we used to." Sis put her hand up to her aching head and closed her eyes.

"Was that the only secret, Sis?"

"Yeah."

"No. What about the day Sweetypie was born? What is it you won't tell me about that day?"

"Not that, Helen. Please, not that."

"I have to know. I have to understand."

Sis looked up at Helen. "Jeez! Dog with a bloody bone again. Alright. But it's ugly and I never wanted you to have that inside your head."

"I'll deal with it. Just tell me."

Sis looked down at her work worn hands and sighed deeply, deciding to tell the story and be done with it. It couldn't get worse than it already was. "Alright. But sit down first, Helen. This ain't something that any good mother will want to hear. It still makes me feel sick when I think of it and it'll be the same for you."

"Godalmighty, Sis, what is it?" Helen pulled up a chair next to the bed and took Sis's hand in her own.

Taking a deep breath, Sis began. "It was when he got home for tea, that day when Sweetypie was born. He'd beaten Mum badly then gone out again, remember? Poor Mum had made a real effort to clean up herself and the house, she was so terrified of him, but he ignored her when he got home. Instead, he told us to get ready for a bath."

311

CHAPTER TWENTY-TWO

Dad called out to Sis, "Get yourself and Helen ready for a bath. Yeah, I know it's early, but do it!"

Sis and Helen jumped to obey. They ran down the steps and under the house to the stone bathhouse. Dad had recently replaced the pump with taps and a pipe that gravity-fed water directly from the river. They liked turning the taps on and watching the clear water gush out. When enough water covered the bottom of the claw-foot bath, they discarded their grubby clothes and climbed in.

And waited.

They knew what to expect when Dad said he would bathe them. Sis hoped he would be quick today because she wanted to get back to Mum and the baby.

They hadn't expected him to bring Sweetypie with him.

He unwrapped the sleeping infant, dropped the towel to the floor and cradled her in one arm. With his free hand he undid his belt and his fly buttons, letting his trousers and Y-fronts

312

drop to his knees. "Your turn today, Helen. Come on now, soap up your sweet little hands and make Daddy's soldier stand to attention." Helen did as she had been taught to do. "Too quick. Slower," he instructed and she obeyed.

It was boring, it was always boring, especially when he wanted it slow. It was better when he wanted it fast, his soldier would sneeze quickly and he would go away, leaving them to play again.

Sis stood apart, knee deep in water, watching her father. His soldier was standing up very straight and it would sneeze any minute now. She waited for that funny look on his face, the look when his eyes stopped being shiny, when they looked flat and dull, he made that weird grin with his lips stretched back and the gold filling in his front tooth glinted, when he breathed funny and his soldier sneezed and then he would look dopey and sigh, like he was waking up after a sleep.

She watched and waited. But he was doing something different now. He reached down and grabbed Helen's hand, rubbing some of the soapy froth onto his own, then he began to caress the baby's belly and legs, sliding his hand up and down her in rhythm with Helen's movements below.

Sis knew. She just knew.

"Don't, Daddy, she's too little. Please don't. You'll hurt her."

As if snapped out of a blissful reverie, Harry looked down at Sis and said with obvious irritation, "What? What was that?"

Fearlessly, Sis repeated her words.

Harry flicked his hand across the top of Helen's head, knocking her out of the way, and dragged Sis to him by her black hair. "Don't you talk to me like that, you little wog bitch. Here, you do it."

Sis obeyed fearfully. She hated this, hated it with all her heart. It hurt her mouth and the taste of the soap made her gag and, if she wasn't quick enough, Daddy's soldier sneezed inside her mouth and made her want to vomit. So she tried to do it properly because that was the quickest way to end it.

But as soon as he took his hand from her head, she pulled back and looked up. He was stroking the baby with soapy fingers and now he parted her tiny legs. The baby jerked and squealed with pain, but he persisted until Sweetypie was impaled, writhing and screaming.

Sis pulled away from him and cried, "Stop it, Daddy, you're making her bleed!" But he didn't seem to hear. He continued probing, ignoring the writhing that threatened to slip the little body from his grasp. Sis saw the glazed eyes and the glinting gold tooth and screamed over her baby sister's screams, "Stop it, don't, don't, don't!" She knew he wasn't hearing her and in panic and fear she slapped at his erection twice, sharp little slaps that stung and got his attention.

He looked down at her with black contempt and the cry died in her throat. Before she knew what was happening, he'd put Sweetypie on the stone floor and raised his fist above her. Then he brought it down across her face with such force that it lifted her out of the water and slammed her into the side of the bath. The impact crushed her nose, broke her front teeth and knocked the breath out of her. She almost lost consciousness, but Helen's screams next to her stopped her from drifting into the blackness completely. Had he hit Helen too, or was she screaming from fear? Only one thought flashed through her mind – she had to stay awake because who else was there to defend Helen or Sweetypie? Who else in the whole wide world was there to stop the monster who was her father from hurting her beloved little sister and the precious new baby?

No one!

In the blinding flash of time it took to make the decision to fight her way back from the blackness that threatened to engulf her to full consciousness, she understood with illuminating clarity who she was and what her role in the family was to be.

314

She understood in that instant who the enemy was and that the fight would never end. She understood what hate was and that it would become the equal partner of love, the love she felt for her sisters. And she understood that the searing pain she felt now would not be the last time, that it was the price she would pay to protect Helen and Sweetypie. She understood and accepted.

The room stopped spinning and she was lying on her back in the bath, blood coursing from her nose and mouth, turning the water red, her head resting in Helen's lap where she had fallen. Tears poured down Helen's terror stricken face and the baby lay squalling on the floor.

They waited there in the bloodied water, waited until full consciousness and a semblance of sanity returned, waited until the bleeding eased, until the pain abated enough for Sis to get her breath, for her to be able to move, until the cool water started her shivering and drove her to her knees. She could see that Helen wasn't hurt, only traumatised. Then her first thought was for Sweetypie who had screamed and cried herself into exhaustion and who lay on the cold stone floor taking in huge sucking gulps of air.

Sis climbed out of the bath, her eyes already swelling into slits, every movement sending a shock of pain through her head. Helen tried to follow her, but the weeping and fear had left her weak and shaky. Sis pulled her over the edge of the bath and left her in a wet heap on the floor while she went to the baby.

She parted the little legs carefully. Dad had such big hands, his fingers were rough and his nails always sharp and ragged. She had felt his cruel fingers tearing her soft membranes many times. Now she saw the savage evidence of Dad's violation in Sweetypie and she was filled with rage.

Poor little baby. Poor helpless, tiny creature. How dare he! Didn't he know how much it hurt? How could he not care?

She picked up the baby and held her tight until the jerky sobs calmed. She held her tight until the infant drifted into sleep. She held her tight and thought and thought. She wasn't aware of the cold stone floor or Helen crying softly next to her. She wasn't aware of the scraping of Dad's chair on the veranda above her or the padding of Mum's footsteps up the passage to her bedroom. She was only aware of the baby in her arms and the small child at her side, and she thought hard about what to do.

She'd keep the baby in her room for a start. Mum couldn't be relied on to protect her. She hadn't protected Sis or Helen. They'd get the keys to the bedrooms from the drawer in the kitchen and keep their rooms locked. When Dad wanted to make his soldier sneeze, she'd offer herself rather than allow Dad to touch the baby. It didn't matter if it hurt or made her cry, just as long as she kept Sweetypie safe.

At six years of age, Sis Downing saw her future as clearly as if someone had laid it out before her. There, on the washhouse floor, she made a commitment to the sleeping infant in her arms and the toddler leaning into her for comfort, and she locked it into place. There was no going back. She would protect her baby and her little girl at all costs. Her purpose in life was sealed with love and a fierce protectiveness that would shape the rest of her days.

Holding the baby in one arm and Helen's hand with the other, she went quietly upstairs, walked past Dad as if he wasn't there, and began.

CHAPTER TWENTY-THREE

Sis couldn't go on. Her face twisted in painful memory and her eyes bulged with unshed tears.

Helen's breath came in ragged gasps. "He was a monster! I wanted to know because I wanted to understand, but I don't understand! How could he ... how could he!" The horror overcame her and she collapsed onto the side of Sis's bed. "Oh, Sis, I didn't know. I just didn't know."

"I shouldn't have told you," Sis said with a tremble in her voice.

"Yes, you should have, because it is the final piece in the puzzle of our lives. It explains why you never ran away and left us. You could have if you'd wanted to. It explains why you took the punches for us, why you sacrificed yourself on so many occasions in our place. Would we have survived at all without you? Probably not. And there's the other thing, the obvious thing."

Sis stared at her wordlessly.

"Don't you see? He initiated both of us into the world in exactly the same way. From the day each of us was born, we never had a chance."

Helen could hold the tears in no longer. They burst from her in a noisy howl.

Sis was shocked. "Hey, jeez, stop that. I ain't seen you cry since ..." Suddenly, the memory of Sweetypie's sixth birthday caught at her throat, the memory of an innocent, beautiful child with her whole life before her, so trusting, so quick and clever, so full of promise, so sweet and warm, sitting between them on the swing, her pretty pink dress flowing out around her and those wondrous pink shoes flashing in the sunlight.

"I tried to save her," she cried, "but I couldn't! If I had, if I'd been stronger and quicker and cleverer, she'd be normal. Normal and alive! It's my fault she lost her mind. My fault!" She raised a fist and slammed it into the bed, the years of repressed emotion threatening to erupt like an explosion.

Helen gripped the clenched fist and cried, "No! It was never your fault, or mine. It was his! His alone!"

"Damn his soul to hell!" Sis cried at the top of her voice and the emotion finally erupted from her. But unlike Helen's damburst at the cubby which was full of grief and despair, Sis's emerged as fury unleashed like a thunderbolt. It picked her up off the bed and made her cry out, "The bastard! The stinking rotten bastard! He did this, he did all of this! Even now he reaches out from the dead and controls us! Damn him to hell! Damn him ..."

A nurse and a doctor came rushing into the room. Within minutes, believing Sis and Helen were grieving for the loss of their missing sister, they were jabbing a needle into Sis's arm to calm her, but it was another ten minutes of cursing and crying out before it began to take effect. Finally, without a single reserve of energy left, she collapsed back onto the pillow.

And then the tears came. Softly and helplessly, her eyes staring blindly at the wasted sad years of her life and the empty meaningless future without Sweetypie, until finally the drug took hold and she drifted off to sleep.

Helen stayed with her until she was sure she was alright, then drove home, poured a Johnny Walker to steady her shattered nerves and made some plans.

CHAPTER TWENTY-FOUR

Three days later, after the police had left the house with no news to give her about Sweetypie, she removed the mirror from where she had hung it over the hole and opened up the rest of the wall with the sledgehammer. When she could walk through, she took the tarpaulin she had found in the shed, placed it on the floor and rolled Dad's remains onto it. She wrapped the tarp around him and dragged it from the house, bouncing it down the steps and sliding it across the wet grass to the water's edge.

She went back to the house and got the sledgehammer. Standing over the wrapped remains, she raised the sledgehammer high above her head and brought it down with a crunching blow where his head lay under the tarp. She did it again and again until the tarp was flattened and no recognisable piece of bone remained. And with each blow, she thought, this is for what you did to us the day we were born, this is for the birthday party, this is for not buying Sis shoes

for the party, this is for beating her, this is for Mum, this is for
…

She rained blow after blow on her father's corpse until the lives of herself and her sisters were purged. Exhausted, she flopped onto the wet grass and waited for her breathing to return to normal. When she could stand again, she pulled the tarp back and surveyed the crushed remains. They were unrecognisable as ever being anything remotely human. Then she spat contemptuously on them four times, once for each of them and once for Mum, flipped the tarp and scattered the remains into the current. She sat again and watched her father wash away with the river.

As he disappeared, she remembered the day he died.

How she had loved his violent suffering that day! How well it had satisfied the need for revenge that had built up inside her twisted youthful mind and body over the years of torture and abuse. And now, seeing him finally sink into the water, she felt only an end to it, a sort of "well, that's that" feeling.

She could never change any of it, but she could let it go. She hoped Sis could do the same.

She washed the tarp down, replaced it in the shed and returned to the house.

Holding a lit cigarette to Sis's elaborate mosquito net, she waited long enough to see the rush of flames lick the timber walls and take hold, placed the cigarette casually on the bedside table, then walked calmly down to the hire car parked near the bridge. Prince and Lady were waiting with wagging tails in the back. She watched the glow of the flames in the rear vision mirror, watched it until she reached the bend and then focused on what was before her.

Bill Stewart led the dogs onto his front veranda and grinned when they responded to his "sit" command. "Tell Sis," he said, "that's it's about bloody time she took a break. The dogs will be happy here. And I'll have those papers to you within the week."

At the hospital, the staff were not expecting her. Neither was Sis. A smaller bandage adorned her healing head and colour had returned to her face, despite the deeply blackened eyes. "I'm taking her for a walk," she told the nurse as she helped Sis into a wheelchair. Outside in the car park, she said, "Get in the car, Sis, we're going for a drive."

"Where're we going? I could use a beer and a decent feed. Will we be long?"

Helen smiled as she pulled out of the hospital grounds and headed north along the highway. "Where we're going, you'll get some of the best food and wine in the world."

"Yeah? Somewhere posh, is it? Well, I ain't exactly dressed for it," she remarked, plucking at the hospital dressing gown and touching her bandaged head.

Helen handed her a shopping bag. "Change into this," she said simply. It contained a pair of navy blue linen pants, top and gold leather sandals.

"Ha! You must be joking. Bit bloody flash for me, don't you think?"

"Not at all," Helen retorted, "they'll go nicely with the bandages on your head and they'll look good with Nonna's rings which, I have noticed, you haven't removed from your right hand since I gave them to you."

Sis looked down at her gnarled weathered hands and gave the rings a self-conscious twist. "Yeah, well, it kinda got to me, you know, having something from a grandmother I look like and was named after. Sort of made me feel in touch with the women who have gone before me."

Helen pondered that for a moment. "I know what you mean," she said. "I deeply regret not giving you the opportunity to meet her. Do you know that if you were to walk into the village near our vineyard in Tuscany, there'd still be a lot of people who would think Nonna had risen from the dead, the resemblance is so strong?"

"Yeah? Really? Shit, I think I like that."

Helen smiled. "Good," she said, turning right at a set of traffic lights, "because in a few months, Tuscany is exactly where you'll be."

"Whadya talking about, Helen?"

"In exactly half an hour, we'll be on a flight to Sydney. My daughters and Aunt Maria will be at the airport to meet us. We'll stay a couple of weeks until Christmas is over, and I'm warning you, you can expect to be the main attraction on Christmas Day. Christmas in the Benotti family is a big occasion. There'll be about two hundred of us at Aunt Maria's. We have doctors and nurses in the family and they will be waiting at her house today to look you over and make sure you are alright. Between Aunt Maria and your nieces, cousins, second cousins and all their families, you'll be getting plenty of tender loving care. We are a large and close knit family, Sis, even though we are scattered all over the world. We'll begin by visiting all the Australian relatives – they've worked out a schedule for us that will take us to the end of autumn and you will have seen all of Australia by then. I thought I should spare you winter in Europe the first year, it will be too much of a shock for a tropical bird like you. Then I'm taking you and Aunt Maria home, to Tuscany. You will adore Italy, it's in your blood. And then we'll plan our trips. I'm going to show you the world, darling. I believe we have at least ten good years left in us and we're going to make the world our playground while we can. We have money to burn and we are going to use it. You'll finally be able to buy those gorgeous white things you love so much and wear them." She laughed. "You're finally going to learn how to buy hats."

Sis was staring at Helen, wide eyed. "Jeez woman, what are you talking about? I got a farm to run …"

"Bill will have it on the market within the week. He'll fax the papers down to us in Sydney. He already has an offer from a syndicate. We have solicitors in the family, they'll take care of it from there."

"But the dogs and …"

"Bill has the dogs and he sends his blessings."

"But I can't just get on a plane and go."

"Why not? And hurry with those clothes. We're almost there. There's a handbag under the shoes - yes, it matches - with your wallet inside. We'll get you a passport in Sydney."

"Passport? I'm gunna have a passport? Never thought I'd need one of those, " Sis mumbled as she pulled the top over her head and slipped the trousers up over her legs.

"Yes, darling. Now, quick with the sandals or we'll miss our flight. Are you alright to walk or shall I get a wheelchair?"

"Course I'm alright to walk. It's just a bloody headache. Hang on, don't walk so fast, I'm a bit more wobbly than I thought, suppose it's these jazzy sandals. Jeez, they look far too posh for me. Oh, it's so cool in here. Hells bloody bells, what do I do now?"

"Don't panic, just follow me, darling, I've spent half my life in airports, there's nothing to it."

"This way? Yes yes, I'm coming. What's this, a boarding pass? What do I do with that? Oh, I see. Oh shit, it's like being swallowed by a fish …"

"There's your seat, darling, first class, only the best for us."

"By the window?"

"Yes. If we are lucky, there will be something special for you to see as we take off."

Suddenly, Sis gripped the arms of her seat. "Helly."

"Yes, Sissy?"

"I'm scared bloody shitless! I never been in a plane before."

Helen laughed, a tinkling sound as light as air. "You scared? Oh Sissy, dearest Sissy, after what you've been through?" She stopped laughing, took Sis's hand in hers and leaned close to her sister's ear, saying in a low voice, "Fear was hearing his footsteps coming up the passage at night. Fear was watching his fist come at your face. Fear was seeing the way he looked at Sweetypie in her pretty pink dress. Fear was witnessing our mother lose her mind and her life. Fear was feeling Sweetypie as cold as death between us. Fear was where he was. Fear was him. And then he was dead and I was free. I have lived my life without a moment's fear for five decades. But not you, he was not gone for you. You lived with his presence in that house for fifty years. Every day you walked past him in the passage, you lived with him in the house, he was always there. But never again, darling, never again."

"But he's still – oh, what was that?"

"We're taking off. Just sit back and swallow until your ears pop. Don't worry. You'll love it. Now we're turning south. No, you're not going to fall out of the plane. Look down, Sis, look down now, quickly before we get into the clouds. See? Down there. Yes. Right there."

Sis saw. Below them, a ball of flame sent black smoke funnelling up into the sky. She looked hard and then she gasped. "It's ..."

"It's gone. It's over."

"But he's still ..."

"He's in the river, where he belongs. I took care of it. It's over forever, Sis."

Sis stared out of the window in silence as she tried to take it all in, her hand gripping Helen's hard enough to strangle the circulation. Helen returned the grip, passing her strength and confidence to her sister, telling her more through that handhold than she could have with words.

Helen was in charge now, that was clear, and difficult as it was to do, Sis wanted to let go, to relinquish control, to let someone else do the worrying, the planning, the organising.

For the first time in fifty years, Sis sighed the sigh of the irresponsible and let it happen. Helen felt it and leaned back in her seat.

The plane climbed through the thick cloud and came out into brilliant sunshine on an endless expanse of fluffy, snow-white cloud tops. Sis stared and stared. She had never seen anything so beautiful. With her gaze fixed on the sight as if it might be snatched away at any minute, she said, "Will it ever be?"

"Be what, dearest?"

"Truly over."

"I don't know. It has made us who we are, we carry that much with us forever. But there is life out there, Sis, I promise you that much, there is life out there to be sampled, embraced and enjoyed. And if I hadn't been so messed up myself, if I'd had more courage and been less self serving, you'd have experienced it all by now."

Sis continued to stare out of the window as the cloud mass gave way to clear skies and she saw the coastline below her emerge. It was happening so fast, so suddenly, this change. It would take a while to adjust.

Helen heard Sis murmur something. "What was that, Sissy?"

With her back to Helen, she said, "You did good."

"In what way did I do good?"

"You did good not telling the family about me or Sweetypie. If you had, my pretty little baby would never have had her happy days fixing the track, swimming in the waterhole, away from critical eyes and interfering do gooders. It would have been different if you'd told them. There would have been too many others involved, you know, thinking they knew best for her, like that stupid doctor. I reckon you gave her a life by not telling anyone, by leaving us alone. You did good."

Sis turned to Helen. "What if they don't like me?" she suddenly asked, thinking of the people waiting for them at the airport.

"What if you don't like them? That's more to the point. That's what they'll all be worrying about."

"I'm not real good with people."

"Oh, darling, just be yourself. They'll love you. They already do. You're the woman of mystery, the secret sister hidden away up north for fifty years, and you've got more personality than anyone they'll have ever met. They'll adore you."

Sis gazed at Helen for a moment. Even with her hair cut so short, her sister was beautiful. She touched her own iron grey hair and suddenly remembered how glorious she thought Helen's hair looked when she first came up the steps a few days ago. "Can I grow my hair?"

Helen laughed with surprise. "We can both grow our hair!"

"Mine used to be black. Can I have it dyed, like yours?"

"Oh god yes. My hairdresser will take you in hand, don't worry about that. Anything else?"

"Yeah," she said wistfully, remembering how she had stared at the girls at church in her youth, secretly envying their pretty clothes and soft shiny hair, but most of all their full red lips. That was the one symbol of femininity, above all others, she had most desired, but most feared. Hence the dozens of unopened bright red lipsticks hidden away on the shelf in her bedroom. And now, reaching out for her denied womanhood, she said simply, "Lipstick. Lipstick would be nice."

THE END

A PLACE IN TIME
By C. A. HOCKING

Dan Campbell is a troubled man who sinks into depression as each birthday approaches. Thirty years earlier, on his 11th birthday, he'd witnessed his father's murder and saved his mother from a deranged stranger, but something is wrong with the memory of that terrible day. Something he can't quite see, something just out of focus.

When his annual depression threatens his family's wellbeing, he goes back to his childhood home to confront his memories and find answers to the mystery of his father's death. Dan is swept back in time to the day of the murder and what he discovers there will turn his world upside down, for no one and nothing is as he remembers. And the truth is more shocking than he could ever have imagined.

HOME TO ROOST
By C. A. HOCKING

Australian Prime Minister Marian Hardwick has achieved everything she ever desired to become the most powerful woman in the country. She is admired by some, but seen as ruthless, calculating and manipulative by others.

Only two men really know her – her husband and her brother – but one loves her and the other hates her. When one threatens to destroy her by revealing a secret buried deep in her past, the other can save her, but first he must break her completely.

Marian's life unravels as everything she ever believed in is exposed as a lie. If she is to survive, she must confront the greatest challenge of all – the truth about herself.

SARAH ANN ELLIOTT Book 1: 1823-1829
By C. A. HOCKING
An Epic Family Saga based on a true story.

Sarah Ann Elliott was born in 1823 into a family of weavers whose lives were entirely dependent on the textile mills of the booming Northern England town of Stockport. Her family is much like any other with highs and lows, joys and sorrows, but when 10,000 spinners and weavers go on strike for nine months in the infamous 1829 Stockport Turnout, the Elliotts are plunged into a life of hardship and turmoil from which no one is spared.

Little Sarah Ann is swept along with the events that surround her and it is only the love of her family and her indomitable spirit that will carry her through.

Sarah Ann Elliott Book 1 is a poignant and harrowing story of one family's struggle to survive the grim mill towns of 19th century England, and is the first book in The Sarah Ann Elliott Series.

OLD FARTS ON A BUS
By C. A. HOCKING

What happens when you put 30 eccentric senior citizens who don't know each other on a bus in a foreign country?

Quite a lot actually.

And it's more fun than a barrel of monkeys!

AUNT EDNA and the Lightning Rock
By C. A. Hocking
Book 1 of the Aunt Edna Stories

When Aunt Edna learns that her 11 year-old orphaned niece, Isobel is coming to live with her, she has a panic attack. Goodness, whatever will she do with a niece? After all, Aunt Edna is an Eternal with magical powers and Isobel is a Mere Mortal.

And what will Diggidydog, Grumblebumkin, The Great Smoking Beastie and Barking Wood Stove make of a niece? Not to mention the five Ghosts on the veranda and Frozen Bert in the freezer.

An Australian Children's Fable of Weirdness and Wonder!